MÜNCHHAUSEN'S PIGTAIL

MÜNCHHAUSEN'S PIGTAIL

or Psychotherapy & "Reality"
Essays and Lectures

PAUL WATZLAWICK

W·W·Norton & Company
NEW YORK LONDON

Printed in the United States of America.

The text of this book is composed in Alternate Janson, with display type set in Ultra Bodoni and Bulmer. Composition and manufacturing by the Haddon Craftsmen, Inc.

Book design by Tere LoPrete

First Edition

Library of Congress Cataloging-in-Publication Data

Watzlawick, Paul.
    [Münchhausens Zopf. English]
    Münchhausen's pigtail, or Psychotherapy and "reality" / Paul Watzlawick.—1st ed.
    p. cm.
    Translation of Münchhausens Zopf, oder, Psychotherapie und "Wirklichkeit".
  Includes bibliographical references.
    1. Psychotherapy.   2. Adjustment (Psychology)   I. Title.
    II. Title: Münchhausen's pigtail.   III. Title: Psychotherapy and "reality".
  RC480.5.W344   1990
  616.89—dc20   89—36580

ISBN 0-393-02825-9

W. W. Norton & Company, Inc., 500 Fifth Avenue, New York, N.Y. 10110

W. W. Norton & Company Ltd., 37 Great Russell Street, London WC1B 3NU

1 2 3 4 5 6 7 8 9 0

CONTENTS

PREFACE

In this anthology, I have attempted to present the development of a thought model, as I have experienced it as a member of the Mental Research Institute (MRI) in Palo Alto, California, and as presented in essays and lectures. It is a development that is inseparably connected to the influence of four extraordinary pioneering personalities.

At the beginning of the fifties the anthropologist and communication researcher Gregory Bateson began, within the framework of a large-scale research grant, to replace the concept of linear causality (from cause to effect) of classical psychotherapy with an anthropological, circular point of view. In other words, instead of asking "Why?" (for example, "Why, on the basis of what determining factors in his individual past, does this person now behave in this irrational manner?"), Bateson asked: "Which effects of an effect influence their own cause?" or "What must be the nature of the present interpersonal context, to which the behavior in question is adjusted, in which it makes sense, and may even be the only possible reaction?" With these fundamental questions Bateson became one of the first scientists to introduce communication theory, and therefore *systemic* concepts, into psychiatry. (Chapter 5 of this volume will discuss this subject in greater depth.)

As in the course of its general research the Bateson group's attention turned more and more toward behavioral (pragmatic) effects of human communication and interaction and also toward the phenomena of disturbed behavior, it became clear that the assistance of an expert in this field was imperative. Bateson found this expert in the person of the psychiatrist and psychoanalyst Don D. Jackson, who by then had already acquired an international reputation. The choice could hardly have been more fortunate. At that time Jackson had already distanced himself from classical analysis (seeking causes in the past) and had begun to work with relationship systems (couples and families), instead of individual patients. What especially distinguished him was his unusual ability to recognize problem-causing and problem-maintaining interaction patterns in the Here and Now and to influence them by specific, direct, active therapeutic intervention. A number of pioneering publications, especially the first formulation of the Double-Bind theory, grew out of the Bateson/Jackson collaboration.

In the year 1959 Jackson founded MRI. At first it was a department of the Palo Alto Medical Research Foundation; then in 1963 it became independent. Bateson's research grant ran out in 1962, but until that time the two groups (his and MRI) maintained close collaboration; indeed, it was often thought to be *one* organization with the fantasy name "Palo Alto Group."

The seminal influence of two other personalities on the development of the MRI approach to problem formation and problem resolution—the famous hypnotherapist Dr. Milton H. Erickson and the internationally known bio-cybernetician Professor Heinz von Foerster—will be referred to in the introductions to Chapters 4 and 7, respectively.

Paul Watzlawick   Spring 1989

MÜNCHHAUSEN'S PIGTAIL

C H A P T E R
1

The Nature and Structure
of Human Relationships

Chapter 1 is based on the work of the "Palo Alto Group," described in the Preface to this book, and deals also with the further development of the cybernetic, system-theoretical, and pragmatic aspects of human communication and their problems.

•

Cybernetics, General System Theory, and Pragmatics as a Basis for the Study of Human Relationships

Imagine a man, who knows nothing about chess, in a foreign country and observing two people engaged in an activity that is obviously symbolic: They move small carved pieces on a board. Since the man does not speak the local language he cannot ask for an explanation of their behavior. He can, however, deduce all the rules governing chess if he watches the actions of the two players long enough (presumably over the course of several games); and he will be able to recognize checkmate as the goal of the game. He will have reached this point by examining the redundancies in the players' behavior and by determining that certain behaviors (moves) appear frequently with certain pieces and never with others. This suggests to him that the players are following specific rules which can be deduced by observation.

Remember here that the observer arrived at his conclusions without being able to ask any direct questions. He reached his conclusion without having to attribute any deeper meaning to the game itself or even to arrive at explanations in the traditional sense of the term. Rather, the result of his observations is a set of simple rules (a "grammar" or an algorithm, calculus, code, program, or *plan*) [116] which covers the myriad possible behavior variants between the players. And finally the observer succeeded in deducing the game's rules without the need for insight into the motives, intentions, feelings, or personalities of the players. An attempt to position this procedure can be undertaken by considering three mutually complementary factors:

1. Insofar as the totality of the possible behaviors is taken into consideration and the patterns of the appearance or non-appearance of these forms are examined, the method is *cybernetic.* The fundamentally new aspect of cybernetics is, after all, that it does not examine the characteristics of separated elementary particles or artificially isolated variables, but rather the interaction between these components.

In his chapter on transformations (i.e. changes of internal states), Ashby [9, p. 11] points out that from a cybernetic point of view it is a question neither of defining what the transformation "really" consists of nor of analyzing the reasons for the change; what matters is only the giving of a set of operands and a statement of what each is changed to. Consequently the transformation is concerned with *what* happens, not with *why* it happens.

2. Insofar as the observer sees the two players and their reciprocal behavior as a whole, his approach is *system*-oriented. Wherever totalities become the subject of investigation, it becomes apparent that their structure, effect, and possible failures are governed by natural laws which are more, and different from, the sum of their individual components. This is the basis of Bertalanffy's [22, pp. 134–165] General Systems Theory, involving his well-known research into isomorphies in the behavior of complex entities, no matter whether the latter consists of atoms, molecules, cells, cell clusters, organisms, individuals, societies, cultures, or whatever.

3. The order inherent in all systems presupposes, however, that their components stand in specific relations to one another, *i.e.*, that they *communicate*. Insofar as the observer studies the communicative behavior of the players (their moves), i.e., the use of symbols (the chess pieces) and their effect on those who use the symbols (the players), his activity falls into the area of *pragmatics*.

Of the three disciplines mentioned above, pragmatics is without doubt the most significant for the understanding of human relationships. Morris [121] defined it as that branch of semiotics (the general theory of signs and languages) which deals with the use of symbols and their effect on those who use them. Morris refers to Peirce [130], Gallie [56], James [77], Dewey [42], and Mead [113], among others, while his own work in turn influenced the Vienna circle of logical positivists [90], among whom Carnap [33, 34] is particularly noteworthy. Carnap agrees that researching a language means studying not only its formal structure (its syntax), but also its relationship to the objects it denotes (semantics) and to the individuals using it (pragmatics).

The interdependence of these three areas is succinctly expressed in George's formulation of semiotics [61, p. 41] where he points out that "in many ways it is true to say that syntax is mathematical logic, semantics is philosophy or philosophy of science, and pragmatics is psychology; but these fields are not really all distinct." Speaking on the same topic in his eminently readable book on communication research, Cherry remarks that these three segments are not disconnected but "overlap one another, just as chemistry overlaps geology or physics" [36, p. 120].

Up to now the rather sparse literature about pragmatics has dealt almost exclusively with the relationship between the user of a symbol (the sender or the receiver) and the symbol itself. We feel, however, that it is not only permissible but imperative to see the triad—sender-sign-receiver—as the smallest unit of every pragmatic investigation and to treat it as indivisible. It is not the purpose of this study to answer the question of the good bishop Berkeley, whether a tree falling in a lonely forest makes a sound even when nobody is there to hear it. We believe that it is idle, even from the standpoint of basic research (let alone practical communication research), to analyze the relationship between sender and sign without taking into consideration the receiver and his reactions, or to study the relationship between receiver and sign while ignoring the sender—just as it would hardly make sense to study a chessplayer's behavior (his moves) without reference to the moves of his partner. Peirce [130] has already pointed out that signs do not exist in a vacuum but that every sign triggers another sign in the receiver, which in turn triggers a third in the original sender, and so on. And with this realization a conclusive step has been taken: Our focus shifts from the individual to the *relationship between* individuals as a phenomenon sui generis—and as soon as this is the case we come into conflict with the time-honored views of man and his behavior. (We are dealing, as the reader will see, almost exclusively with dyadic relationships. This is merely to simplify the presentation and does not mean that our statements cannot be applied to multiple relationships. For similar reasons we rarely mention nonverbal communication at all. Should this create the impression that pragmatics deals only with verbal messages, we would like to make it quite clear that in all communicational structures, both verbal and nonverbal communication can arise. And, finally, this discussion is based mainly on Anglo-American material, with full awareness that this is one-sided, leaving European authors and sources insufficiently represented.)

Basically, human perception entails two very different elements: objects and relationships. As far as objects in their widest sense are concerned, that is objects of the outside world, it may be best to consider them, as did Leibniz, as monads and to examine their characteristics. Should opinions differ, these can often be resolved by objective analysis, even if these analyses occasionally prove exceedingly difficult. In the end it may then be possible to conclude that one of these opinions was right and the other wrong. The tradition of occidental thinking is based on this monadic concept; it divides the world into subjects and objects, is reflected in the structure of Indo-European languages, and has since Aristotle been the foundation of classical logic.

In contrast to objects, however, human relationships are not phenomena which exist objectively, in their own right, as it were, nor is it possible to have a consensus about their properties. Above all, if there are differences of opinion about the characteristics of a human relationship, it cannot be proved that one of the partners is right and the other wrong, or, to anticipate one of our main topics, that one partner is "normal" and the other "crazy." Relationships, the contents of our *interpersonal*, pragmatic reality, are not real in the same sense as objects are; they have their "reality" only in the perception of the partners, and even this reality is shared only partially by the partners. When A defines his relationship with B by the statement: "I know that you don't like me," and B answers with his definition of their relationship by saying: "You always think the worst of me," then, in the nature of human communication, there is no possibility of solving this controversy by objective proof. Pragmatic events cannot be determined monadically. If this is attempted anyway and if relationship phenomena are either ignored altogether or seen as epiphenomena, the monad will inevitably acquire hypothetical properties, which either do not exist at all or cannot be proved. It is especially significant that this problem runs like a red thread through the conceptions of man and his behavior, no matter how incompatible these views might be in every other respect. Since the soul is objectively unfathomable, the human monad is especially susceptible to having unprovable properties ascribed to it, which makes it only too easy for logical, linguistic, and semantic absurdities to play havoc. This danger is omnipresent even in the exact sciences; one only has to remember classical astronomy's seemingly innocent and simple assumption of the simultaneity of two events as the starting point of fundamental but useless theoretical deductions. For us laymen it is still hard to comprehend that this assumption is considered scientifically useless because it cannot be proven. Ayer, whose theoretical position is close to that of the Vienna circle, points out in his *Language, Truth and Logic* [11, p. 152] that Einstein's definition of simultaneity made it clear "how necessary it is for the experimental physicist to be furnished with clear and definitive analyses of the concepts which he employs. And the need for such analyses is even greater in the less advanced sciences. For example, the failure of present-day psychologists to emancipate themselves from metaphysics, and to coordinate their inquiries, is principally due to the use of symbols such as 'intelligence' or 'empathy' or 'subconscious self,' which are not precisely defined. The theories of psychoanalysts are particularly full of metaphysical elements which a philosophical elucidation of their symbols would remove."

If we do attribute certain characteristics to the human monad, then it becomes quite obvious to draw upon them as principles for the explanation of behavior. In a monadic sense, behavior has meaning because there is a cause behind it (as for example a desire, an act of volition, repression, a character trait). The mirage-like nature of these concepts, which become less and less clear the more carefully they are examined, has given rise to extensive skepticism especially in the last few years. On the other hand, studies of animal behavior have shown that it is possible to systematize behavior processes without such concepts, by employing methods of observation based exclusively on behavior redundancies, which "explain" nothing in the traditional meaning of the word and which correspond to the chess analogy mentioned above. Our imaginary observer could, of course, have attributed to the game as a whole—and to each chessman in particular—a "deeper" or "symbolic" meaning; but such a mythological or metaphysical interpretation of the game would add as little to the understanding of the players' behavior as astrological interpretations contribute to the understanding of astronomy.

And here we believe we have outlined the fundamental difference between the monadic and pragmatic approach. From a monadic viewpoint we ask about reason, cause, motive, in other words, *why?* From a pragmatic standpoint we ask *what* is happening here and now.

Do we seem proponents of a superficial and soulless philosophy which denies the dignity and freedom of man and thereby the reality and richness of his inner world? This, of course, was not our intention. What we are proposing is a process that tries to keep innate limitations in mind. As in modern physics, the point of view of the observer is decisive. In *personal* experience the monadic view will always be the only possible one, and constitution, early experiences, feelings, convictions, etc. will always remain decisive. In his private world even the most radical pragmatist will be deeply convinced of his subjective free will and therefore of his ethical accountability. Philosophers have attested to this again and again, as for example Sartre, for whom the only freedom which we do not have is not to be free. For the purposes of behavioral research, however, all these concepts, no matter how venerable, are useless, because they elude objective analysis. The researcher must therefore content himself with quite a different standpoint: He must analyze human behavior without the aid of all those criteria toward which his subjective personal experience is constantly prompting him. This limitation helps us to avoid the unfortunate consequences of jumbling subject and object, monadic and pragmatic principles, and opens for us—as we will show—new, fertile perspectives. This has been the case for some time in all other disciplines which have moved from the concern with monads to the study of interaction between monads. Morris pointed out, as far back as 1938, that "it is not necessary to deny 'private experiences' of the process of semiosis or of other processes, but it is necessary from the standpoint of behavioristics to deny that such experiences are of central importance or that the fact of their existence makes the objective study of semiosis (and hence of sign, designatum, and interpretant) impossible or even incomplete" [121, p. 84].

Regularities and Pathologies of Relationship Systems

At its current state, our understanding of the nature of relationships is fragmentary. On the one hand this is understandable, because the absence of a nonmonadic language seriously impedes every investigation into, or even thoughts about, relationship phenomena. But when one considers that relatedness is one of the most immediate aspects of human existence, the degree of our ignorance is astounding and proves once again that what is most immediate is often the most difficult to grasp. It would exceed the scope of this chapter to discuss how little our perception of reality rests on "facts" and how much that which we call "real" is either the result of interpersonal agreements or the outcome of contexts that, as members of a certain culture, social class, family, etc., we were literally born into. Real *is,* after all, what is *called* real by a sufficiently large number of people. In this extreme sense, reality is an interpersonal convention, just as use of language depends on the unspoken and mostly quite unconscious agreement that certain sounds and signs have specific meanings. The "reality" of a banknote, for example, does not lie primarily in the fact that it is a printed, multicolored piece of paper, but in the interpersonal agreement that this object represents a specific value. Bateson (personal communication) reported that the inhabitants of a certain coastal region in New Guinea availed themselves of heavy millstone-shaped rocks for larger transactions (for daily cash they used seashells). One day one of these rocks, as payment for a major purchase, was transported from one village to the next across a broad estuary. The boat capsized in the surf and the rock disappeared into the deep water, never to be seen again. Since this event was common knowledge, the rock kept functioning as currency, even though it now existed, as it were, only in the heads of the people concerned.

Epictetus declared that we are not disturbed so much by things themselves as by our ideas about these things. And modern anthropology, from Durkheim to the present day, has furnished very convincing evidence on how much these ideas are of interpersonal origin.

In spite of the difficulties mentioned above, it is possible at least to sketch the fundamentals of the pragmatics of human communication—the science of human relationships—and to furnish clinical evidence for typical disturbances of human relations. (A detailed presentation of the following material can be found in Watzlawick [176]. Some of the examples in the present essay were taken from that work.)

The following outline of the principal aspects of pragmatics makes no claims to either completeness or optimal formulation.

1. Even though there can hardly be doubt that behavior in the present is determined by past experiences, the nature of human relationships—as proposed by Wertheimer—is more than, and different from, the sum of all attitudes, conduct, dispositions, expectations, etc. which the partners bring into the relationship from their individual past. The nature of a relationship proves to be a complex phenomenon sui generis with its own rules and its own pathologies, whose characteristics cannot be attributed to one or the other partner. Analogies from other disciplines offer themselves: Water is more and different from the mere summation of the properties of hydrogen and oxygen; biologists speak of emergent qualities, and economists have long given up trying to grasp the economic behavior of large populations by adding or multiplying, as it were, the behavior of individuals.

It is in the transpersonal nature of relationship phenomena that their structure can be relatively clear to outsiders but not to the partners involved—rather like the impossibility of seeing one's own body in its entirety, because the eyes, as the organs of perception, are themselves part of the body being perceived. But when conflicts arise in a relationship, the blame for the trouble is "necessarily" attributed to the madness or badness of the *partner*, because "obviously" blame does not lie with oneself, and a *third* possibility does not seem to exist between *two* partners. Understandable as this one-sided view of human conflict may be in the case of the partners themselves, it becomes exceedingly questionable when used as the basis for psychopathological explanations. As long as human behavior is examined monadically, however, this distortion cannot be avoided, and we therefore speak of "patients," "mental illness," and so forth. It is one of our hypotheses that there are disturbed relationships but not disturbed individuals, or, to put it more precisely, that behavior disorders are a function of human relationships but not of sick minds. (It is hardly necessary to point out that this hypothesis extends only to so-called functional, not organically caused, disorders.) The following two examples will illustrate this hypothesis:

When both partner A and partner B see their essential fulfillment in giving, their relationship will in all probability lead to a very specific conflict. Since every giver needs a taker, without whose existence he could not be a giver, both will try to induce the other to take, and both will construe the attempt of the other to monopolize giving as a proof of coldness and rejection. This form of interpersonal conflict is particularly intensified by the feeling of both partners that the other's "coldness" does not show itself openly but is diabolically camouflaged behind a façade of good will and helpfulness. In "reality," however, they both feel how little the partner loves them.

On the other hand, a relationship, based more or less exclusively on A's help for B can develop, according to its nature, in only two directions. In one, the efforts of B remain unsuccessful, in which case the relationship will founder, because sooner or later B will feel used, become discouraged, and withdraw from the relationship. If, however, A is successful, and B is therefore no longer in need of his support, the relationship loses its reason for being and falls apart.

The following holds true for both examples: For the understanding of, and, as we shall see, any influence on such relationship disorders, it is immaterial how, when, or why the described basic behavior patterns of the partners originated. What matters is that the reason for such conflicts cannot be attributed to one or the other partner. As in chemistry, this is a matter of a *compound* of two elements; alone or in combination with partners of different mind, these particular disorders would not arise.

2. In the presence of another person all behavior—active or passive, intentional or unintentional—takes on meaning and therefore becomes communication. Since there is no such thing as *non-*behavior, one cannot *not* communicate. This seemingly trivial statement has pragmatic significance. It is not hard to imagine interpersonal situations in which one would love to stay uninvolved. But, as we have seen, in the nature of human communication noninvolvement is impossible. This then leads to specific evasive solutions, which we will call *disqualifications.* This term covers all those behaviors whose purpose it is to deprive one's own or the partner's statements of clear meaning, so that it cannot be nailed down to a specific meaning and one cannot be held responsible for it. Elsewhere [176, 184] we have described such maneuvers, as, for example, contradictions, inconsistencies, sudden topic changes, incomplete sentences, misun-

derstandings, unclear or idiosyncratic formulations, meaningless generalizations, switches of meaning from the literal to the metaphorical or vice versa, etc. The communications of many individuals diagnosed as schizophrenics exemplify these categories. When we observe their behavior, here and now, independently from traditional etiological conjectures, these people will appear trying *not* to communicate. But since even gibberish, muteness, immobility (bodily silence), and practically every other form of avoidance or negation of communication is very much itself communication, they face a practically unsolvable and theoretically infinite regression of negations. And again it is unnecessary to ask ourselves what psychic mechanisms and what causes in their earlier lives have determined this behavior; what is essential, from the pragmatic standpoint, is *that* this is the case and that such behavior must lead to this specific dilemma.

3. Another important characteristic of interpersonal reality grows from the unavoidable fact that every message has two aspects. To begin with, every communication (verbal or nonverbal) conveys information which constitutes its *content*. But beyond that it also has a metacommunicative aspect, i.e., it is a communication as to how the receiver is supposed to interpret it. This second aspect is sometimes reinforced by an additional remark, for example, "This is an order," or "I'm only kidding, of course." As these two examples show, metacommunication also defines at the same time the way in which the sender sees his relationship to the receiver; we therefore call it the *relationship* aspect. "This is an order" means obviously that the sender sees the receiver as a subordinate. Such express reinforcements are used only rarely; the relationship definition contained in every communication is usually sufficient. For example, the two statements: "It is important to change gear smoothly" and "Just

let the clutch go, it's very good for the transmission", mean practically the same thing, but they obviously define a very different relationship between driving instructor and learner.

Obviously, these two aspects of human communication are of incisive importance for the nature of relationships. Depending on whether, and on which of the two levels, agreement or disagreement exist, specific and clearly definable patterns and disturbances of relationship will ensue. To select only one of the possible variants:

Suppose the partners agree on the content level but not on the relationship level. This relationship will remain stable as long as outside necessities require this accord on the content level. As soon as this is no longer the case, the two people will no longer be able to ignore their so far latent relationship conflicts. Here we find those marriages which fall apart just when outside difficulties have been overcome, which until then had forced husband and wife to work together in a common effort. The same holds true for political or international coalitions between ideologically different parties or states, as for example the United States and the Soviet Union until their joint victory in 1945. And finally we must mention yet another factor that in this context is often very important for the maintenance of equilibrium in families: the scapegoat role of a child with problems (school failure, neurosis, psychosis, juvenile delinquency), which forces the parents to work together and gives their marriage a seeming stability that does not really exist. In clinical practice it can be seen again and again how an improvement in the behavior of the child is followed by a marital crisis of the parents and very often seems to force the child back into his old role.

4. As we have shown, every communication has both content and relationship aspects, but the latter is is by far the

more significant. We all know from experience that in daily life we exchange much less information than relationship definitions with those close to us (purely factual information as in business meetings at least partially excepted). This raises the question of the function of this communicative behavior. Developmental psychology, as well as modern experiments with sensory deprivation, have taught us that human beings cannot survive total lack of communication either physically or emotionally. The claim of the mysterious Kaspar Hauser,* that as far back as he could remember he had always been held alone in a dark dungeon, is simply unbelievable. In contrast, the description of an early psycholinguistic experiment sounds absolutely believable, although, or maybe just because, it goes so far beyond the phenomena of marasmus and hospitalism, as described by Spitz [168]. According to the chronicles of Brother Salimbene of Parma [150], Emperor Frederic II wanted to determine the original language of man by having several children raised from birth by nurses who had orders to take care of them in every way except to talk to them or to talk in their presence. In this way the emperor hoped to find out whether the children would spontaneously begin to speak Hebrew, Greek, or Latin. In spite of its excellent research design, the experiment unfortunately produced no positive results: "it was all in vain, for the little ones all died." According to Frey [53] Herodotus reported similar attempts in Egypt in the fifth century B.C.

Why communication is a life-or-death necessity for

---

*He surfaced in Nürnberg on March 26, 1828, with an anonymous letter of recommendation to the authorities. He declared that he was born in 1812 but except for remembering his confinement in darkness, he could give no explanation whatever about his past. He soon became the subject of many romantic theories, and the riddle became immortalized on December 14, 1833, when he came home with several stab wounds, supposedly inflicted by an unknown assailant, and died three days later.

human beings (and presumably to a certain degree all mammals) cannot be answered definitively at our present state of knowledge. But *that* we depend upon it is without question. When we analyze our everyday communicative behavior it becomes clear that it consists of a never-ending process of offering, accepting, rejecting, disqualifying, or redefining relationship definitions. Our own investigation confirms the results of many other researchers [e.g., 15, pp. 90–105; 79; 94; 97; 98; 105; 193], who found that acknowledgment of our interpersonal perceptions, i.e., the acceptance and confirmation of our relationship definitions by our partner, is essential for our mental health. To be understood by someone else means that the other person shares our own view of interpersonal reality and thus ratifies it, so to speak. In healthy, viable relationships, the partners seem to have come to a far-reaching, tacit agreement; while in "sick" relationships, those burdened with many conflicts, the partners struggle desperately against being subjected to the other's definition. Being defeated seems to be literally linked to mortal terror. The statements of schizophrenics that they are "empty," "puppets," or "robots" express this only too eloquently.

5. As we mentioned before, relationship definitions are neither true nor false but are at best shared more or less by the partners. This "more or less," however, has profound meaning. Typically we know much more about the pathological than the positive characteristics of human communication on the metacommunicative level, where, in Bateson's apt words, "reality is a matter of faith" [14, ch. 8]. Below, we shall try to divide these ego-disqualifying, pathogenic communication patterns into three groups, without regarding this division as exhaustive or claiming that there is a qualitative difference between these and "more normal" patterns of

communication. As everywhere else, there are only transitions, not sharply defined boundaries.

a) If partner B reacts to a message from A with a statement, which on the one hand confirms having received the information but on the other hand ignores its content as well as its relationship aspect, we speak of what Ruesch [149] has called a *tangentialization*. In one of his examples a child proudly shows his mother a worm he has just found. The mother looks at him and says in a cold, disapproving voice: "Go wash your hands." Considering only the dirty hands, she leaves her child's message hanging in the air, as it were, and introduces a new communication process which has no reference to that of the child. If the mother had said: "Yes, that's a beautiful worm," then had paused, she could have introduced the new message: "But now go and wash your hands."

A series of similar communication patterns, called *interpersonal disqualifications (transacciones descalificadoras)*, were described by an Argentine research team under Sluzki [161]. Their common denominator is a situation in which the statement of one partner is disqualified by the other's response, whose relationship aspect is ambiguous or unclear and which stands in contradiction to the content of the statement or the context in which the communication process is taking place. These disqualifications can produce laughter or fury, but more probably confusion, because partner A is not clear whether B agrees with the content of his statement, whether he rejects it, resents it, makes fun of it, or knew about it already. In one of the examples a son complains: "You treat me like a child," and the mother answers: "But you *are* my child." Such an answer can have a positively paralyzing effect, for it virtually amounts to an example of Erickson's "confusion technique" in hypnosis [47, pp. 183–

207]. In order to overcome the effect of this disqualification and get the conversation halfway back on the firm ground of logic, the son would have to undertake a not uncomplicated, metacommunicative explanation and point out that he used the word "child" in the sense of "immaturity," whereas his mother used it in the sense of "son." The son, especially if he is a so-called patient, might have great difficulties with this correction, while it would be easy for the mother to interpret his reaction as further proof of insanity and ignore it lovingly. A similar example from our own research is that of a mother whose psychotic son suddenly started shooting a gun in their apartment. When asked what she had done in this dangerous situation, she answered: "I told him for the hundredth time not to play *in* the house."

   b) In the second group, the *mystifications*, the contradiction lies not between message and answer but rather between the message and the context in which the communication process is taking place. In its most abstract form *mystification* signifies: "What you see (or think, hear, feel) is wrong. *I* will tell you what is real (or what you should see, hear, or feel)." This will have little effect on people who have learned to trust their own perceptions. In vital relationships, however (especially between child and parents), or in extreme situations (as in political persecution or brainwashing), mystification can put the receiver into an untenable position. For if he cannot, or may not, demystify the situation by suitable metacommunication, he is caught in a hopeless predicament, for this trap can be made virtually inescapable by extending the mystification to cover his perception of the mystification itself. As the psychiatrist Laing [95, pp. 343–363], who introduced this concept into psychopathology, puts it, "Every mystified person is, by definition, confused; which does not also mean that he must *feel* confused."

In their investigations at the Mayo Clinic, Johnson et al.
[79, pp. 143–148] found practically the same communication
structure in the families of schizophrenic patients:

> When these children perceived the anger and hostil-
> ity of a parent, as they did on many occasions, immedi-
> ately the parent would deny that he was angry and
> would insist that the child deny it too, so that the child
> was faced with the dilemma of whether to believe the
> parent or his own senses. If he believed his senses he
> maintained a firm grasp on reality; if he believed the
> parent, he maintained the needed relationship, but dis-
> torted his perception of reality.

In other words, the parents' statements put the child in a
predicament by creating an unsolvable dilemma between
the content and the relationship aspect of their communications.

In a similar context, one of Laing's examples [95] illustrates the case of a mother's attempted (but rejected) mystification of her schizophrenic daughter, which leaves the
girl the choice between insanity and ill will:

MOTHER: I don't blame you for talking that way. I
            know that you don't really mean it.

DAUGHTER: But I do mean it.

MOTHER: Now dear, I know you don't, you can't help
            yourself.

DAUGHTER: I can help myself.

MOTHER: Now dear, I know you can't because you're
            ill. If I thought for a moment you weren't ill,
            I would be furious with you.

An important variation of this theme arises when A defines his relationship to B first in one specific way and then,

as soon as B has accepted this definition, he suddenly changes it and accuses B of madness or badness because he has not seen their relationship in this light from the beginning. As soon as B submits to the second definition, A can then condemn him for not having accepted the original relationship definition. Processes like these were first described by Searles [157, pp. 1–18]. He mentions six variants, which he has observed frequently in his work with schizophrenics, their parents or spouses, and occasionally even their psychotherapists. For example, A may discuss one and the same topic first in a humorous and then in a deadly serious manner, and then reproach B either for having no sense of humor or for not showing the necessary seriousness. In a similar way A can behave in a sexually provocative way in a situation which precludes sexual advances and then accuse the other, depending on his reaction, of being either inhibited or shameless.

c) Finally there is a form of communication which contains its own contradiction. Basically it resembles the classical *paradoxes* of logic. Wittgenstein [191, p. 179] was probably the first to point out the pragmatic significance of paradox: "The various half-joking guises of logical paradox are only of interest in so far as they remind anyone of the fact that a serious form of the paradox is indispensable if we are to understand its function properly. The question arises: what part can such a logical mistake play in a language game?"

Let us analyze first the classical paradox of the liar, i.e., his assertion "I am lying" (a simplified version of the famous self-definition of Epimenides, the Cretan, who was supposed to have said that all Cretans were liars). This sentence has an unusual structure, because on the one hand it makes a statement ("I am lying"), and on the other it makes a statement about its own statement, that is, "I am lying, and therefore I am also lying when I say 'I am lying.' " It now becomes clear that an injunction of identical structure can only be followed by not being followed or that, when a relationship is defined in such a paradoxical way, it can only be in compliance with the definition when it is not in compliance and vice versa—and thus there are no limits to the confusion of interpersonal reality. Unfortunately the complex nature of these patterns makes it impossible to present detailed descriptions, but at least its most frequent appearance shall be mentioned briefly, namely the so-called Be spontaneous! paradox. It is a request for behavior that by its very nature can only be engaged in spontaneously, but is now impossible, precisely because it has been demanded. The receiver is thereby put into an untenable situation; he is supposed to do something spontaneously which is *demanded* of him and this is impossible both in formal logic as well in the nature of human communication.

An example of this paradox is a frequently observed situation in marriage where the wife is dissatisfied with the passivity and lack of initiative of her husband and demands in one form or another: "I wish you would be more aggressive." Seen superficially this may seem an understandable request, but in reality this demand puts both into an untenable position. Only two alternatives are open to them now, and both are unsatisfactory. If he remains passive she will, of course, be dissatisfied; but if he begins to be more active it will not make her happy either because he is only doing what he was told, instead of doing it on his own initiative. He may act the way she wants him to, but this should have come about "spontaneously" and not because she demanded it. In other words, he is doing the right thing for the wrong reason.

The following is a somewhat different example of inter-personal paradox: A marriage is threatening to fail because of the unreasonable jealousy of the wife. Oddly enough the husband is excessively rigid, moralistic, and ascetic—from a monadic standpoint as unlikely an object of jealousy as one could imagine. Especially important to him is his often re-peated claim that throughout his life he has never given any-one reason to doubt his word. His wife, clearly a much more relaxed and lighthearted person, seems to have resigned her-self to his attitude with one exception: She is not prepared to give up her (very moderate) enjoyment of alcohol, which, from the beginning of their long marriage, has caused much discord between them. About two years ago the husband threatened in a fury that if she did not give up this vice he would acquire one of his own and implied that he meant affairs with other women. Since the hoped-for deterrent ef-fects failed to materialize, he decided a few months later to officially sanction her cocktails. It was at this point that her jealousy broke out because, as she saw it, he was absolutely trustworthy and therefore *must* have followed through with his threat and become untrustworthy, i.e., unfaithful.

Paradoxical communications were first studied in the fif-ties by the research team under Bateson, who called them *double binds*. The results of this work were published in 1956 in a paper entitled "Toward a Theory of Schizophrenia" [18, pp. 251–264]. In their most abstract form double binds are composed of the following:

1. a complementary relationship (as, for example, between parents and child);
2. a self-referential statement, i.e., one that denies what it states and states what it denies;
3. a situation that cannot be avoided, coupled with the in-ability or impossibility of solving the paradox by meta-communication.

Since the above exemplifications of pathogenic communication patterns are extremely sketchy and anecdotal, and in order to avoid misunderstanding, it is especially important to remember that they are not "one-way streets" but vicious circles in which all partners are caught. Depending on how the participants "punctuate" the sequence of their interaction (or how this sequence arises out of the fundamentally monadic and not interactional nature of human language), the illusion of a beginning is created, which of course does not exist in a circle. Each one of the patterns described not only *causes* a certain reaction in the partner, but then helps to perpetuate the pattern. As the last two examples show, once a paradoxical statement has been made, it is difficult if not impossible to undo its pragmatic effect, and therefore *both* partners are caught in the predicament.

Pathogenic Communication Patterns

Every attempt to influence pathogenic and pathological relationship systems comes up against the stubborn inertia of these structures, which seem to resist all reason and have, in monadic thinking, given rise to hypotheses of sadomasochistic tendencies or manifestations of a death wish. Why are so many relationships maintained even though the partners are deeply unhappy and dissatisfied, and why do they not only not break up the relationship but ensure their continuation by constant painful adaptations? Again we ask "why?" and our thinking is almost unavoidably directed into the monadic, individual past. Two modern views, however, contradict this way of conceptualizing. Bertalanffy [23, pp. 1–20] postulated the concept of *equifinality* as one of the typical characteristics of open systems (i.e., those which are in constant interrelation with their environment). By this he means that in these systems, very different initial conditions or beginning states can lead to the same results. In our experience with human relationship systems, this seems to imply the opposite as well: identical initial conditions can result in very different final conditions. (We are aware that this hypothesis throws doubt on the value of many psychological long-term and comparison studies, standardizations, calibrations, etc.). The other conclusion is that of Jackson [75, pp. 79–90], who extends the concept of *homeostasis* to human relationship systems. Accordingly, a system, once it is constituted, maintains its stability with the help of regulation processes which are isomorphic with the homeostatic processes in physiology studied by Claude Bernard, Cannon, and many others. These systems are autonomous and have their own regularities and therefore need no longer stand in a causally determined relation with their conditions of origin.

As we have emphasized before, from this point of view it is wasted effort to try to find out when, why, and how any of these processes were introduced into the system; what is essential for basic research as well as for exerting a practical effect on such a system is that its behavior, seen purely empirically, seems to be rule-governed and that any change of these hypothetical rules causes reactions which are system-specific and can, after sufficient observation, be predicted. As far as these rules are concerned it appears that well-functioning systems distinguish themselves by greater flexibility and a greater repertoire of rules, while "sick" or conflict-ridden systems have few and rigid rules. This empirical fact is not necessarily contradicted by the often chaotic surface manifestations of these systems.

In addition to this basic difference, these systems lack another important quality which seems to be inherent in the structure of viable ones: pathological systems do not have adequate meta-rules, i.e., rules for *changing* their rules. This implies that such a system will be unable to cope with a situation for which its rules (its behavior repertoire) are inadequate, while at the same time it is incapable either of generating new rules or of changing the existing rules in such a way that the problem can be solved. Instead it will become trapped in a *circulus vitiosus,* a Game without End. This phenomenon reveals another general system quality which is by no means restricted to human systems. It can be observed in analogous forms as the so-called halting problem in mathematical decision procedures, when a computer is expected to calculate a value which is outside the domain of its program. Typically the computer will then run through all possible solution searches again and again without getting anywhere and without ever reporting that the problem is not solvable [40, p. 10]. It is the latter aspect of this phenomenon which seems most significant to us. Analogous problems appear in international relations, as is shown in Osgood's example [129, pp. 155–228]:

> Our political and military leaders have been virtually unanimous in public assertions that we must go ahead and stay ahead in the armament race; they have been equally unanimous in saying nothing about what happens then. Suppose we achieve the state of ideal mutual deterrence . . . what then? Surely no sane man can envisage our planet spinning on into eternity, divided into two armed camps poised to destroy each other, and call it peace and security! The point is that the policy of mutual deterrence *includes no provisions for its own resolution.*

There is reason to hope that communication research will sooner or later open new ways for the researcher to understand these Games without End in human systems. We will mention only three hypotheses with regard to the occurrence of certain mystifications, disqualifications, and double binds in families. Greatly, perhaps excessively, simplifying, and again inevitably proceeding as if a specific starting point existed, we postulate these hypotheses:

1. If someone is reprimanded for his *perception* of reality or of himself by significant others (usually a child by his parents), he will tend to mistrust his own senses. Once this uncertainty has been created, he can then be told to try harder, to see things the way they "really" are, which sooner or later leads to the imputation: "You must be crazy to to see the world in this way." Consequently it will become increasingly difficult for him to orient himself in impersonal as well as interpersonal contexts, and he will tend to search fruitlessly for those significances which seem so perfectly clear to others but not to him. From a monadic point of view and disregarding the pragmatic situation, his behavior will correspond to the clinical picture of schizophrenia.

2. If someone is reprimanded by important others for having *feelings* which he should *not* have (or, conversely, for not having certain feelings which he *should* have), he will eventually feel guilty for his inability to have the "right" feelings which would make him acceptable to the others. This guilt feeling can then in turn be labeled as one of those feelings he should not have. A dilemma of this kind often results when parents interpret the occasional normal sadness (or crankiness, or tiredness) of the child as unspoken criticism of their parental value. The parents will then tend to dispute the child's right to these moods by saying things like: "After all we have done for you, and all the sacrifices we have made for you, you ought to be happy and content." Sadness is thereby associated with ingratitude and badness.

In his unsuccessful attempts to feel what he "should" feel, the child will display behavior patterns which correspond, from the monadic standpoint, and again disregarding the pragmatic situation, to the clinical definition of depression. Depression seems to arise in a similar way when someone is made responsible for something over which he has no control (for example, his parents' marital disagreements, the illness or failure of a family member, or parental expectations which exceed the physical, intellectual, or emotional capabilities of the child).

3. If someone is instructed by important others to behave in ways which require *actions* that are both demanded as well as prohibited, he is put into the paradoxical situation in which he can only obey by disobeying. The prototype of such a demand is: "Do what I tell you, not what I want you to do." An example would be parents who want their son to respect law and order and be a dare-devil at the same time. Another example would be parents who place such importance on making money by any means, fair or foul, but at the same time impress on the child that one must always be honest. Similarly, a mother may begin to warn her daughter at an unusually early age of the dangers and ugliness of sex, but insist on the need to be "popular" with boys. From the monadic point of view, and disregarding the pragmatic situation, the resulting behavior corresponds to the social definition of delinquency or social deviance.

These hypotheses are an attempt to apply pragmatic perspectives to clinical nosology. But even this attempt is questionable because, very likely, an improved understanding of relationship phenomena will eventually require a revision of relationship disorders and their therapy from first principles. The mere fact that in this essay we ourselves are con-

stantly forced to use monadic terms, such as psychpa-
thology, schizophrenia, and neurosis, shows that we have a
long way to go before we will reach this revision.

Conclusions Concerning Behavior Modification

With this we come to what may be the most fascinating aspect of the pragmatics of human relations: the question of
behavior modification. If it is true that a system is pathological to the extent that it cannot generate rules for changing
its rules, then it is obvious that the task of effective therapy
is to introduce these rules into the system from the outside.
When the members of such a system enter into communication with an outsider who is not caught in their Game
without End, this expanded system can, from the outside so
to speak, gain a perspective of its original structure and can
effect a change. For what makes this Game without End
into a vicious circle is its inability to see from the inside the
alternatives not contained within it. Again it appears to
have been Wittgenstein [191, p. 100] who first described this
situation, although in an entirely different context:

> Let us suppose, . . . that the game is such that who-
> ever begins can always win by a particular simple trick.
> But this has not been realized;—so it is a game. Now
> someone draws our attention to it;—and it stops being
> a game. . . .
> That means, . . . the other man did not *draw our
> attention* to anything; he taught us a different game in
> place of our own.—But how can the new game have
> made the old one obsolete?—We now see something
> different, and can no longer naively go on playing.

Wittgenstein obviously does not deal with questions of behavior modification, but what he mentions in the second paragraph of the quote is of immediate significance for our considerations. The other person did not draw our attention to anything but instead taught us a different game in place of our own—and now we can no longer naively go on playing the old one. No matter how different the classical schools of psychotherapy may be from each other, they have one thing in common: the therapeutic effect which they attribute to interpretation, confrontation, and explanation—in short to the drawing attention in the sense of the above quotation—and to the *insight* which supposedly follows. There is, however, no practical proof for this cornerstone of all psychodynamic theories of human behavior—it is a dogma and therefore a part of a *theory* of man, but not of human nature itself.

From a pragmatic point of view, as mentioned before, two things are questionable: the attribution of importance to the causal connection between certain factors in the past (pathogenesis) and certain other ones in the present (symptomatics); and the insistence on the need to become aware of this connection (insight) as a prerequisite for change. In everyday life insight is rarely the companion, let alone the precursor of change and maturation. At best, we may suddenly realize with hindsight that half a year ago in a particular situation we would have reacted quite differently. On the other hand, one frequently encounters people who, after lengthy psychotherapy, have every conceivable insight without in the least profiting from it. Of course, one could always argue that these people have not yet gained the right insight and are still in need of further analysis. The fundamentally different way in which changes of interpersonal realities can take place spontaneously is illustrated in the following example, which has recently come to our attention:

On her first day in nursery school, a four-year-old girl began crying so desperately when her mother tried to leave that the latter had no choice but to stay with the child. The same problem repeated itself the next and all following mornings. The mother could not leave, and the situation became not only a problem of time but also an emotional burden. After about two months, and before the school psychologist had an opportunity to look into the case, it was the father who, for reasons unknown to us, brought the girl to school one morning and then took off for work. The child did cry for a while but soon quieted down. On the next day the mother brought the child to school and to her great surprise there was no scene, as on the previous day, and this is how things stayed.

One could engage in all kinds of speculations about the simplicity of this spontaneous solution. What seems to matter, however, is that this system needed only a very small and apparently completely accidental change of its "rules." One could argue, after the fact, that we here are "obviously" not dealing with a severe, profound disorder. But there is no question that the case would have run a very different course if the apparatus provided for these problems had been put into action. The case would have been diagnosed as a "school phobia," and depending on the scientific orientation of the therapist the pregenital fixation of the child, the neurotic needs of the mother to maintain her daughter in dependency, or some other intrapsychic monadic aspects would have become the subject of extensive and iatrogenic analyses. In all probability nobody would have come up with the simple idea of having the father bring the girl to school, because this measure does not appear to explain the causes of an already clearly diagnosed psychic developmental disorder.

Pragmatic behavior modifications have as their goal, in Wittgenstein's sense, "to teach a different game" instead of the old one. If new behavioral rules are introduced into human relationships systems, behavioral changes become possible, which, in monadic thinking, would have required insight. Of course, these interventions are complex measures and not only statements of desired change, like "be nice to each other." This subject, too, can only be touched on briefly in the context of this presentation. Of the many possible interventions, paradoxes offer themselves as the most typical examples. They are the most effective techniques we know. In their structure they are mirror images of pathogenic double binds. In principle, in each therapeutic double bind, the behavior which the patient wishes to change is "prescribed." Since we are dealing with symptomatic behavior and since every symptom may be considered spontaneous, i.e., uncontrollable behavior, these so-called *symptom prescriptions* are full-fledged "Be spontaneous!" paradoxes. In other words, a therapeutic double bind consists of (a) prescribing the (spontaneous, symptomatic) behavior, which is to be changed, (b) depicting this behavior prescription as a means of change, and (c) creating a paradox because the patient is required to be spontaneous on command. If, for example, contrary to all "common sense," one would tell a married couple locked into a pattern of continuous bickering to start a deliberate fight at eight o'clock each evening in addition to their daily arguments, the partners would probably not only be unable to pick this fight but would find it much more difficult to argue at all. Intuitive therapists have used and described such interventions for a long time, for example, Frankl [51] as paradoxical intentions, Rosen [145] under the title "Repetition of the Psychosis," and Jackson [76, pp. 306–307].

Our world of relationships is interlaced with paradoxes. For example, the stability of a relationship becomes considerably more secure when the partners realistically discuss the possibility of separating. On the other hand, most lovers who feel that they cannot live without each other cannot live with each other either. The husband whose wife is constantly threatening to kill herself can help her and their marriage much more if he asks her calmly and in detail about her wishes for her funeral rather than increasing her depression by his panic.

We even know about a spontaneous remission of an agoraphobia which happened when the patient imposed a double bind on *himself* and thereby managed to escape the vicious circle of his symptomatic Game without End:

During the course of several years the neurosis of this man had become an increasingly unbearable burden. Every attempt to counteract the constant shrinking of his anxiety-free territory only increased his panic. One day, in desperation, he decided to commit suicide and decided to drive to a mountaintop some thirty miles away—convinced that, as he moved farther and farther away from his home, a stroke or a heart attack would put an end to his misery. To his indescribable amazement he not only arrived safely at the top of the mountain but felt, for the first time in many years, completely free of anxiety. In the last six years his phobia has not returned, nor has it been replaced by any other symptoms. Using this same method, he even succeeded (as confirmed by the psychiatrist with whom he collaborated) in helping several other patients with severe phobias. (The reader who is familiar with Zen literature will recognize the similarity between this example and the teaching that enlightenment comes only after the seeker has ceased all efforts to attain it.)

Outlook on Further Developments in Communication Research

We are convinced that in the coming years an increasing interest in the phenomena of relationships will encourage further study and new, fruitful, and interdisciplinary perspectives. The ideal goal would, of course, be a comprehensive systematization of pragmatics, so that a grammar or calculus of human relationships could be formulated. This may seem a utopian goal, especially if one considers that the investigation of the syntax of a natural language already presents great difficulties, while the hope of a systematization of semantics meets with increasing skepticism. How much more unrealistic therefore the hope to reach this goal in the even more complex area of pragmatics! We believe that success or failure will depend on the solution of two fundamental problems. The first concerns nonverbal communication, whose analysis will require much more difficult and costly methods than that of the purely verbal one. The second problem has to do with the lack of a language to express and describe metacommunicative phenomena. Whereas mathematicians have numbers and algebraic symbols with which they can express mathematical propositions (equations, formulas, etc.), and while they can use natural languages to express metamathematical statements, we have only *one* language for communication as well as for metacommunication. This difficulty is more incisive than this brief remark might lead one to believe. We can furthermore expect that the problem of unresolvability in Gödel's sense [67] will become increasingly incisive. Gödel has demonstrated that no formal system, at least as complex as arithmetic, can prove its own completeness and logical consistency without making use of concepts which are more general than the system itself and therefore are no longer part of the system. The result is a theoretically infinite regress.

But even if these difficulties should prove to be insurmountable, we can assume that partial solutions will bring fruitful results. The present chapter is an attempt to illustrate the application of pragmatic principles to the goal of understanding and modifying human relationships. This does not mean, however, that they are limited to those areas. Rather, these principles should be understood as systems characteristics, valid in other relationship systems as well. The modern discipline known either as conflict resolution or peace research is largely based on similar suppositions. And perhaps it is not overly optimistic to assume that pragmatics will open up new views of the nature of the reality which surrounds us and of our position in this reality.

C H A P T E R
2

Psychiatry's Changing Image
of Man

The transition from the monadic, introspective, retrospective, and intrapsychic basis of the classical schools of therapy to a systemic view also creates a new image of man. In Chapter 2 an attempt is made to show how this transition runs parallel to the historical expansion of the scientific view of the world, which, proceeding from classical antiquity's concept of static matter, *was tremendously enriched by the inclusion of the concept of* energy, *and has lately acquired new, additional dimensions through the* introduction *of the concept of* information.

•

In a textbook published in 1911 the author, one of the outstanding representatives of European psychiatry in this century, quotes the letter of a schizophrenic to his mother:

Dear Mother: Today I am feeling better than yesterday. I really don't feel much like writing. But I love to write to you. After all, I can tackle it twice. Yesterday,

Sunday, I would have been so happy if you and Louise and I could have gone to the park. One has such a lovely view from Stephan's Castle. Actually, it is very lovely in Burghölzli. Louise wrote Burghölzli on her two last letters, I mean to say on the envelopes, no, the "couverts" which I received. However, I have written Burghölzli in the spot where I put the date. There are also patients in Burghölzli who call it "Hölzliburg." Others talk of a factory. One may also regard it as a health-resort. . . . All people have eyes. There are some, too, who are blind. These blind people are led about by a boy. It must be very terrible not to be able to see. There are people who can't see and, in addition, can't hear. I know some who hear too much. One can hear too much. There are many sick people in Burghölzli; they are patients. One of them I like a great deal. His name is E. Sch. He taught me that in Burghölzli there are many kinds, patients, inmates, attendants. Then there are some who are not here at all. They are all peculiar people.

The author of the textbook, Professor Eugen Bleuler, comments:

A non-schizophrenic informant would tell us what in his immediate environment affected him; what may have made him feel comfortable or uncomfortable; or, perhaps, something that might interest the reader. There is complete absence of any such purpose here. The common denominator of all of the patient's ideas rests in the fact that they are present in his awareness, but not because they have any close relation to him. . . . Although nearly all the ideas expressed are correct, nevertheless the letter is meaningless. The patient has the goal of writing, but nothing to write about. [24, p. 17]

Seventy years ago, these conclusions were compelling and convincing: the letter is the expression of a deranged mind. Nowadays it is difficult for us—laymen or professionals—to interpret the meaning of the letter in this way. A change has occurred in our thinking, and we are much more inclined to see clues in this letter, innuendoes, which deal with the *relationship* between the writer and his mother and, in a broader sense, his fellow man, and with the institutional milieu. The following quotation, from a book published in 1970, makes this change even more obvious:

There must be something the matter with him
    because he would not be acting as he does unless there
        was
    therefore he is acting as he is
    because there is something the matter with him.

He does not think there is anything the matter with him
because
    one of the things that is
    the matter with him
    is that he does not think that there is anything
    the matter with him
therefore
    we have to help him realize that,
    the fact that he does not think there is anything
    the matter with him
    is one of the things that is
    the matter with him

This is a quotation from the aphoristic book *Knots* by the London psychiatrist Ronald Laing [96, p. 5], which—with tongue in cheek—one could also call a textbook of psychiatry. His frame of reference, however, is quite different. He does not deal with the manifestations of a disturbed mind but rather with a disturbed relationship, or, more precisely, with one's own assumptions about the assumptions of someone else. These assumptions are, however, mere constructions and not ascertainable facts, much less platonic truths. The way a relationship is experienced by the relationship partners defies all objective verification. What can be verified, however, is the degree of harmony between the partners, which grows from a more or less concurring definition of their relationship, or the *folie à deux*, if it deviates too far from the way others define the relationship, or the severe conflicts which arise from the partners' disagreement about the definition of their relationship.

In these few sentences much has been touched upon which must be further documented if we are to do justice to the subject of this talk.

It is well known that for thousands of years psychiatry's image of man was dominated by religious, magic, demonic, or superstitious conceptions. We will not discuss these ancient concepts here, even though it might be tempting for the chronicler, familiar with the subject matter, to point out those undeniable though embarrassing parallels between certain "treatment" methods practiced in those dark ages and certain therapeutic techniques still applied in our day.

The Age of Enlightenment, with its search for objective reasons, brings about an important change also in the way mental disturbances are conceptualized. Instead of demons, *déesse raison* now reigns and sets the tone in scientific circles. The installation of reason as the highest authority is logically followed by the wish to objectivize natural phenomena, i.e., to rid the scientific view of the world of unprovable dogmas, prejudices, assumptions, myths, and so forth. The first step in establishing an objective order in the kaleidoscopic complexity of nature consisted in finding commonalities, similarities, and linking elements, to divide the objects of observation into groups and subgroups, and to name these groupings—in a word, to classify them. For this purpose things were categorized according to the nature of their physical properties. At the risk of oversimplifying, one could say perhaps even that *matter* (in the classical sense) became the object of research—at least with respect to the above-mentioned properties and their appearances.

Like any other discipline, psychiatry relies on the epistemology considered valid at any given time. It is remarkable, however, that it never manages to be at the cutting edge of progress, but tends to cling to outdated paradigms, long after other disciplines have abandoned them. Whatever the reasons for this might be, we find, *grosso modo*, that psychiatry's image of man bases itself at first on the concept of predisposition: We are endowed by nature with certain characteristics that gradually take shape and develop in the course of our lives. Although *matter* can only be spoken of metaphorically in this context, we are nevertheless dealing with material properties, such as one's constitution. To understand people in their suchness, physiognomy is practiced—a system of classification which probably goes back to Aristotle and in the eighteenth and nineteenth centuries was linked with names like Lavater and Carus. At the beginning of the nineteenth century Gall and his disciple Spurzheim developed a method, called phrenology, which deduces the genetic characteristics and therefore also the character of a person from the shape of his skull, especially its irregularities, and from them attempts to draw conclusions regarding the underlying areas of the brain. Somewhat

later, Lombroso spoke about the *reo nato,* the criminal born
with an organic inferiority, a human being whose behavior
is determined once and for all, like the color of his eyes.

While the image of man was still sought in such static
properties, other disciplines had long abandoned this mat-
ter-oriented viewpoint. The decisive change, whose roots,
however, also reach back into antiquity, occurred through
the introduction of the concept of *energy.* This development, culminating in the first law of thermodynamics, was
responsible for the breathtaking progress of technology in
the last three centuries. In the interaction of matter and energy, of material states and their dynamic exchanges, new
categories of understanding were created which had not
been available to a world-view based on the static properties
of matter. With Freud—disregarding for brevity's sake his
important predecessors—the concept of energy also enters
into psychiatry. Emotional states are now seen as dynamic
processes. Like the physicist, the physician of the mind begins to think in terms of an albeit hypothetic, metaphorical
energy, the *libido.* Freud speaks of a *libidinal quantum,*
postulating that mental energy is available in a certain fixed
quantity, but can undergo transformations of its manifestations. It is no accident that one of Jung's most important
works from this epoch is *Transformations and Symbols of
Libido.* Hydraulics plays godfather to the psychoanalytical
model: libido acts somewhat like a viscous fluid, which never
quite detaches itself from positions once reached, but which
can be be dammed up or diverted by obstacles from its
strictly determined path. An obstacle may regressively re-
vive tributary branches which had earlier been largely abandoned; but it may also, by way of sublimation, activate possibilities of flow at higher levels. The metaphor has
unprecedented heuristic value. It makes possible an image of
mental functioning that deepens our understanding of the

causes of human behavior and suggests previously unknown therapeutic possibilities. Man turns out to be deeper, more complex, but also more torn and predetermined than anyone had dared to imagine. The sublunar world of madness and dreams is illuminated and given a scientific explanation.

But like every metaphor, psychodynamics also has it limits. The image of causally determined man, pushed by his instincts, (to which Jung juxtaposes his image of the individual as pulled forward by finality) proves to be unsatisfactory exactly at the point where the very epistemology on which psychoanalysis is based begins to reach the limits of its heuristic usefulness. Such issues are, for example, the undeniable fact that from lower forms of organization and function there can arise higher complexities. There is a contradiction here somewhere, a need for additional principles of explanation, which the world-view of classical science cannot provide. Bergson attempts an explanation by postulating the workings of an *élan vital;* Jung reaches back to the old idea of entelechy. Even more tempting is the return to the postulate of the workings of a higher principle of order, itself not subject to its own laws of cause and effect—just as the omnipotence of God is not really disproved by that touching old scholastic dilemma, although he cannot create that fateful rock that is so big that He Himself cannot lift it.

And yet, the answer was not only already known but had even been put into practice a long time ago, albeit in a context that apparently had nothing to do with our image of man. When in the eighteenth century, James Watt was working on his plans for the steam engine, it was pointed out to him that the idea was impracticable. According to the strictly linear causal thinking of his time, an authority outside the machine, a *spiritus rector* as it were, would have had to control the steam supply. To put it into more prosaic terms: for the machine to function it appeared necessary to have an operator who at the right moment would close one of the two valves and open the other in order to bring about the back-and-forth-movement of the piston. Watt, of course, solved the problem by using the movement of the piston *itself*, which opens and closes the steam inlets and exhausts by means of a slide valve. Today this solution seems obvious, as it is only a very early application of the now routine principle of self-regulation, namely, the feedback of an effect to its own cause in the form of a circular causality. But to the strictly deterministic, linear-causal thinking of that time it seemed inconceivable that an effect could influence its own cause and thereby create a mechanism whose behavior strikes one as "intelligent." An even more surprising application of the principle was Watt's invention of the governor, a device which keeps the revolutions and the output of the machine constant even when the load varies.

After the Second World War, when the results of secret wartime research became public knowledge, it turned out that the development of new weapons systems had led to even greater changes in the scientific view of the world. Although we may hope that war is not the father of *all* things, in this case the impetus came from purely military objectives. Examples are the development of firing predictors to shoot down high- and fast-flying planes, or the necessity to equip tanks with a gun whose carriage can compensate for the random movements of the vehicle on uneven terrain, so that it can aim and fire at targets even while the tank is moving at high speeds. Here energy is no longer the problem; it is available to these complex systems wherever necessary. Here, as with the governor of the steam engine, a completely new principle comes into play. Again, feedback of an effect upon its own cause is established, or, more precisely, a small part of the effect of an event is fed back on the event itself—not as a plus or minus of energy, but rather as a signal, as *information*. This new principle expanded the classical scientific image of the world as composed of matter and energy by a third, independent principle. Greatly simplifying again, it can be said that the electronic revolution, the development of cybernetics and of systems theory, as well as the exploration of human communication, began with the inclusion of this principle.

As mentioned earlier, psychiatry follows the scientific paradigms of its time at a respectful distance. However, in our field the beginnings of their practical application have been with us for quite some time.

In child psychiatry it has been recognized for several decades not only that the behavior of a mentally disturbed child presents severe problems for his parents and therefore affects the whole family, but also that the behavior of the parents has an undeniable, obvious influence on the degree of the child's disturbance. This insight was at least partly due to the fact that in the frame of outpatient treatments, the mother brings the little patient to the clinic, waits for him, and takes him home again. Much more than with adult patients this gives the doctor the almost accidental opportunity to observe the interaction between mother and child and to witness that disturbed behaviors are often triggered by the mother and not the child. Taking into consideration the extreme asymmetry of the mother-child relationship, a relationship in which the child is almost totally dependent on the mother, this observation led to the apparently logical definition of the mother as the cause of all the child's problems. A new vantage point seemed to have been won—in reality, however, only the direction of the causal sequences had been turned around; the positions of cause and effect had simply been reversed.

The view of causality underlying this new conceptualization had remained the same, as is true of antipsychiatry's image of man, which caused such a furor in the sixties. Here, too, cause was considered effect and effect became cause. Before, the patient had been considered crazy and society innocent and normal; now society and the family were regarded as the prime evil and the so-called patient as the only normal being in a sick and pathogenic environment. Again, the basic paradigm had not changed; only the attribution of guilt had been reversed.

The inclusion of the concept of information, however, brought about a significant change. The new conceptualizations which had already gained a foothold in other disciplines were too obvious to be ignored. The view of the human monad, the individual, as the measure of all things, and along with this the idea that all human mental disorders were of a purely intrapsychic nature, became more and more untenable. Even if a disorder originated purely from psychodynamic processes, its effects would nonetheless be interpersonal, i.e., it could only be ascertained from the behavior of that person. For how does the diagnostician arrive at his diagnosis? Only by observing behavior, which of course includes verbal communication, i.e., dreams, free associations, and even apparently objective test results such as the Rorschach, the TAT, intelligence tests, and so on.* In classical psychiatry, however, a person's behavior, although

---

*A reported dream, for example, is not simply the report of a dream. Rather, it is the report of a dream by a person who knows that he is supposed to report dreams to his psychiatrist. He also knows, or at least assumes, that certain dreams are somehow considered positive, others negative, that the psychiatrist will react to them in one way or another, and that he, the dreamer, will have to react to this reaction, etc., etc. This phenomenon was well known to Freud; he called these dreams *Gefälligkeitsträume* (hypocritical dreams). Something very similar holds true for projective tests, which for a long time were considered the instruments through which the inner world projected itself to the outside. More recent investigations (e.g. Rosenthal [148] and Mischel [117]) prove that a person's responses are greatly influenced by interhuman factors in the test situation and that the attitudes, expectations, and prejudices of the person administering the test can only too easily turn into self-fulfilling prophecies.

admittedly the basis and the starting point of all exploration, is nevertheless considered no more than the surface manifestation of inner states. That which is to be explained thus suddenly becomes its own explanation. This brings to mind Plato's analogy of the people sitting in a cave with their backs to its entrance and trying to understand what is going on outside by watching the shadows projected onto the back wall of the cave. The reason why the psychiatrist, as observer of these shadow plays, does not take the fairly obvious step of turning around and leaving the cave, instead of speculating about shadowy states of mind, lies in his view of the individual as his ultimate object of study and as a monad, independent of his or her environment. The idea of the individual human being as the measure of all things makes this kind of epistemological acrobatics inevitable. Where, if not within the human being, can the human be found?

But with the apparently self-evident logic of inside and outside we enter new territory. What is man's physical boundary? Is he demarcated by his skin? To use one of Bateson's [14] analogies: Is the tip of a blind man's cane his connection with the outside world, or is it the handle in his hand? Or is it halfway between the two ends of the cane? Does the hammer of the hammering cobbler belong to his inner or to his outer world? These simple examples shed light on the questionable nature of our concept of the individual and his psychic processes. The blind man's spatial orientation must incorporate the space around him, as well as his cane, as the link between himself and that space. Not even this simple process can be explained by the concepts of the monadic human image. Instead, we are dealing with a circular process of information, consisting of the blind man, the cane, the sidewalk, the feedback of the various tappings of the cane, and presumably numerous other elements. No single one of these elements and processes has prime importance; they are all equally indispensable. Together they form a circuit through which information passes continuously, and in which the smallest quantitative or qualitative change at any one point is immediately passed on to all other points of the circuit, changing their function. Modern science considers these circuits to be the smallest indivisible units. If one tried to divide them further into "simpler" components, one would have to attribute properties to these components which they do not possess.

It cannot be emphasized enough, however, that phenomena which, at least in the vocabulary of our standard language, are given definite mental or intelligent properties require no participation of man, nor that of a supposed *spiritus rector*. Everything which in earlier times was believed to be purpose and resolve breathed into dull matter by God can now be explained as a necessary consequence of certain systemic processes in nature. Norbert Wiener gave this theoretical orientation and its technical applications the name "cybernetics." The following example convinces by virtue of its triviality: Everyone is familiar with the heating regulator (thermostat) in the modern house. In terms of modern electronics, this is a device of the most banal simplicity. The thermostat measures the temperature in the house; if it exceeds the desired degree, the heat is turned off; if it gets below the set mark, it is turned on again. In either case, the deviation from the desired norm is put into the service of its own correction. The amazing thing is that this ridiculously simple instrument has the capacity to equilibrate the fluctuations in weather conditions, which are caused by factors of such unpredictability and complexity, that meteorologists have not yet succeeded in devising a suitable mathematical model of these complicated causes and their interactions. This means that causal-genetic thinking is to no avail here.

The thermostat, on the other hand, neither an expert in meteorology nor having read the latest weather report, achieves something undeniably intelligent and "mental" in the traditional sense of these terms. And how does the thermostat manage to do this? Not by trying to grasp the astronomical complexity of the interacting factors from a causal point of view but by taking up *one* single factor, the deviation from the desired norm, and by putting this deviation— just as Watt did—into the service of its own correction.

Most of us are willing to accept this calmly—as long as we are dealing with physiology, steam engines, refrigerators, steam irons, and a hundred other everyday applications of this principle. But as soon as it begins to invade our image of man it becomes the subject of heated controversy.

The classical perception of the soul and its processes, whose localization had already created problems for the Greek philosophers, must, in modern thought, yield to the image of an information-processing network containing and going beyond the human monad. And this is where resistance flares up. To dethrone the individual as the center and ultimate measure of humanity is at least as unacceptable to our self-esteem as the relegation of our planet, at the time of the heliocentric revolution, from being the center of the universe to a third-rate satellite of the sun. The inevitable impression is that what we consider the essence of our human nature has been mechanized and degraded. It would undoubtedly be tempting for a philosopher of science to draw a parallel between those doctrinaire arguments which left Galileo with only a muttered *"eppur si muove . . ."* for an answer and the objections which indignantly reject this new image of man as "mechanistic," "mindless," "superficial," and robbed of the old venerable "depth" of the soul.

This is what it is basically all about. Our long-winded introduction may be reduced to a simple formula: the difference between the properties of a monad and those of a relationship. Another trivial example can help us here: The sentence "This apple is red" obviously refers to a property of the object, the apple. It can therefore be entirely attributed to the object in question. The sentence "This apple is bigger than that one," however, cannot be attributed to the one apple or the other; it does not specify an individual property but expresses a statement which makes sense only in regard to the relationship between the two apples. The "being bigger" floats, as it were, in the space between the two apples, relates to both of them, and yet does not deal with either the one or the other *alone*. To get back to our starting point: In the example quoted, Bleuler discusses a pathology which exists, isolated, in the monadic mind of the patient; Laing emphasizes the entanglements which result from the snares of contradictory definitions of a relationship.

What do we know about relationships? Basically, still very little. The psychology of perception made us realize that only relationships can be perceived. We see a figure because it stands out from the background. A monotonous, unchanging sound is difficult to perceive; thus fire engines use the oscillating sound of sirens. If we try to stop our pupils from moving constantly from one point to another, visual perception becomes extremely difficult if not impossible; hence the traditional technique of fixing the eyes on a shiny point when trying to induce a trance. If we explore the properties of a surface by touch, we move our fingertips back and forth; keeping them in one place would give us little or no information. We perceive the world primarily through differences; only secondarily do we reify these differences into supposedly unchanging properties of the objects perceived.

While the difference in size between apples can be measured objectively, an exact definition of human relationships is not possible. As already mentioned, its supposed "nature" is a mere construct—a matter of opinion, shared, more or less, by the partners. These constructs are the basic material of human communication and the origin of most human conflicts. This statement may be surprising since we are accustomed to regard communication primarily as an exchange of objective, factual information. But even what seems the most impersonal communication contains an implicit expression of how the sender sees his relationship with the receiver. In an old Viennese joke, Count Bobby's maid looks out the window and says: "Your lordship, we may be getting rain." Bobby stiffens and sets her straight in no uncertain terms: "Mitzi, *I* may get rain, and *you* may get rain." In other words, by using the much too familiar "we," the maid violates Bobby's definition of the relationship as a strictly formal one between a nobleman and a servant. All this has nothing whatever to do with rain.

But why do we humans (and the higher species of animals, too) invest so much time and effort in defining our relationships to others? Exactly because we are not discrete, self-contained monads. As will be shown, the uncomfortable results of the research on communication suggest that our consciousness does not sit like a little man in the main office of the skin-encapsulated human being with another little man in his head who has consciousness of his consciousness, and then refuses to answer our question of who then has consciousness of consciousness of *his* consciousness. No, the observation of severely disturbed behavior in its natural context, namely, the family, and not the totally alien environment of the psychiatric clinic, leaves no doubt that we human beings feel ourselves to be real—and therefore "have" consciousness—only to the degree to which the definitions of our relationships to the key people in our human

environment have been accepted by them and thereby rati-
fied, as it were. A lecturer, for instance, defines himself to his
audience as such by specific behaviors, and his listeners confirm in his role by behaving like an audience. If they were to
begin singing the Marseillaise or start to do physical exer-
cises, the speaker's sense of being "real" would disintegrate.
In other words, our self, our reality, is not contained in our
monadic skull—although individually we experience it as
being located there—but between me, the individual, and
them, the others, just as the property of being larger is not
the individual characteristic of *one* apple.

Martin Buber [32, pp. 97–102] points to this phenomenon:
"In human society, at all its levels, persons confirm one another in a practical way, to some extent or other, in their
personal qualities and capacities, and a society may be
termed human in the measure to which its members confirm
one another."

And William James [77, p. 89] is said to have remarked:
"No more fiendish punishment could be devised, even were
such a thing physically possible, than that one should be
turned loose in society and remain absolutely unnoticed by
all the members thereof."

Such conflicts arise, however, in the interactions of
human systems, especially in families, but also in expanded
systems such as working environments, in larger social or
political organizations, and even in international relations.
The ratification of our reality by others is a matter of life and
death for us, just as they need our confirmation of their
reality. *"L'enfer, c'est les autres"* is the quintessence of eternal
damnation in Jean Paul Sartre's play *Huis clos.*

The following example illustrates this need. In the classical experiment of the psychologist Asch [7, pp. 31–35] seven
participants sit in a half-circle facing the experimenter.
Their task is to tell which one of three parallel lines on a card

is just as long as a single line on a second card. In Asch's words:

> The experiment opens uneventfully. The subjects announce their answers in the order in which they have been seated in the room, and on the first round every person chooses the same matching line. Then a second set of cards is exposed; again the group is unanimous. The members appear ready to endure politely another boring experiment. On the third trial there is an unexpected disturbance. One person near the end of the group disagrees with all the others in his selection of the matching line. He looks surprised, indeed incredulous, about the disagreement. On the following trial he disagrees again, while the others remain unanimous in their choice. The dissenter becomes more and more worried and hesitant as the disagreement continues in succeeding trials; he may pause before announcing his answer and speak in a low voice, or he may smile in an embarrassed way.

The explanation of his strange behavior lies in the fact that the other subjects were instructed before the experiment to give false answers unanimously starting with the third round. The dissident, the only real subject, thus finds himself in the bizarre situation in which five people before him and one after him casually and matter-of-factly give an answer which is in direct contradiction to his own perceptions. He now has two options: either he trusts his perceptions, which, however, brings him into conflict with the group, or he avoids this social stigma, albeit at the price of having to distrust his senses and his normalcy. Asch was able to show that under these circumstances 36.8 percent of the subjects succumbed to the group opinion, although with strong feelings of unreality, depersonalization, and anxiety. According to an unconfirmed but not incredible rumor, one subject even experienced a schizophrenic episode. Aside from that episode, however, the subjects were clinically normal people. Where, then, lies the pathology? In their minds, in the answers of the others, or in the test situation? The answer is everywhere, and therefore not at any *single point*.

A further property of relationships suggests itself from the above and is therefore worth mentioning even in this summarized description. Relationships have *gestalt* characteristics, i.e., they are more than, and different from, the mere sum of the elements brought by the partners to the relationship. Outside psychiatry this phenomenon has long been recognized. Experts in the fields of genetic research, endocrinology, molecular biology, neurology, and many other disciplines know that in the organic world interactions of even the simplest components lead to phenomena of enormous complexity, phenomena which resist every attempt to reduce them to single and separate components. If such terrible simplifications were attempted all the same, properties would have to be attributed to the components which they do not possess, and scientific nonsense would be the result. Here, then, classical reductionist causal thinking—the reduction of phenomena to their causes—is bound to fail. This sobering fact is slowly penetrating even psychiatry's image of man. What from a monadic point of view may be seen as a specific illness of a specific mind, in the categories of these modern conceptualizations reveals itself as the result of complex interactions *between* people, as one of many possible results of the circular causality of every relationship, which, once established, has no beginning and no end. In this view every cause has an effect and every effect becomes itself a cause.

Where does the "cause," the "fault," lie in the case of the

Central European who enters a restaurant ahead of his American companion, opens the door, and holds it open for her from the inside? She is offended by his rudeness (in America the man lets the woman go first even in this situation), and he is annoyed by her sudden mysterious chilliness. Both see the fault in the other and, as long as they maintain an angry silence (which is what they are most likely to do), and not in the transpersonal nature of their relationship, i.e., the clash of two behavioral rules which are in and by themselves normal and correct, but contradictory with respect to each other. Or: A writes B proposing some joint venture; B responds with enthusiasm but his letter is lost in the mail. Now both wait with growing resentment for the other's response and A finally decides to punish B for his impoliteness by ignoring him. These examples are clinically trivial, but not so the following ones, which have the same basic structure:

For whatever reason a person suffering from melancholia may see the world in dismal colors, his behavior and that of the people around him will unavoidably lead to the establishment of a feedback loop which maintains and intensifies his depression. His sadness motivates others to cheer him up, to point out that life and the world are not all that tragic, and to suggest that he pull himself together. This well-meant advice has exactly the opposite effect: it intensifies his feelings of hopelessness and inferiority, and especially of being ungrateful toward his loved ones, who try so unselfishly to help him. When on top of that he notices that their inability to cheer him up makes them feel helpless, a devastating sense of guilt compounds his melancholy, as he sees himself pulling them down with him.

Where does the pathology lie? Seemingly in the individual patient. Studies of the communication patterns in families with a depressive child suggest, however, that these depressions do not necessarily exist from birth, but that in these human systems unusual significance is attached to even the most normal forms of occasional sadness or passing indispositions. It seems as if the system had a transpersonal rule which assigns an especially negative value to every despondency. This is not to deny that in a depression the vague concept of predisposition or concrete physiological factors may play a decisive role. It is just that only too frequently the term "predisposition" stands for rules of behavior passed on from generation to generation and eluding observations that are limited to the individual, since these rules are of a systemic and not an individual nature. As far as physiological, metabolic, or endocrinologic factors are concerned, they too are self-regulating, and one cannot determine offhand whether physiological processes give rise to affects, or, conversely, whether mental states cause the physiological processes. In terms of cybernetics this question is meaningless; the body-mind dichotomy belongs to the monadic view of the world.

The second example is taken from a one hundred-year-old work whose authors anticipate the modern interactional concept of psychiatric illness by expanding the frame of observation beyond the individual patient. It is the classic study by Lasègue and Falret [102] about the *folie à deux*. They first describe the patient and then continue:

> The above description belongs to the insane person, the agent who provokes the situation in *délire à deux*. His associate is a much more complicated person to define and yet careful research will teach one to recognize the laws which are obeyed by this second party in communicated insanity. . . . Once the tacit contract that ties both lunatics is almost settled, the problem is not only to examine the influence of the insane on the

supposedly sane man but also the opposite, the influence of the rational on the deluded one, and to show how through mutual compromises the differences are eliminated.

In order to avoid misunderstandings it should be emphasized that the above examples are not meant to be "explanations" of depression or schizophrenia. Rather they are descriptions of patterns of interaction which make the terms "depression" and "schizophrenia" meaningful only when restricted to the identified patient, and then require an explanation based on linear causality. It is not possible to discuss here the questionable nature of this procedure, i.e., its serious personal and social consequences for the so-called patient.

All these considerations raise the question as to what extent the concept of emotional or mental disorders can be defined at all. Classic psychiatry has a clear answer: Mental sanity or insanity depends on the degree of a person's reality adaptation. But at least since Kant it has been assumed that the "real" reality is not accessible to us and that we live with mere *interpretations* or *images* of reality, which, however, we naively assume are objectively real. This imaginary knowledge of objective reality and the seemingly logical conclusion that normal people see the world the way it really is, while madmen do not, has therefore always been untenable. This problem is of equal importance to the researcher as well as to the clinician. When we talk of reality we usually mean two things. First, we perceive the physical properties of objects—form, color, properties, etc. Let us call this the reality of the first order. At this level, differences of opinion can—at least theoretically—be settled objectively. A whale is not a fish because it is a mammal. Whether a particular object is red or green can be decided spectro-

scopically on the basis of the wave lengths of the light reflected from that object. It is understood, of course, that this
is only possible among people for whom terms like "fish,"
"whale," "red," "green," and their symbolic representation
by written characters have the same meaning, i.e., between
people who speak the same language. This basic prerequisite
of all communication shall not concern us here.

In addition to the purely physical properties of the objects
of our perception, another aspect of reality comes into play,
namely, the meaning, significance, and value we attribute to
these objects. This universe of meaning, significance, and
values attributed to objects shall be called second-order reality. And in this universe, as already mentioned in our discussion of relationship definitions, there are no objective criteria. Reality of the second order is the outcome of highly
complex communication processes [178]. We are born into
this reality and we naively assume that it is the real reality
until, for instance, the exposure to another culture abruptly
shakes this simple assumption. We then realize with surprise—and often with contempt—that different countries
have different views of reality, and we usually conclude:
"that's crazy," just as the people in those countries look
upon our idea of reality as crazy. In ancient Greece homosexuality was held to be an especially sublime form of
human love; a person who might be considered holy in India
would be diagnosed as catatonic in the West. Eccentricity,
craziness, malice are thus no longer properties of the monad
but the result of irreconcilable realities of the second order
and of the inadmissible reduction of the conflict to *one* individual while disregarding the interpersonal context. This
is not to deny that a psychiatric disorder may very well
also involve and cause perceptual distortions in one's reality
of the first order. But long before this happens, severe di-
vergencies between that individual's view of the world, his

second-order reality, and his human environment are already present.

Furthermore, it has to be remembered that disorders of the first-order reality do not exist in a vacuum but are bound to have profound interpersonal consequences. Most importantly, the very symptoms which are considered particularly psychotic can be generated without any great difficulties through hypnosis in clinically normal, mature, and well-adapted people, for example, positive or negative hallucinations, split personalities, amnesia, and distorted orientation in space and time. These well-known facts are especially interesting because hypnosis is an interaction between two people.

An additional objection against this view of man is of an ethical nature. Does it not lead to a relativization of all morals, does it not amount to a warmed-over version of determinism and fatalism? What about my responsibility, my free will? But this is not a new problem and therefore not the exclusive shortcoming of this perspective of the human being. In 1946 Max Planck [134, p. 75], like others before him, defined it as follows: "Observed from without, the will is causally determined. Observed from within, it is free. This finding takes care of the problem of the freedom of will. This problem came into being because people were not careful enough to specify explicitly the viewpoint of the observation, and to adhere to it consistently."

The truth of this insight has not changed. On the contrary, our deeper understanding of human interaction teaches us that the position of the observer is of fundamental importance. From within the system it is impossible to grasp it as a whole, just as we cannot perceive our body as a whole because our eyes are themselves part of the body to be perceived. Our eyes cannot see our back, nor can they see *themselves*. "Life is like any eye which cannot see itself, like a sword which cannot cut itself," a Zen master is supposed to have said. Thus, *within* a relationship we are individually accountable, and probably always shall be. But from *outside* the frame of a relationship a general overview of its approximate totality can be reached. And the psychotherapist stands outside the relationship—or at least he should, if he is not to lose his perspective and his ability to intervene.

What is the image of man to which all this will lead us? In order even to attempt to answer this question, we need to expand the limits of our examination. This inevitably leads us into the field of epistemology, the theory of the nature and the origin of knowledge. In other words, we are no longer dealing with the classical question about the nature of the objective world, from which, in accordance with the classical dogma of absolute objectivity, everything subjective has to be banished. Heisenberg has taught us that it is impossible to separate the observing subject from the observed object, and that a completely objective, subject-free universe would be altogether unobservable. The question about the nature of man—psychiatry's central question—is further complicated by the fact that here man is subject as well as object, observer as well as observed, describer as well as description. Here psychiatry falls headlong into the problems of recursiveness (see p. 168ff), and the question is no longer *"What* do we know?" but *"How* do we know?" in other words, epistemology.

The fluidity of the boundaries between man and his environment has already been referred to in the example of the blind man and his cane. Cybernetics, the epistemology of our time, must be credited with having dealt extensively with interdependence. The cybernetician Heinz von Foerster [49, p. 401] defines it as follows:

> After this we are now in the possession of a truism that a description of the universe implies one who de-

scribes it (observes it). What we need now is the description of the "describer" or, in other words, we need a theory of the observer. Since to the best of available knowledge it is only living organisms which would qualify as being observers, it appears that this task falls to the biologist. But he himself is a living being, which means that in his theory he has not only to account for himself, but also for his writing this theory.

In the final sentences of his *Calculus of Self-Reference,* the Chilean biologist and cybernetician Francisco Varela [171, pp. 5–24] writes:

> The starting point of this calculus . . . is the act of indication. In this primordial act we separate forms which appear to us as the world itself. From this starting point, we thus assert the primacy of the role of the observer who draws distinctions wherever he pleases. Thus the distinctions made which engender our world reveal precisely that: the distinctions we make—and these distinctions pertain more to a revelation of where the observer stands than to an intrinsic constitution of the world which appears, by this very mechanism of separation between observer and observed, always elusive. In finding the world as we do, we forget all we did to find it as such, and when we are reminded of it in retracing our steps back to indication, we find little more than a mirror-to-mirror image of ourselves and the world. In contrast with what is commonly assumed, a description, when carefully inspected, reveals the properties of the observer. We, observers, distinguish ourselves precisely by distinguishing what we apparently are not, the world.

In these remarks, taken from a field which has nothing to do with psychiatry, a new image of man which at the same time is a new view of the world takes shape. In this view man and world are complementary. The world is no longer something that stands in opposition to us. This complementary nature of man and world is still as difficult to grasp as Heisenberg's complementarity of waves and particles.

The almost mystical nature of this outlook adds to our reluctance to embrace it. For until now the immediate experience of the unity of subject and object in rare and unusual moments was left to the mystics, who then tried to describe this experience in the inadequate language of the very world which they had transcended. And yet—from Wittgenstein's *Tractatus* to Varela's *Calculus*—there exists now a whole spectrum of new conceptualizations which will enter the language of psychiatry and thereby shape its image of man.

It is an image that has always been familiar to poets. In one of T.S. Eliot's *Four Quartets* we find the following simple description:

> We shall not cease from exploration
> and the end of all our exploring
> will be to arrive where we started
> and know the place for the first time.

Depression Following Stroke: Brief, Problem-focused Family Treatment

(in co-authorship with James C. Coyne)

Does the system-theoretical orientation offer new and specific approaches to the solution of emotional problems? This is the question that the next chapters will explore.

There can be no doubt that the clinical picture of depression is the result of the convergence and the interference of numerous interdependent factors of the most diverse origins. But it is this very complexity of the condition which permits a variety of different therapeutic approaches, none of which can so far claim to be exclusively effective. This chapter describes the application of the systemic model to the treatment of a depression. Although the identified patient refused to participate in the family therapy sessions, a significant improvement of his condition was achieved through the active modification on the part of the therapist of the behavior and, above all, of the solutions attempted by the other family members.

Members of a family were seen in the treatment of a fifty-eight-year-old man suffering from depression secondary to two strokes. The identified patient did not attend any of the five sessions. Therapeutic interventions emphasized interdicting the self-defeating efforts of family members to be supportive and encouraging. It is proposed that successful therapeutic interventions often involve changing the behavior of persons other than the identified patient but that traditional therapists have avoided the full implication of this. Ethical concerns about this mode of treatment are considered.

•

The Mental Research Institute group [185, 186] has developed a brief problem-focused approach to therapy that conceptualizes clinical problems as aspects of ongoing interactional systems. It is assumed in this approach that psychological distress and symptoms arise from the mismanagement of life transitions or other disruptions of patients' interactional systems and that severe symptomatology may reflect the exacerbation of initial difficulties by the reasonable but inappropriate problem-solving efforts of patients and those around them.

Therapeutic interventions characteristically focus on attempted solutions—what is being done to deal with the patients' difficulties—rather than on the difficulties themselves [185, p. 81]. The interventions involve deliberate attempts to prevent the occurrence of problem-maintaining behavior, typically by reframing or redefining the problems, as well as the original motives and beliefs of involved persons, thereby bringing about very different behavior. The emphasis is on getting those involved to act in relevant new ways through the use of homework, direct and indirect, suggestion, and paradox. Therapeutic goals are typically small, but definite changes in behavior are intended to instigate change of a more generalized nature [179].

Two important aspects of an interactional systems orientation are frequently misconstrued. First, the approach emphasizes the involvement of others in the perpetuation of disturbed behavior; it does not assume that there are any individual gains for them, but that interactional patterns, once established, have a tendency to maintain themselves on account of their homeostatic function (i.e., they maintain the stability of the system *in its present form*). Clinical experience suggests further that in dysfunctional systems, the existing patterning represents a miscarried problem-solving effort. Second, an interactional system approach does not require that all persons composing the system attend therapy sessions; appropriate change in a subsystem (e.g., one family member) can bring about major changes in the entire system. Indeed, in the present case study, the depressed patient did not attend any of the five sessions.

It should also be pointed out that this case was chosen for study because the identified patient's depression was secondary to a purely physical condition (stroke). Family psychotherapy is by no means limited to strictly psychological conditions but has a wide range of applicability and effect over the course and the severity of primarily physical illnesses, an approach for which Weakland [187] has coined the term "family somatics."

Presenting Problem

Twelve months prior to therapy, the identified patient, Mr. B., a fifty-eight-year-old former engineer, suffered his second stroke. After physical and speech therapy, he showed only a few residual deficits: some slurring of speech and problems in the use of his left hand and leg. He could no longer work and began spending up to fourteen hours a day in bed, watching television. He seldom left the house except when pressured by his wife to go for a walk around the block. His general behavior was described by his family as that of a "vegetable." However, as is not infrequent with this condition, he would, for brief periods of time, be "his old self" again. At his retirement party, for instance, he stood up and gave a perfectly clear speech, afterward relating warmly to the well-wishers and shaking their hands. On another occasion, when his wife had mistakenly ingested sleeping medication instead of a tranquilizer and he found her half-unconscious on the floor, he took reasonable and appropriate initiative and also informed one of their three sons by telephone of what had happened, assuring him that Mrs. B. was all right. After each of these brief interludes, however, he would quickly lapse back into his state of abulia and hopelessness.

Along with his wife and their sons, he was seen in a video-taped interview at the Stanford Medical Center. Discussion revealed the extent to which his depression had halted recovery from his stroke and even reversed some earlier gains. Much of the interaction involved either the wife or sons making a hopeful prognostic statement or indicating that he had functioned better shortly after the stroke than he did currently, followed by a terse denial by the patient. When he attempted to speak, they often finished sentences for him and occasionally answered for him. But the most remarkable, recurrent pattern of interaction consisted of their combined efforts to encourage Mr. B. to pull himself together, try harder, and see his situation more optimistically—whereupon he invariably responded with increased helplessness, pointing out to them how little they understood the severity of his physical handicaps and of his dejection, to which they then responded with increased, obviously well-meant optimism and encouragement. The family thus seemed to be caught in a typical Game without End—an interactional impasse in which more of a problem-perpetuating "solution" by one party is countered by more of the same reaction by the other. Although this pattern was obvious to the observers, the family was unaware of it and only conceded that they had not dealt well with his predicament. Family therapy was suggested, Mr. B. agreeing that it might be beneficial but indicating that he would not himself participate. With his consent, the family was referred to the Brief Therapy Center of the Mental Research Institute.

THE CONDUCT OF THERAPY

The first session was attended by Mrs. B. and two sons. All three sons no longer lived at home but visited frequently enough to participate in efforts to assist Mr. B.'s recovery.

The therapist obtained a detailed description of the family's problem-solving efforts. After the stroke, Mrs. B. had attempted to comfort him and to be of as much assistance as possible. She had helped with his speech and physical therapy until he had lost interest in them. When he cried, she gave him pep talks, but she often would begin crying herself. She repeatedly reassured him that the doctor had predicted nearly complete recovery and that he would soon be "the man he once was."

The wife and sons reported vacillating between two extremes in their expectations for his recovery. At times they would become quite hopeful and encouraging, but when his progress did not keep pace with what they had anticipated, they would fall back upon increasingly coercive strategies to motivate him. He would become hostile and more depressed, and they would then lose hope. In such periods of despair, they expected very little of him and would often do things for him that he was capable of doing for himself. The cycle of hope and demoralization had been repeated a number of times, with growing resentment and resistance by Mr. B. to any influence whatsoever.

Although many of the limitations on Mr. B.'s activities were self-imposed, the influence of Mrs. B. was also clear. She reported that it was she who no longer wanted to go to restaurants, because she was uncomfortable seeing other couples unburdened by such problems and enjoying themselves. She had become aware of the fact that many of her husband's deficits seemed to be limited to interactions with her; both she and the sons reported dramatic changes in his behavior when others visited.

The family was aware that the patterns they had developed "somehow" contributed to Mr. B.'s problems, but they felt helpless; each effort to get him to resume normal activities seemed only to make matters worse. At this point the therapist felt that it might be useful to refer to the pattern that had emerged so clearly from the videotaped interview. Even though Mrs. B. and her sons had just referred to it in their own terms, they were surprised to hear how often and how predictably Mr. B. had responded negatively to their optimism. From there it was a relatively easy step to enlist their willingness to reverse this self-defeating "helpful" behavior by dealing with Mr. B.'s undeniable difficulties in a new way. They were encouraged to think about some concrete but very small change that they might be able to bring about in Mr. B.'s behavior. They were told that the targeted change need not be a chore but should be an everyday activity that he had ceased to engage in. They were urged not to attempt to implement it, however.

The family readily accepted the goal of some small

changes in Mr. B.'s behavior that would indicate he was resuming normal activities. The therapist's goal, however, was to interdict their helpful efforts.

Between this session and the next, the above-mentioned incident with the sleeping medication occurred, and the therapist utilized it to stress the completely different effect Mrs. B.'s helplessness had had on her husband's behavior, compared with the effects of her encouragements and pep talks. He pointed out that usually she was the active, competent member of the pair, and if Mr. B. did not do something, he could depend on her. She was helpful and encouraging, but hard as she had tried to bring about something positive to make him see he was not as handicapped as he thought, the result had been the opposite. In this particular incident, however, she was unable to be competent or encouraging, and she had finally succeeded.

In the ensuing discussion, the family considered deliberate efforts to recreate a situation in which their usual strategy was suspended. Mrs. B agreed to prepare an elaborate breakfast early the next morning but to fall asleep on the living room couch without calling Mr. B. When he finally came for breakfast she was to apologize profusely. She was told not to discuss the plan, but she was free to admit she was overwhelmed. Other deliberately staged problems were also planned. She was to fail to clean the kitchen after meals and to forget to make coffee in the afternoon. Furthermore, she was to repeatedly serve pork roast, a meat Mr. B. detested. The rationale given to him was to be that she had trouble making the decisions necessary to plan a menu, but she remembered that they had seldom eaten pork roast.

In the third session, the family reported some partial success in completing the assignments. Although Mrs. B. was skeptical as to whether it was a direct result of the interventions, Mr. B. began to come to breakfast without being called. He assisted in cleaning the kitchen, made coffee, and had suggestions for dinner menus. Mrs. B. reported that he had kissed her spontaneously before going out for a walk, something that she could not recall him doing in quite a while.

The therapist stressed the need to avoid falling into old patterns, pointing out how difficult this would be and how difficult it would be for Mr. B. to forget her training of him. The more the therapist insisted that he was probably asking too much of her, the more she insisted that she could do whatever he thought might be useful in order to help her husband.

Mrs. B. revealed more of the extent to which she had assumed responsibility for Mr. B. She reminded him to take walks and to wear his jacket and attempted to regulate when he went to bed at night.

The latter issue became targeted for change. Mr. B. often complained of pain, indicating that he was therefore retiring early, and a struggle would follow. Rather than resisting Mr. B., Mrs. B. was urged to sympathize with him and help him to get to bed even earlier.

However, there also were reports of her (and her sons') slipping back into the old, familiar, "commonsensical" attempts to motivating Mr. B. positively. At this point the therapist, mindful of one of the basic rules of interactional therapy, namely to talk to clients in their own "language" [179], hit upon a formulation that seemed to make more sense, especially to Mrs. B., than all the explanations and advice he had given so far. Realizing that they basically only talked and understood the language rather than the process of *helping,* he first led them into fully agreeing with him that Mr. B. was a proud and even stubborn man and that such people are easily discouraged and made to feel worthless when others try to help them. He then concentrated his instructions into the paradoxical formula: *"You must encourage him by discouraging him."*

The fourth session began with a report of further successes. Mr. B.'s assistance with housework had become more routine. He took three longer walks, and Mr. B. described his interaction with relatives as more pleasant, talkative, and enthusiastic. Mr. B. had also become more concerned about an issue with his former employer, a large industrial concern. Before his stroke, the company had adopted a money-saving suggestion he had made, but papers had not been processed for him to receive the remuneration to which he was entitled. Although he stated that he was not hopeful about receiving a settlement, he felt it would be enough satisfaction to have made clear his case. He was enthusiastic about dictating a detailed complaint letter to the company.

The therapist again stressed the need to avoid overconfidence and suggested that Mrs. B. must paradoxically encourage Mr. B. with appropriate discouragement. Although she could thank him for his increased involvement in household chores, it would be best to discourage his new initiatives with, "Don't do it, because it is too much for you." Mrs. B. volunteered again that stubbornness had been one of his enduring traits and that he usually dealt well with a challenge.

In the fifth and final session, Mrs. B. reported that they had attended church for the first time in months and afterward had driven a considerable distance to a resort town for dinner. He had cleaned his shop area and began using his tools again. He had also rented a boat with his sons and discussed purchasing his own small boat. The therapist again stressed the difficulty of avoiding old patterns and the need for randomness and flexibility in helpful discouragement. He stressed the loyal sacrifice of the family in their compliance with therapeutic homework.

In the three-month follow-up after this fifth session, Mrs. B. reported that her husband had been doing very well for a month but that he had suffered a third stroke and that this time his physicians felt there was little chance for significant recovery. During that first month, however, he sometimes arose before she did, dressed himself, took walks, and talked to the neighbors. They had been going out to dinner, and he and the sons had bought a boat.

DISCUSSION

A recent prospective study has revealed the extent to which the recovery of depressed persons is dependent upon the response from the environment [173]. Traditional therapy has given minimal consideration to this, however. "The persistent assumption has been that the support and information available to depressed persons are incongruent with their depression and that, therefore, the continued display of symptoms is evidence of their distorted view of the environment" [38].

In treating the depressed patient only through contact with his family, this presentation has adopted an alternative interactional view. It was not assumed that the family was uniformly supportive of the patient's recovery or uniformly hostile toward him. Rather, it was assumed that the particular helping strategy they adopted made his resumption of normal activities less likely and frustrated them all. Although it was considered important to interdict this pattern, it was also considered important to recognize the good intentions of the family and to utilize them for change.

Other than the complete absence of the patient from therapy sessions, the case illustrates typical features of the brief, problem-focused approach to therapy. Of particular interest is the manner in which initial therapeutic endeavors, i.e., merely selecting appropriate target behaviors, were assimilated within the family's existing problem-solving strategy of coercion. The brief, problem-focused approach to therapy reframes or redefines key elements in the problem situation in order to shift the behavior of relevant persons. It remains unclear whether the effectiveness of the approach in the present case was due most directly to the situations presented to the patient as a result of the family's homework or to the fact that their usual strategy had been disrupted and therefore he did not need to resist them.

From a traditional perspective, concern can be raised around the issue of contracting with a set of persons to change the behavior of someone else. The interactional perspective does not minimize the issue but invokes the counterargument that most clinically relevant behaviors occur in the context of significant relationships and changes in these behaviors are associated with changes in the relationships. Successful therapy, even of the traditional individual variety, typically involves changing the behavior of persons not present. The full ethical implications of this are not frequently debated, and traditional therapists have avoided the issue by construing their responsibilities in myopically unecological terms [39] or by "playing at not playing a game" [96]. The interactionist perspective assumes that the identified patient and those around him or her are unavoidably influencing each other. The therapist is therefore left with the responsibility of deciding how this is to be taken into account in the most humane, ethical, and effective manner.

C H A P T E R
4

Hypnotherapeutic Principles
in Family Therapy

The third personality who had a decisive influence on the development of the MRI model was the famous hypnotherapist Milton H. Erickson.

From 1936 to 1939, during his fieldwork on the island of Bali, Bateson had observed and become very interested in the phenomenon of spontaneously occurring trance states during the ritual temple dances. Upon his return to the United States he contacted Erickson, and the contacts were renewed in 1953, mainly by Bateson's collaborators John Weakland and Jay Haley.

At that time Erickson had already studied the effects of those interventions, now known as behavior prescriptions. *Although they originated within the frame of traditional hypnotic or post-hypnotic suggestions, they were no longer based on prior trance induction but given as simple requests or injunctions to behave differently in the particular problem situation. On the strength of countless examples, Erickson was able to show that by using such overt suggestions he was able to bring about unexpected, rapid, and, above all, lasting changes.*

The reader will not find it surprising that these active interventions have a different linguistic structure than those of the classic, traditional interventions, which rely almost exclusively on description, explanation, and interpretation.

•

The title of this chapter might give the impression that it deals with the hypnotherapy of entire families. What I want to present, instead, are thoughts on *language* and *reality* in family therapy, with particular attention to the behavioral effects of certain uses of language that have been part and parcel of hypnotic techniques for a long time. It may be unnecessary to point to the fact that what follows can at best amount to an overview.

Hypnosis is the *enfant terrible* of psychotherapeutic orthodoxy. On the one hand, the often surprising results of hypnotic interventions are undeniable; on the other hand, it is difficult, if at all possible, to reconcile them with the postulates of the classical theories of therapeutic change. In the psychodynamic model, hypnosis at worst represents the anathema of purely symptom-oriented treatment; at best it has some usefulness as a tool for lifting repressed material into consciousness, for instance, by means of time regression in the service of facilitating insight.

Different and even incompatible as the respective tenets and techniques of the classical schools of psychotherapy may be, they have one thing in common: the use of language as a means of description, explanation, and, above all, interpretation. This language is called *indicative* or—in terms of the lateralization theory of the brain—*left-hemispheric*. For a long time, in fact until the middle of our century, it was considered the language of science par excellence. But even at best, this language can only provide an intellectual, rational understanding of meaning or of cause–effect relations that have so far remained outside somebody's comprehension. This alone accounts for the well-known fact that indicative language is ill suited for the communication of those experiences whose nature cannot be expressed rationally. The brain researcher Galin [54] once pointed to this difference by contrasting the experience of listening to a piano concerto (which cannot be "described") with the appreciation of the sentence "Democracy requires informed participation" (which can be communicated only in the indicative mood).

It is obvious that therapy is concerned far more with conveying experiences than with intellectual appreciations. A good joke can achieve much more than an exhaustive (and exhausting) explanation, although—or maybe because—the point or the punch line of a joke violates the rules of indicative language and its underlying logic. The famous hypnotherapist Milton H. Erickson was known for his ability to resort to suggestions that violated the rules of grammar, syntax, or semantics, to juggle with puns or other plays on words (which in the traditional perspective would have been attributed to slips of the tongue or even primary-process thinking), and to take full therapeutic advantage of the confusion he thereby managed to create. And long before him—in fact, for millennia—the powerful effects of specific uses of language for the purpose of providing immediate emotional experiences were already known and utilized in rhetoric, drama, poetry, and ritual. Consider the second half of Hölderlin's poem "The Middle of Life" (in Michael Hamburger's translation):

> But oh, where shall I find
> When winter comes, the flowers and where
> The sunshine
> and the shade of the earth?

The walls loom
speechless and cold, in the wind
weathercocks clatter.

Or permit the opening lines of Leopardi's poem "The Evening after the Fair," translated by John Heath-Stubb, to influence your mood:

The night is soft and clear, and no wind blows;
The quiet moon stands above roofs and orchards
Revealing from afar each distant hill.

The clinical usefulness of this language, its potential for conveying completely different experiences, for achieving very different emotional effects, rather than the dry, objective language of explanation and interpretation, has for a long time been confined to hypnosis. What I would like to suggest is that more than any other particular therapeutic skill, a familiarity with this language may provide new, effective approaches to solving human problems, handling resistance, and modifying behavior. Therefore, these approaches can be helpful in family therapy. Let us examine at least some of them.

What is a suggestion? Although many divergent definitions have been proposed, it is safe to say that it is a communication that changes—even if at times only temporarily—somebody's view of his reality. Basically, any suggestion amounts to the request: Behave *as if* such and such were the case. Thus it is a behavior prescription, often, but not necessarily, given in covert form. For instance, the suggestion, "Imagine that you are biting into a thick, juicy slice of lemon," will provoke immediate salivation in most of us; in other words, it will elicit a physiological reaction that we cannot produce for ourselves voluntarily in any other way. The decisive difference lies in the as-if character of the situation. In other words, the recipient of the suggestion is invited to create in his mind a different reality (after all, he does not "really" bite into a lemon), and this imagination leads to a concrete effect. At first sight this outcome may seem hardly remarkable, but on closer examination it reveals its practical usefulness for bringing about therapeutic change. Admittedly, this perspective is not at all new. As early as 1911, the German philosopher Hans Vaihinger presented his *Philosophy of "As If"* [170], a work of over 800 pages that greatly influenced Alfred Adler and to a lesser degree Sigmund Freud. Vaihinger presents countless examples in support of his contention that, not only in our individual lives but also in the natural sciences as well as in the humanities and in the wider social contexts, we always act on the basis of unproven and unprovable "as-if" assumptions. And even though these assumptions can make no claim to being "true" or reflecting "reality," they are more or less useful fictions that produce desirable or undesirable *concrete* results, whereupon the fiction need no longer be part of the situation and "falls out," to use Vaihinger's expression.

What practical conclusions can be drawn from this for therapy? First, it enables us to dispense with the naive notion that to have any effect at all an interpretation must be in some sense "true," since the theory on which the interpretation is based is itself considered to be true. That this delusion of "truth" then makes it possible to declare all other theories and hypotheses to be "untrue" and provides the basis for endless and useless "scientific" debates is mentioned here only in passing. Not truth, but only effectiveness toward a given purpose, can be the goal of science. What matters, here and elsewhere, are not interpretations or explanations as such, but the realization that imaginary assumptions provide fictitious bridges to practical results.

What are the optimal preconditions for this technique of change? Let us recall the essence of every suggestion: the demand to imagine and/or to behave *as if* something were the case that "is not" the case in the world image of that person. But since this world image is itself but a composite of as-if fictions, a new "reality" is thereby constructed [183]—provided, of course, that the new fiction is acceptable to the recipient of the suggestion. This means that it must not be too alien or contradictory to the way this person has so far constructed his or her "reality." Out of this necessity grows one of the basic rules of the Ericksonian approach: *Learn and use the client's language.* This is a significant departure from the techniques of the classic therapies, whose first phase is largely taken up by the task of teaching the *patients* a new "language," that is, the constructs and conceptualizations of that particular school of therapy, with a view to getting the patients to see themselves, their problems, and their causes as well as their present situations in this new conceptual framework. The very opposite takes place in hypnotherapy. There it is the *therapist* who tries to learn, as quickly as possible, the subject's "language," that is, the subject's way of conceptualizing the world. The only language spoken and understood by an overprotective mother is the language of maternal responsibility and sacrifice; with the engineer or computer expert one must try to speak the crystal-clear language of binary logic (rather than attempting to bring him into touch with personal feelings—something his spouse has already tried in vain for twenty years); with the starry-eyed, esoteric youth we may have to speak the language of Eastern thought. Of course, any one of these languages is only the form, the "package" used to introduce the particular as-if fiction.

Another characteristic of hypnosis is the avoidance of so-called *n*-words, that is, of negations (no, not, nobody, nowhere, never, etc.). According to a plausible paleolinguistic hypothesis, negation is a relatively late acquisition of human (digital) language. This would account for the undeniable fact that in a state of hypnotic regression negations are often not "received" and that a suggestion containing an *n*-word can easily have the opposite effect. Similarly, a child is more likely to forget the admonition "Don't forget to . . ." than the equivalent positive formulation "Remember to. . . ." Applied to psychotherapy in general, this means that negations (and in a wider sense, therefore, also negative remarks and judgments) by the therapist may produce unintended and contrary results, causing resistance and an unwillingness to go along with the as-if fiction of the therapeutic intervention. Thus, rather than criticize an attempted solution as pointless or counterproductive, it may be considerably more effective to remark: "You seem to have tried just about everything possible to get rid of your problem—maybe together we can come up with something *additional* that might be done."

Closely related to this is the *use of resistance* in hypnotherapy. Instead of following the classic procedure of interpreting it in terms of its supposed origin in the past and thereby at best reinforcing it, it is considerably more effective to *prescribe* it. Prescribed resistance ceases to be resistance, for it leaves the clients only two possibilities: either to continue that particular form of resistance, which now, however, owing to its having been prescribed, amounts to compliance rather than resistance, or to stop that behavior in order to resist the request to engage in it. In terms of the pragmatics of human communication, a therapeutic double bind is thereby created.

A still more complex pattern of communication is the *creation of resistance* in the service of therapeutic change. Essentially this consists of explaining to the family what kind of problem solution might be most effective under the circumstances, but immediately defining it as something that the family members will most probably be unable to carry out. The more condescending, authoritarian, and pessimistic the therapist manages to sound when expressing this opinion, the greater the likelihood that the family members will feel challenged by this pessimism and will be motivated to prove to him how wrong he is.

A separate essay would be necessary to present yet another form of intervention taken directly from hypnotherapy, *reframing*. It is the most immediate practical application of an as-if fiction. The family presents the problem in their view; the therapist puts it into another perspective, another frame, which may be equally applicable or even more plausible. The much-quoted example is that passage from Mark Twain's *Tom Sawyer* where Tom succeeds in reframing his punishment (to paint a fence) as an unusual privilege, so that his friends—who at first tease him for having to work on a Saturday afternoon—eventually are eager to pay him for permission to paint the fence themselves.

The references to poetry at the beginning of this chapter may give the unintended impression that the therapist should use poetic language. This would be asking a bit too much. But the *telling of stories* is an age-old technique of opening new perspectives and facilitating change. Tales, especially witty or wise ones, may not only appeal in and by themselves, but also facilitate identification. And since they are always about other times and circumstances and deal with fictitious people, it is entirely up to the listener to decide how much of the story appears to be similar to his own life situation. He can identify himself with a story *à distance*, as it were, that is, apparently without commitment and therefore with a minimum of resistance. Milton H. Erickson was known for his frequent use of stories—either from his personal life [146] or others that he freely invented at the spur of the moment to fit a given situation—in order to conceal in this "wrapping" a suggestion that would probably have been rejected or disqualified if given in a more direct and overt form. For those interested in the use of such archetypically therapeutic stories, books like Peseschkian's *The Merchant and the Parrot* [131], or the writings by Idries Shah [159] too numerous to be listed here by title, can be recommended.

The common denominator of all the interventions mentioned so far is the fact that the therapist plays an *active* role. He deliberately influences, even though at times—as in storytelling—this influence may be covert. This active stance becomes particularly obvious in the so-called *direct behavior prescriptions*. While a suggestion attempts to communicate to its recipient an as-if fiction that is different from the way he has so far *seen* his situation, the behavior prescription attempts to get him to *act* as if he lived in a reality that is quite different from the one he has so far constructed for himself—as if, for instance, his problem were already solved. In this connection it cannot be stated too strongly that those as-if behaviors should be very simple. Their often trivial simplicity accounts for their surprising, almost "magical" effects. And yet they are behaviors that were possible at all times but were not resorted to, because in the frame of the family's reality construction there was no room for, or sense in, resorting to them. This, incidentally, may also be the reason why such unorthodox ways of dealing with somebody's "reality adaptation" are rejected by many therapists. Yet it is known that such surprisingly abrupt and unplanned problem solutions may emerge spontaneously in the course of treatment. The famous somersault by one of Michael Balint's patients is a classical example [13]. He was working with a patient, "an attractive, vivacious, rather flirtatious girl in her late 20's, whose main complaint was an inability to achieve anything." This was due, in part, to her "crippling fear of uncertainty whenever she had to take any risks." After two years of psychoanalytic treatment

> she was given the interpretation that apparently the most important thing for her was to keep her head safely up, with both feet firmly planted on the ground. In response, she mentioned that ever since her earliest childhood she could never do a somersault; although at various periods she tried desparately to do one. I then said: "What about it now?"—whereupon she got up from the couch and, to her great amazement, did a perfect somersault without any difficulty.
>
> This proved to be a real breakthrough. Many changes followed, in her emotional, social, and professional life, all towards greater freedom and elasticity. Moreover, she managed to get permission to sit for, and passed, a most difficult postgraduate professional examination, became engaged, and was married.[13, pp. 128–129]

(Whereupon Balint uses almost two pages to explain that this breakthrough does not contradict object relation theory, and that such an unexpected and unplanned remission does not "replace interpretation, it was in addition to it" [p. 134].)

A further characteristic of the language of behavior prescriptions is its *injunctive* and *performative* nature, occasionally also referred to as *deontic.* To define these terms very briefly: *Injunctive* comes from the Latin *injunctio* (order, admonition) and is defined in this sense for instance by George Spencer-Brown [166] as that class of communications which requires the recipient to engage in a certain action which, in turn, may lead to a totally new experience. The second term, *performative,* was coined by the British philosopher of language John L. Austin [10], who introduced the important distinction between utterances that state or explain something (called *constative*) and other "speech acts" through which something is actually achieved or accomplished and thus, in a very real sense, *performed.* If the president of an assembly utters the words, "The meeting will come to order," he has not made a remark about (i.e., described) something but has thereby created a specific, concrete interpersonal situation. *Deontic,* finally, is a term introduced by the philosopher Ernst Mally in his *Logic of Will* [111], a logical system dealing with the structure and interpersonal effects of command sentences.

The three logical domains just mentioned intersect and overlap, even though on closer examination they seem to be going in different directions. But their common denominator remains their pragmatic, reality-creating effect, which has always been an important part of hypnotic technique but is equally applicable to human relationship systems, such as couples, families, and even larger contexts.

The brief therapy model developed at the Mental Research Institute in Palo Alto relies on interventions of this kind. They entail a reversal of the classical principle of insight as a *precondition* of behavioral change. In the MRI model, what matters and produces change are actions carried out by the family in compliance with specific behavior prescriptions. The most elegant and complex applications of this technique are *family rituals,* as described by Selvini [158] and van der Hart [71], whose performance leads to the experience of a new "reality." Here, then, insight is the *consequence,* the *effect* of a behavior change, very much in accordance with Heinz von Foerster's Aesthetical Imperative: "If you desire to see, learn how to act" [50, p. 61].

5

Brief Therapy of Schizophrenia

Even more than depression, schizophrenia is considered a mental disturbance which requires long-term treatment, if it is considered amenable to psychotherapy at all. But this view presupposes that it (just like any other clinical picture) exists and can thus be identified objectively. This view then leads to the rejection of all techniques of psychotherapy which are not based on these supposedly objective facts and are, therefore, considered "wrong." The problem with this position is that it never questions the conviction that the ultimate criterion for judging the sanity or insanity is a person's reality adaptation, by which it is tacitly assumed that there exists an objective reality which is accessible to the sane mind. What is involved here, then, is not simply one of many scientific paradigms in Thomas Kuhn's sense, but a firm belief to have grasped, once and for all, the true, "scientific" nature of the world.

The present chapter deals with this fallacy. It not only questions the supposedly definitive validity of any dogmatic assumption (and its consequent rejection of any other, different assumption), but considers the therapeutic possibilities which de-

rive from a critical examination of a given premise itself—*and not only of its practical application.*

•

The juxtaposition of schizophrenia and brief therapy seems absurd, as it is generally agreed that schizophrenia is a severe mental disturbance whose treatment is long and of uncertain outcome. In this chapter an attempt will be made to show that the difficulties surrounding the treatment of schizophrenia are partly the result of the views held about the condition and not due to its intrinsic nature. This approach is based on the work of the Bateson group in the 1950s and on subsequent developments of this model by the staff of the Mental Research Institute in Palo Alto.

In his *Introduction to Cybernetics,* first published in 1956, the famous cybernetician Ashby writes:

> Suppose I am in a friend's house and, as a car goes past outside, his dog rushes to a corner of the room and cringes. To me the behaviour is causeless and inexplicable. Then my friend says, "He was run over by a car six months ago." The behaviour is now accounted for by reference to an event of six months ago. If we say that the dog shows "memory" we refer to much the same fact—that his behaviour can be explained, not by reference to his state now but to what his state was six months ago. If one is not careful one says that the dog "has" memory, and then thinks of the dog as *having* some*thing,* as he might have a patch of black hair. One may then be tempted to start looking for the thing; and one may discover that this "thing" has some very curious properties.

And Ashby then goes on to say:

> Clearly, "memory" is not an objective something that a system either does or does not possess; it is a concept that the *observer* invokes to fill in the gap caused when part of the system is unobservable. The fewer the observable variables, the more will the observer be forced to regard events of the past as playing a part in the system's behaviour. Thus "memory" in the brain is only partly objective. No wonder its properties have sometimes been found to be unusual or even paradoxical.

And then, in one simple sentence, he draws the only logical conclusion:

> Clearly the subject requires thorough examination from first principles. [9, p. 117].

This sounds deceptively simple. In actual fact, scientists share with all higher animals an inability or unwillingness to reexamine their conceptual models "from first premises." If it were not so, there would be no such thing as an experimental neurosis in a laboratory animal whose "world-view" is shattered when the experimenter turns the reward-and-punishment context upside down, or the fate of Galileo Galilei, with ether, phlogiston, the dilemmas of plane geometry, the inheritance of acquired characteristics, and a thousand other, similar "facts" lying somewhere between these extremes. Worse still, what is involved here is an inability not just to question one's assumptions but to accept the possibility that one's "first premises" are just that: mere assumptions, paradigms in Kuhn's sense [93], and not eternal truths discovered once and for all.

In the case of psychiatric theories this trend is, if anything, even more pronounced. The question of what is abnormal and what is normal, and how the former can be changed into the latter, is complicated by the fact that psychiatric theories are held by their authors and subscribers with much greater fervor than, say, those of the physicist or the economist. Since they do not involve merely impersonal issues but the human being as such (including, therefore, those who accept them), they are almost in the nature of religious beliefs. And the basic belief must not, may not, be wrong.

Take a book like *Freud or Jung?* by the eminent psychoanalyst Edward Glover [65]. The author painstakingly fills 195 pages in order to prove what can be said in one sentence: Jung's ideas do not coincide with Freud's. In fact, this is what Glover does in his conclusion (p. 190): "As we have seen the most consistent trend of Jungian psychology is its negation of every important part of Freudian theory." A statement of this kind would not be worth making if the authors and his readers did not believe Freud's ideas to be the basis of the final, true explanation of human behavior. Then *and only then* does it make sense to point to the fallacies of somebody else's thinking. (The same holds for Marxism or any other ideology which through political power *fiat* has been declared to be the scientific and therefore ultimate and eternally true explanation of the social and economic laws governing human existence and human values.)

If this is so and if actions taken in accordance with the theory are unsuccessful, the fault must be sought in the *applications* of the theory but not in the theory itself. This means further that in a very real sense the point of therapy may be to save the theory, not the patient. And it finally means also that within the framework of any theory, certain deductions are consistent with its premises and others must be ruled out as inconsistent. Symptom removal, for instance, is inconsistent and incompatible with the tenets of psychodynamic theory and must "therefore" not be attempted on pain of symptom substitution or exacerbation. But since as practitioners we are not trained as philosophers of science, we are likely to remain blind to the fact that this limitation is in the nature of the *theory* and not in the nature of the *human mind*. Hypnotherapy, behavior therapy, certain forms of family therapy, and a number of brief therapeutic techniques successfully practice what in the psychodynamic framework would be symptomatic treatment pure and simple.

When in 1904 a panel of thirteen eminent scientists certified that a stallion, since then known as Clever Hans [132], was a genius, capable of the most amazing intellectual feats, the same mechanism seems to have been at work. What was involved in this weird miscarriage of scientific thinking was a simple process of nonverbal interaction between the horse and the experimenters. But nonverbal communication had no place in the scientific paradigm of that era and, therefore, exactly in Ashby's sense, the observers had to fall back on an absurd explanation "to fill the gap caused when part of the system is unobservable"—or, more to the point, when the observers are blind to that part. *If* a horse can do arithmetic and *if* deception can be ruled out, then this horse *is* a genius—this is how the panel of experts must have seen it.

In arriving at their fantastic but (for them) inevitable conclusion (which was led *ad absurdum* three months later by a graduate student who simply looked in the right direction), these scientists had actually committed the mistake which Molière had spoofed 250 years earlier in one of his comedies: He has a panel of learned doctors investigate the reason why opium makes people sleep. After careful consideration they arrive at the conclusion that this is so because opium contains a "dormitive principle." A word thus leads to a reification, i.e., is made into a thing *(res)* and—to quote Ashby once more—"one may then be tempted to start looking for the thing; and one may discover that this 'thing' has some very curious properties." For it seems naively obvious that if there exists a name, then the thing thus named *must* exist. That a disembodied name should flutter around in our conceptual universe, like those little bodiless angels in baroque paintings, is an almost intolerable thought, Alfred Korzybski notwithstanding. He never tired of insisting that the name is not the thing and the map not the territory [89].

It should by now be fairly clear what all of this has to do with schizophrenia. When in 1911 Eugen Bleuler published his famous monograph, *Dementia Praecox, oder die Gruppe der Schizophrenien* (which was not translated into English until 1950 [24]), he coined the term "schizophrenia" because he was dissatisfied with the then current name, *Dementia praecox,* which he considered misleading. In his *Textbook of Psychiatry* [25] he explains: "As the disease need not progress as far as dementia and does not always appear *praecociter,* i.e., during puberty or soon after, I prefer the name *schizophrenia.*"

As is known, the new name found rapid international acceptance. What was accepted together with the term was the unquestioned reification that it referred to a split or equivalent deficit of the mind. This was perfectly in keeping with the traditional, monadic approach in psychiatry. It did not, however, mean that there existed (or exists) consensus about the *thing* to which this name refers. To quote Arieti:

> Although I admit that in what we call the schizophrenic syndrome there is still much that is indefinite, variable, inconstant, accessory, I feel nevertheless that there is a more or less homogeneous core which makes

us recognize the schizophrenic person as such and
leads us to some conclusions, some of which have pragmatic value. The fact that the nature of this core has not
yet been fully or uncontroversially determined points
to the incompleteness of the concept of schizophrenia
but does not prove it is a fallacy. [6, p. 501.]

Since on the strength of available evidence little can be
done to heal the supposed split of the mind, it is not surprising that a controversy continues to rage between the advo-
cates of heredity or constitution, endocrine or cardiovascu-
lar causation, biochemistry or neuropathology, degenerative
processes, and a large number of psychological and other
hypotheses.

But every once in a while a case like the following, treated
by the director of the Mental Research Institute, Carlos
Sluzki, finds its way into the literature:

A 29-year-old man—diagnosed schizophrenic for
the prior 6 years—is seen with his mother and two of
his siblings. The family history includes the fact that
his father left them when the patient was 6 years old.
The patient, a very passive, mild-mannered man, was
married, had three children and eventually had an af-
fair that was discovered, and his wife expelled him—or
he abandoned his family—over 6 years ago. A short
time after this he began to produce delusional symptoms and hallucinations, and engaged in bizarre behavior such as masturbating in public and defecating in the
living room of his house. From then on his history is a
series of hospitalizations, remissions, releases, and re-
lapses. In the course of the interview it becomes evident that when the patient behaves psychotically the
family withdraws from him, but when not, swamps

him with infantilizing concern, only to withdraw again as soon as he behaves symptomically. At the end of the interview the psychiatrist tells them: "It is evidently most important for you (the patient) and your family to differentiate clearly between your betraying, abandoning father and you yourself by declaring you insane and therefore not responsible for any action that may make you look like your father. Therefore, we shall suspend any attempt at curing you, for what you are doing is needed by you and your family." In fact, no further family meeting was proposed and the patient's individual therapy was discontinued. He was offered to request medication each day if he wished so, "for needing medication is as good a way of defining you insane as your symptoms."

About a month after this session he requested his discharge from the hospital and has so far remained free of symptoms for 12 months, a time span unheard of in his past. [160, pp. 278–279]

Clearly, this is an outcome for which none of the existing theories and therapies of schizophrenia, divergent as they may otherwise be from one another, can account. This being so, the claim of having achieved a long-term remission in a chronic schizophrenic in a single family session is bound to be rejected in negative unison. The rejection is most likely to involve an ex-post-facto reasoning: Since it is *known* that schizophrenia is a serious mental illness of uncertain origin and difficult treatment, any condition that can be influenced by a brief intervention at the end of just one therapy session cannot, *for this reason,* be schizophrenia. This form of syllogism is well expressed by Salzman in his critique of a book dealing with the successful outcomes of behavior therapy with phobias: "(The author) defines the condition (i.e., phobias) in a way that is acceptable only to conditioning theorists and does not fulfill the criteria of the psychiatric condition of this disorder. Therefore, his statements should not apply to phobias, but to some other condition." [151]

The history of science is full of such mental acrobatics. "If the facts contradict the theory, so much the worse for the facts," Hegel is supposed to have said more than 150 years ago. In other words, once a theory has been accepted as "true," any facts contradicting its truth must be irrelevant or wrong, or—worse still—are likely to lead to a refinement of the theory, but not to its revision "from first premises." Only a "scientific revolution" in Kuhn's sense [93] can make such a revision possible.

It is my contention that the controversy raging over the subject of schizophrenia or, for that matter, any functional disorder as well as over their treatment is of exactly the same kind. Endless time and tens of thousands of pages of learned books and journals are put into the service of establishing, once and for all, that one theory is right and the others therefore wrong. But the purpose of scientific investigation is not and cannot be the discovery of truth. Eternal truth has no place in science—least of all on a subject as intangible and self-reflexive as the human mind. The only sensible criterion is the greater *efficacy* of one approach rather than of another.

What relevance does all this have to the subject matter of this chapter? Apparently very little. Apparently this is nothing but a dilettantish excursion into epistemology rather than the description of a therapeutic technique that could be of some use to the clinician who has to deal with the stark manifestations of schizophrenia.

But this objection *is* the problem. It demands information on practical applications, and it refuses to question the assumptions underlying these applications. In this sense it is analogous to the joke about the judge who asks the defendant: "Have you stopped beating your wife? Answer yes or no," and threatens him with contempt of court when he tries to explain that neither "yes" nor "no" applies, because he has *never* beaten his wife.

In other words: If it is assumed that the cause of schizophrenia is explained by one of the existing theories, then there is no need to look elsewhere and the unsatisfactory results of treatment are due to shortcomings of technique. If, on the other hand, all these theories were concepts "that the *observer* invokes to fill the gap when part of the system is unobservable" or—more likely—is observable but considered irrelevant to or inconsistent with the premises of a particular theory, then the theory *itself* is in need of revision.

A case like the one reported by Sluzki can be shrugged off as irrelevant in terms of existing theories; or it can be seen as the example of an outcome that becomes possible when observable facts are not a priori censored according to their theoretical relevance or irrelevance. Essentially this is an anthropological and not a psychiatric approach. As is known, the training in these two professions is different to the point of mutual exclusiveness. The psychiatrist typically attempts to unravel a patient's pathology on the strength of his knowledge of psychopathology. He tries to elucidate the *causes* of the psychiatric condition. Ideally, the anthropologist does the opposite: In studying an alien culture he tries to keep his mind as free from preconceived assumptions as possible, and he tries to understand that particular culture *on its own terms*, rather than in terms of its deviance from the norms of his own culture. He tries to understand the *effects* of these culture-specific patterns by observing them in the here and now, rather than by investigating their historic origin.

This approach was introduced into psychiatry by the anthropologist Gregory Bateson and his research group in 1956 through their by now classical paper, "Toward a Theory of Schizophrenia" [18], postulating the concept of the double bind. With hindsight wisdom it can indeed be called a reexamination from first premises. Space limitations do not permit to give here a detailed overview of this revision, but the conclusions of major relevance to this chapter are the following:

1. In spite of its title, the paper is not so much a theory of schizophrenia as a basically new way of looking at the formation of human problems in general. Subsequent studies have not only shown the presence of double-bind patterns in other major clinical pictures [162, 163, 177], but also the potentially therapeutic nature of these patterns [20,185].

2. The patterns are seen as existing in the here and now, as circular action-reaction processes between people, i.e., in human systems.

3. The circular causality of these patterns (with reaction feeding back into and thus modifying action) has a systemic nature of its own. It cannot be reduced to any one of the myriads causes that went into its making in the course of time. In classical Gestalt terms, these patterns are more than and different from the sum of its parts.

4. This being so, the question as to *why* the so-called Identified Patient behaves the way he behaves (which is the question underlying the traditional reductionistic, linear, cause-effect approach to mental problems) is replaced by the question: *"What* is going on here and now?"

5. To ask *what?* instead of *why?* is a cybernetic approach.

In dealing with the phenomenon of change and of the transformations involved in change, Ashby specifically points to the difference between these two questions:

Notice that the transformation is defined, not by any reference to what it "really" is, nor by any reference to the physical cause of the change, but by the giving of a set of operands and a statement of what each is changed to. The transformation is concerned with *what* happens, not *why* it happens. [9, p. 11]

There is another reason for the dwindling importance of the question *why*. Modern biology teaches us that the decisive element that can start a whole train of new, complex developments may be a chance event of the kind which comes about at the point of the fortuitous intersection of two independent causal chains. But once this chance event has occurred, the process set in motion by it usually is of an enormously complex, rule-governed nature. In view of this, the French biologist Jacques Monod [119], for instance, speaks of *Chance* and *Necessity* as the two great interdependent principles of evolution. In fact, during the last twenty-five years intense interdisciplinary studies have been carried out in what is now known as *autopoiesis* (self-organization), i.e., a "newly emerging category of paradigms addressing the issues of self-organization and spontaneous phenomena within physical, biological, and social systems" [196]. This as yet by no means unified approach to the processes of perseverance, change, and perturbations is linked with such names as Francisco Varela, Humberto Maturana, Ricardo Uribe, Ilya Prigogine, Henri Atlan, and Gordon Pask.

As we study the immediate circumstance surrounding the outbreak of a psychotic crisis and as we resist the temptation to fill in the gaps in our understanding of the crisis by taking recourse in the "dormitive principles" of some existing theory, we may discover analogies to the findings of the researchers just mentioned, namely, the effects of chance events on the eruption of seemingly monolithic crises.

This is the basis of the brief therapy approach not just to

schizophrenia but to any problem that may be termed a functional pathology: a careful investigation of the practical, concrete circumstances coinciding with the onset of the crisis. This search will yield a specific event or a set of connected events that either occurred for the first time and were mishandled or—more likely—will reveal the recurrence of particular events for which the same inappropriate and unsuccessful attempts at solving them were again applied, as already in the past. What is meant by just such a set of circumstances and how a chance event can further complicate them is illustrated by the following example:

A young woman in intensive psychotherapy develops the suspicion that her therapist has hired the services of a colleague to spy on her. It turns out that this colleague is a psychiatrist who occasionally substitutes for her therapist on weekends. She, therefore, knows his name (Dr. F.) but has never seen him. In a session she angrily reports that he again followed her around during a recent visit to a park. Her therapist suggests that she make an appointment with Dr. F. to see if this is indeed the man. She accepts the idea, but in order to save money decides that she will just sit in Dr. F's waiting room shortly before the full hour so that she can take a look at him when he dismisses one patient and asks the next one into his office.

It so happens that Dr. F. has an appointment with a new female patient whom *he* has not yet seen and who is late for her first visit. On finding the young woman waiting, he of course assumes her to be his new patient and in a matter-of-fact way says: "Oh, there you are already—I'll be with you in just a moment."

The patient realizes that, on the one hand, Dr. F. is not the man she saw in the park, but on the other hand his remark "proves" to her that he knows her and was expecting her. The suspicion of an ominous coalition between the two therapists is now much stronger and is further compounded by both therapists' attempts to clarify the "innocent" nature of the complication.

The next example has very much the same structure, except that the chance event is replaced by a deliberate action undertaken with the best of intentions:

An elderly woman is in counseling for some rather minor, long-standing difficulties with her daugther and her daughter's husband, in whose home she lives. She has the unpleasant impression (and many incidents to prove it) that the young couple is overprotective and intrusive. In particular she suspects that her son-in-law has recently installed hidden microphones in her part of the (rather large) house. She now feels invisibly surveilled even with doors and windows closed. When she complains and demands to know what is going on, she only gets evasive answers.

Rather than to interpret this idea as a well-documented part of many involutional complications, the psychiatrist decides to have a session with the young couple. Without being asked, they immediately express their concern for the old lady's failing health and their fear that she may fall, fracture a leg or a hip, and then lie helplessly in her part of the house, perhaps for several hours, without being discovered. Therefore the husband, who is an electronics engineer, decided to install microphones in her rooms, but in order to avoid worrying the old lady "unnecessarily," he and his wife decided not to tell her about these installations.

This example is nothing but a more flamboyant version of the numerous stories, known to every clinician, of medication being mixed into somebody's food who promptly develops "delusions" of being poisoned by his family, or of the supposedly "merciful" lies to trick somebody into hospitalization, to say nothing about what we now know about the famous Schreber case [125, 152] and the starkly concrete external facts connected with it. Clearly, in all of these instances the attempt to look for the pathology in just one person in a system of relationships can be accomplished only at the price of attributing "dormitive principles" to that individual.

Of course, to all of this one may point out that an abnormal situation already existed before the trigger event occurred, for otherwise, i.e., under "normal" circumstances, a human system would have no difficulty coping with the event. But by the same logic one might just as well argue that the crisis would never have arisen without the trigger event. This means further that the obvious goal of therapeutic intervention must be that particular event and its immediate consequences, so as to restore that human system to a level of adequate functioning. The purpose of responsible, realistic therapy cannot be a problem-free life but adequate functioning—a term that embraces a wide gamut of more or less successful adaptations to the ups and downs of life but is far from perfection.

Practical experience with these crises teaches us that usually a difficult situation exists for a long time, but without any need for outside expert help, until a trigger event of the kind described above produces a crisis. The direct, practical consequences of this event are then typically dealt with by all concerned in a counterproductive, deviation-amplifying way. These attempted solutions then compound what started as a mere coincidence or a practical difficulty into a problem that is beyond the coping powers of the system and snowballs into dilemmas of bizarre proportions. Experience further teaches us that the difference between acute and chronic pathology is merely one of duration: chronic problems have been mishandled *longer*, but in very much the same way, than acute ones.

Taking these factors into account enables the therapist to

intervene effectively and rapidly, as exemplified by the following case, which was originally described elsewhere and in a different context [185]:

A woman in her fifties came for help because her twenty-five-year-old chronically schizophrenic son seemed on the verge of another psychotic break. Since the age of fifteen he had spent most of his time in mental hospitals and had been in almost continuous intensive psychotherapy. He was asked to come in with his mother on her second visit. Although his statements were riddled with cryptic remarks, unlabeled metaphors, and other speech characteristics of schizophrenia, he did, when pressed for a description of the *present* problem, explain his concrete dilemma: He was living a marginal existence in a rented room, financially supported by his parents. However, he could never be sure how much money he was going to receive from them and when. From the way the mother described the problem, it became clear that the parents found it unfeasible to give him a certain amount on a regular basis because they were convinced that he would foolishly squander it within a few days and then demand more. It also seemed that their way of doling out money to him was determined by their judgment as to how sanely or how crazily he was behaving at any given time. The uncertainty created by this attempted solution contributed to his erratic behavior, which, in turn, convinced the parents that another psychotic episode was imminent.

At this point the therapist made his intervention by instructing the son to *deliberately* utilize psychotic behavior, explaining that since the son felt helpless to contend with his parents' stubborn refusals to comply with his wish for a fixed weekly (or even monthly) living allowance, he had the right to defend himself by threatening to cause an even greater expenditure by his having to go to a mental hospital again. Therefore, the therapist suggested, he should turn on psychotic behavior, which the therapist described very much in terms of the eccentricities displayed by the patient in the course of the session. With this the session was terminated. The mother was seen individually for a few more times, during which she stated that she was now uncertain which of the son's behaviors were "really" crazy and which were feigned.

In the follow-up interview several months later it turned out that the mother had begun to feel much less threatened by her son's behavior and had been paying him a larger amount on a regular basis, making it clear that with this money he could sink or swim. The son, on the other hand, had managed to save enough of this money to buy an old car, which in turn gave him much greater independence from his mother, who until then had been acting as his chauffeuse.

This, of course, is not a "cure" of schizophrenia—but then, what is? The result is a significant, practical improvement of a situation which without the therapeutic intervention would probably have led to another hospitalization with all its additional economic, psychological, and social consequences. To many therapists a small, concrete, limited, and presumably not life-long improvement is not good enough. But he who operates with more grandiose designs may find himself with less grandiose results, or as Robert Ardrey [5] once put it: "While we pursue the unattainable we make impossible the realizable."

The main ideas presented in this chapter were tested on a large scale not at the Mental Research Institute but independently by a group of clinicians and researchers who had arrived at similar practical conclusions. This work began in 1964 at the Family Treatment Unit of the Colorado Psychiatric Hospital in Denver under the direction of psychiatrist Donald Langsley. Their main goal was the avoidance of hospitalization of acutely psychotic patients. They attempted this by investigating the circumstances of the precipitating crisis in the course of the first session in which all available family members were brought together as soon as the identified patient had been admitted to the unit. For research and evaluation purposes these admittances were made on a random basis. To quote from one of their reports:

> The request for hospitalization of one member of the family is assumed to evolve from a series of events. A hazardous event such as a death, maturation of a child, a job change or a host of other "usual problems of living" requires adjustment. Most families master these stresses without serious decompensation, but when the family includes a susceptible individual or when the family has become used to dealing with problems by using psychiatric hospitals, the stage may be set for symptoms of mental illness. [100, p. 146]

In 1968 the Denver Group published the results of the first seventy-five (randomly assigned) cases treated by them and the comparison with a control group of seventy-five other patients who underwent routine psychiatric hospitalization at the same hospital. They reported:

> Of the 75 family crisis cases, none were hospitalized during the crisis treatment. Instead of being hospitalized they were treated by an average of 4.2 office sessions, 1.6 home visits, 4.5 telephone calls, and 1.3 contacts with other social agencies. Of the 75 control cases, all were hospitalized. They were in the hospital a total of 1,959 days, an average of 26.1 days per case. In other words, none of the experimentals and 100 per cent of the controls became mental hospital patients as a result

of the current problems and the treatment approach.
[99, p. 161]

The study also shows that the Denver group did not simply postpone hospitalization, but that the recidivism rate of
their sample was much lower than that of the control group:

> For the controls (hospital cases) 13 (17%) of the sam-
> ple were rehospitalized within a month after discharge.
> Over the next 5 months an additional three of the 75
> cases were readmitted to a psychiatric hospital. By the
> end of six months, 21 per cent of the sample had been
> readmitted to a mental hospital. Of the 75 Family
> Treatment Unit cases, only five were admitted to a
> mental hospital during the first month. This represents
> 7 per cent of the sample rather than 17 per cent. By the
> end of six months, a total of 14 patients had been hospi-
> talized at one point or the other. This does not look
> enormously different for experimentals and controls. It
> would suggest that perhaps we have only delayed hos-
> pitalization rather than prevented it. If we had only
> delayed hospitalization, our subsequent hospitalization
> rate would be much higher than that of the controls. In
> fact it is *lower*. [99, p. 162]

The general approach described in this paper almost necessarily imposes certain departures from routine clinical
practice. To conclude my presentation, I want to list some
of them here without claiming this list to be complete or
exhaustive:

1. If it is accepted that the very first contact with a new
case is decisive, then it stands to reason that it must be made
by the most experienced therapist available. Traditionally,

the very opposite is the case: The intake interview is considered a lowly routine job and left to an intern or first-year resident. This practice is blind to the enormous therapeutic potential of this first contact for the entire course of treatment, to say nothing about the individual, familial, social, and economic consequences of being declared insane. For, as Rosenhan [147] has shown, the diagnostic label routinely slapped on every case constructs a reality all of its own which by the nature of the ensuing interaction perpetuates itself. And once a schizophrenic, always a schizophrenic— because everybody "knows" what that is.

2. If diagnostic terms cannot be avoided altogether, they should at least be used as verbs and not as nouns. It is considerably less heuristic to think of *schizophrenia* as a thing, than to think in terms of *being* or *acting schizophrenic*, i.e., as the sum of behaviors in a specific context.

3. If it is accepted that the chance of intervening rapidly and decisively is lost by the routine application of some standardized intake procedure, it follows that only the immediate past must be concentrated on. What then matters are effects, not causes. Any attempt to explore the remote genesis of the problem in the identified patient's individual life is of little, if any, practical value. A detailed history makes sense in the linear model of intrapsychic treatment, but not in the interactional, system-oriented paradigm. One might even go so far as to suspect that the only effect of a well-taken history is to reduce the therapist to almost the same state of hopelessness and pessimism as his patients and to blind him to the decisive facts and therapeutic potentialities inherent in the here and now.

4. In line with all of this, the question to be asked is not the time-honored *Why?* (i.e., Why does the patient behave the

way he is behaving?), but rather *What for?* In other words, what specific purpose is served by that behavior in the interactional situation of which the patient is a part? This is another way of saying that his behavior may appear bizarre and pathological only when considered in monadic isolation, but when examined in its natural context reveals itself as the best possible—perhaps the *only* possible—adaptation to that context. It thus becomes the royal road toward the understanding of the pathogenic situation itself.

5. Once the dynamics of that situation are sufficiently understood, the task of therapy then consists in the introduction into this system of new behavior patterns which the system was unable to generate from within itself. As explained in detail elsewhere [179,185], these interventions into a disturbed system are *active* ones and do not rely on the classic methods of explanation, confrontation, interpretation, etc., but rather on direct behavior prescriptions, therapeutic double binds, and positive connotations.

6. The goals of these interventions are concrete, practical, pragmatic changes and improvements, and not nebulous constructs like self-esteem, ego strength, emotional catharsis, consciousness raising, or the decoding of the deep, symbolic meaning of the patient's psychotic actions and verbalizations. Admittedly this is a radical departure from established practice, which considers insight the precondition of change. But Heinz von Foerster's conclusion, "If you desire to see, learn how to act," [50, p. 61] is again applicable here.

C H A P T E R
6

Imaginary Communication

*From earlier chapters we know that a relationship is more than,
and different from, the sum total of its components, and thus has
the properties of an* emergent quality, *or* Gestalt.

*So far, however, we have investigated only human relation-
ships, but similar qualities may emerge on a purely* imaginary
*basis—and by no means only as delusions or hallucinations.
Imaginary communication with a not "really" existing partner
may have the heuristic value of a "thought experiment" and
thereby lead to concrete and scientifically as well as philosophically useful insights and results.*

•

In this chapter I want to present examples of communication contexts that are purely imaginary but at the same time
lead to intriguing, albeit contradictory conclusions. My li-
cense for doing this is the same as the mathematician's; his
business, as Nagel and Newman once stated, "is to derive
theorems from postulated assumptions," and "it is not his
concern as a mathematician to decide whether the axioms
he assumes are actually true" [123, p. 11].

Étienne de Condillac, the eighteenth-century philosopher

and economist, used to outline what was to become the basis of so-called association psychology by postulating an at first inanimate statue which became more and more human as he imagined it to be increasingly endowed with perceptual capabilities. But the classic example is Maxwell's Demon, an imaginary tiny doorkeeper who controls the connection between two containers filled with the same gas. The molecules of any gas bounce around randomly and at different speeds. The Demon uses his little door to allow the free passage of any molecule that comes shooting from container A into container B, but quickly closes the door whenever a molecule tries to bounce from B into A. Gradually, therefore, container A is filled with most of the fast-moving molecules, while B contains the slow (low energy) ones. As a result of this discrimination by the Demon, the temperature in container A rises while B gets colder, although they both started out with the same internal temperature. This, however, contradicts the Second Law of Thermodynamics. Although the entire matter was "only" an intellectual exercise, it greatly bothered theoretical physicists for a long time. Maxwell's Paradox, as it became known, was eventually resolved by the physicist Leon Brillouin, who, on the basis of a paper by Szilard, showed that the Demon's observation of the molecules amounted to an increase of information within the system, an increase that had to be paid for by exactly the amount of energy the Demon generated. Thus, while to laymen the entire idea of Maxwell's Demon seems absurd, it led physicists to important insights into the interdependence of energy and information.

Newcomb's Paradox

Every once in a while the long list of paradoxes is enriched by a new, particularly intriguing, mind-boggling one.

In 1960, a theoretical physicist at the Livermore Radiation Laboratories of the University of California, Dr. William Newcomb, hit upon yet another, reportedly while trying to sort out the Prisoner's Dilemma. Through various intermediaries it eventually reached Harvard University philosopher Robert Nozick, who published it in a truly mind-bending paper in 1970 [126]. In 1973 it was reviewed by Martin Gardner in *Scientific American* [58] and produced such a flood of readers' letters that Gardner, after consulting with Nozick, published a column, with a second article on the subject by Nozick [59].

This paradox is based on communication with an imaginary Being; a Being that has the ability to predict human choices with *almost* total accuracy. As Nozick defines the Being's ability (and the reader is urged to pay attention to his definition, since it is indispensable to the understanding of what is to follow): "You know that this Being has often correctly predicted your choices in the past (and has never, so far as you know, made an incorrect prediction about your choices), and furthermore you know that this Being has often correctly predicted the choices of other people, many of whom are similar to you, in the particular situation to be described below."

The Being shows you two boxes and explains that Box 1 contains $1,000, while Box 2 contains either $1 million or nothing. You have two choices: to take what is in both boxes, or to take only what is in the second box. The Being has arranged the following outcomes: if you choose alternative 1 and take what is in both boxes, the Being (predicting this) will leave Box 2 empty; you therefore get only $1,000. If you decide to take only Box 2, the Being (predicting this) puts the $1 million in it. This is the sequence of events: The Being makes his prediction, *then* (depending on his prediction of your choice), he either does or does not put the $1 million in Box 2, *then* he communicates the conditions to you, *then* you make your choice. You fully understand the conditions, the Being knows you understand them, you know that he knows, and so on.

The beauty of this imaginary situation is that there are two equally possible and equally plausible but totally contradictory outcomes. What is more, as Newcomb quickly found and as the deluge of letters Gardner received amply demonstrated, one of the choices will immediately appear to you the "obvious" and "logical" one and you will not for the life of you understand how anybody could possibly even consider the other. Yet a very strong argument can be made for either strategy.

According to the first argument, you can have almost complete confidence in the Being's predictive ability. Therefore, if you decide to take both boxes, the Being will almost certainly have predicted this and will have left Box 2 empty. But if you decide to take only what is in the second box, the Being will almost certainly have predicted this choice as well and will have put the $1 million in it. So it obviously makes sense to choose only Box 2. Where is the problem?

The problem lies in the logic of the second argument. Remember that the Being makes his prediction first, then tells you the conditions, and *then* you decide. This means that by the time you make your decision, the $1 million *is already in the second box or it is not.* Ergo, if it is in Box 2, and you elect to take what is in both boxes, you get $1,001,000. But if Box 2 is empty and you take both boxes, you get at least the $1,000 from Box 1. In either case you get $1,000 *more* by choosing both boxes than by taking only what is in Box 2. The inescapable conclusion is that you should decide to open both boxes.

Oh no, the supporters of the first argument are quick to point out: It is this very reasoning that the Being has (almost certainly) predicted correctly and has therefore left Box 2 empty.

You don't get our point, the defenders of the second argument reply: The Being has made his prediction and the $1 million now is (or is not) in Box 2. No matter what you decide, the money has already been there (or not been there) for an hour, a day or a week *before* you made your decision. Your decision is not going to make it disappear if it is already in Box 2, nor will it make it suddenly appear in Box 2 as a result of your decision to take only what is in Box 2. You make the mistake of believing that there is some sort of "backward causality" involved—that your decision will make the $1 million appear or disappear, as the case may be. But the money is already there or not there *before* you make up your mind. In either case it would be foolish to take only Box 2; for if Box 2 is filled, why forgo the $1,000 in Box 1? If Box 2 turns out to be empty, you will certainly want to win at least the $1,000.

Nozick invites the reader to try this paradox on friends and students, and he predicts that they will divide fairly evenly into proponents of the two contradictory arguments. Moreover, most of them will think that the others are silly. But, Nozick warns, "it will not do to rest with one's belief that one knows what to do. Nor will it do to just repeat one of the arguments, loudly and slowly." Quite correctly, he demands that one must pursue the other argument until its absurdity becomes evident. This, however, nobody has so far succeeded in doing.

It is possible—but has not, to the best of my knowledge, been previously suggested—that this dilemma is based on a fundamental confusion between two very distinct meanings of the apparently unambiguous proposition *if-then*. In the sentence "If Tom is the father of Bob, then Bob is the son of Tom," the *if-then* signifies a timeless logical relationship between the two. But in the statement "If you press this button, then the bell will ring," the relationship is a purely causal one, and all causal relationships are temporal in the sense that there is of necessity a time lag between cause and effect, be it only the millisecond needed by the electric current to flow from the button to the bell.

It may well be that people defending the first argument (to take only what is in Box 2) are reasoning on the basis of the logical, timeless meaning of *if-then:* "If I decide to take only what is in Box 2, then the box contains $1 million." The supporters of the second argument (to take what is in both boxes) appear to be reasoning on the basis of the causal, temporal *if-then:* "if the Being has *already* made his prediction, then he has accordingly put, or not put, the $1 million in Box 2, and in either case I get $1,000 more if I take what is in both boxes." As the reader can see, the second argument is based on the causal time sequence: prediction—(non)placement of the money—my choice. In this perspective my choice comes *after* both the Being's prediction of my choice and his subsequent (non)placement of the money, and my choice cannot exert any backward influence over what took place *before* it.

This possible solution of Newcomb's Paradox requires a thorough examination from first principles that I am alas incompetent to perform but that may provide an interesting challenge to a graduate student of philosophy.

At this point several strands left dangling in the pages of this book begin to converge into a discernible texture. We have seen that the question of whether or not our reality has an order is of the greatest importance. There are three possible answers:

1. It has no order, in which case reality is tantamount to *confusion* and chaos, and life would be a psychotic nightmare.

2. We relieve our existential state of *disinformation* by inventing an order, forget that we have invented it, and experience it as something "out there" which we call reality.

3. There is an order. It is the creation of some higher Being on whom we depend but who itself is quite independent of us. *Communication* with this Being, therefore, becomes man's most important goal.

Most of us manage to ignore possibility 1. But none of us can avoid making some sort of commitment—no matter how vague or unconscious—for possibility 2 or 3. As I see it, this is what the Newcomb Paradox drives home so forcefully: you either believe that reality, and with it the course of events, is rigidly, inescapably ordered, as defined by possibility 3, in which case you take only what is in Box 2, or you subscribe to possibility 2—you believe that you can decide independently, that your decision is not predetermined, that there is no "backward causality" (making future events determine the present or even the past), and take what is in both boxes.

As Gardner has pointed out, this amounts to a restatement of the age-old controversy over determinism versus free will. And this innocent little mind game suddenly throws us into one of the oldest unsolved problems of philosophy.

What the problem boils down to is this: When faced with the everyday necessity of making a choice, any choice, how do I choose? If I really believe that my choice, like any other event, is determined by (is the inescapable effect of) all the causes in the past, then the idea of free will or free choice is an illusion. It does not matter how I choose, for whatever I choose is the only thing I *can* choose. There are no alternatives, and even if I think there are, this thought itself is nothing but the effect of some cause in my personal past. Whatever happens to me and whatever I myself do is

predetermined by something that, depending on my prefer-
ence (oops—I mean, of course, depending on some inescapable cause in my past) I may call causality,* the Being, the
divine experimenter or fate.

If I really believe that my will is free, then I live in a totally
different reality. I am the master of my fate, and what I do
here and now creates my reality.

Unfortunately both views are untenable, and nobody, no
matter how "loudly and slowly" he makes his case for one or
the other, can live by it. If everything is strictly determined,
what is the use of trying, of taking risks, how can I be held
responsible for my actions, what about morals and ethics?
The outcome is fatalism, which itself suffers from a fatal
paradox: to embrace this view of reality one must make a
nonfatalistic decision—one must decide in what amounts to
a *free act of choice* that whatever happens is fully determined
and that there is no freedom of choice.

But if I am the captain of my ship, if I am not determined
by past causes, if I can freely make my decisions—then what
on earth do I base them on?

There does not seem to be an answer, although many
have been offered in the course of the past two thousand
years, from Heraclitus and Parmenides to Einstein. To mention just a few of the more modern ones: for Leibniz the
world is a huge clockwork, wound up once and for all by
God and now ticking away into eternity, with not even the
divine clockmaker himself able to alter its course. So why

---

*The scientific concept that comes closest to Newcomb's Being is, of course,
causality, a very high statistical probability of outcome: If I release my pen in
midair, it will fall to the floor. I expect this because on all previous occasions it (or
any other object, for that matter) has always fallen and it has never (with me or
anybody else, as far as I know) shot up to the ceiling. But according to modern
scientific theory, there is absolutely no guarantee that the next time it will not do
just that. If we compare Nozick's definition of the Being with this definition of
causality, the similarity is evident.

worship this God if He Himself is powerless to influence His own creation, causality? This is the essence of a famous scholastic paradox: God is caught by His own rules; either He cannot create a rock too heavy to lift Himself, or He cannot lift it—in either case He is not omnipotent. Laplace is the most famous advocate of the extreme deterministic view:

> We ought then to regard the present state of the universe as the effect of its anterior state and as the cause of the one which is to follow. Given for one instant an intelligence which could comprehend all the forces by which nature is animated and the respective situation of the beings who compose it—an intelligence sufficiently vast to submit these data to analysis—it would embrace in the same formula the movements of the greatest bodies of the universe and those of the lightest atom; for it, nothing would be uncertain and the future, as the past, would be present to its eyes.
> [101, p. 4]

There is no biographical evidence that Laplace based his own life on this world-view and reached the logical conclusion, fatalism. In fact, he was a very active, creative scientist and philosopher, deeply concerned with social improvements. Monod [119, pp. 82–83] attempts the solution on the basis of the complementarity of chance and necessity. And in a lecture at the University of Göttingen in July 1946, the famous physicist Max Planck suggested a way out of the dilemma by postulating a duality of viewpoints: the external, or scientific, and the internal, or volitional. As he summarized it in a subsequent publication, the controversy of free will versus determinism is a phantom problem:

We can therefore say: Observed from without, the will is causally determined. Observed from within, it is free. This finding takes care of the problem of the freedom of the will. This problem came into being because people were not careful enough to specify explicitly the viewpoint of the observation, and to adhere to it consistently. This is a typical example of a phantom problem. Even though this truth is still being disputed time and again, there is no doubt in my mind that it is but a question of time before it will gain universal recognition. [134, p. 75].

Forty years have passed since this was written, but there is no sign that it has gained universal recognition as a resolution of the free-will dilemma. If it is a phantom problem, Planck seems to have given it a phantom solution.

Dostoevsky, on the other hand, attempts no solution. He places the dilemma squarely before our eyes: Jesus and the Grand Inquisitor represent free will and determinism, respectively, and they are both right and both wrong. When all is said and done, we find ourselves where Ivan Karamazov's poem finishes—unable to follow either Jesus' "Be spontaneous" paradox of free compliance or the deceptive illusion deliberately imposed by the Grand Inquisitor. What we do instead and will continue to do every day of our lives is to ignore both horns of the dilemma by blunting our minds to the eternal contradiction and living as if it did not exist. The outcome is that strange affliction called "mental health" or, funnier still, "reality adaptation."

Flatland

Almost a hundred years ago the headmaster of the City of London School, the Reverend Edwin A. Abbott, wrote a small, unimposing book. He was a classics scholar, and his works—over forty in number—deal mostly with the classics or with religion. But, to borrow James Newman's pithy remark [124, p. 2383] "his only hedge against oblivion" is that little book with the title *Flatland: A Romance in Many Dimensions* [1].

While *Flatland* is written in, shall we say, a rather flat style, it is nevertheless a unique book, not only because it anticipates some developments of modern theoretical physics but because of its astute psychological intuition which the heaviness of its Victorian style fails to squelch. I have often wished that it, or a modernized version, would be made required reading in high schools.

Flatland is told by an inhabitant of a two-dimensional world—that is, it has length and breadth but no height—a world as flat as a sheet of paper covered with lines, triangles, squares, etc. The people move around freely on or, rather, in this surface, but like shadows, they are unable to rise above or sink below that plane. Needless to say, they are unaware of this inability; the existence of a third dimension—height —is unimaginable to them.

The narrator has a mind-shattering experience preceded by a strange dream. In his dream he is transferred to Lineland, a one-dimensional world where all the beings are either lines or points, moving to and fro on the same straight line. This line is what they call space, and the idea of moving to the left or right of this "space," instead of merely to and fro, is totally unimaginable to the Linelanders. In vain the dreamer tries to explain to the longest line in Lineland (the monarch) what Flatland is like. The King considers him deluded, and the narrator eventually loses his patience:

> Why waste more words? Suffice it that I am the completion of your incomplete self. You are a line, but I am a Line of Lines, called in my country a Square:

and even I, infinitely superior though I am to you, am of little account among the great nobles of Flatland, whence I have come to visit you, in the hope of enlightening your ignorance. [p. 64]

Upon hearing these mad insults, the King and all his line- and point-shaped subjects prepare to launch an attack on the Square, who at this moment is awakened to the realities of Flatland by the sound of the breakfast bell.

In the course of the day, another disconcerting event takes place. The Square is teaching his little grandson, a Hexagon,* some basic notions of arithmetic as applied to geometry. He shows him how the number of square inches in a square can be computed by simply elevating the number of inches of one side to its second power:

The little Hexagon meditated on this a while and then said to me, "But you have been teaching me to raise numbers to the third power: I suppose 3^3 must mean something in Geometry; what does it mean?" "Nothing at all," replied I, "not at least in Geometry; for Geometry has only Two Dimensions." And then I began to shew the boy how a Point by moving through a length of three inches makes a Line of three inches, which may be represented by 3; and how a Line of three inches, moving parallel to itself through a length of three inches, makes a Square of three inches every way, which may be represented by 3^2.

Upon this, my Grandson, again returning to his for-

---

*As the narrator explains, it is a law of nature in Flatland that a male child always has one more side than his father, provided the father is at least a Square and not merely a lowly Triangle. When the number of the sides becomes so great that the figure can no longer be distinguished from a circle, the person is a member of the Circular or Priestly Order.

mer suggestion, took me up rather suddenly and exclaimed, "Well, then, if a Point, by moving three inches, makes a Line of three inches represented by 3; and if a straight Line of three inches, moving parallel to itself, makes a Square of three inches every way, represented by 3^2; it must be that a Square of three inches every way, moving somehow parallel to itself (but I don't see how), must make Something else (but I don't see what) of three inches every way—and this must be represented by 3^3."

"Go to bed," said I, a little ruffled by this interruption: "if you would talk less nonsense, you would remember more sense." [p. 66]

Thus the Square, paying no attention to the lesson he might have drawn from his dream, repeats exactly the same mistake he tried so hard to point out to the King of Lineland. But as the evening progresses he cannot quite shake off the prattle of the little Hexagon, and eventually exclaims aloud, "The boy is a fool, I say; 3^3 can have no meaning in geometry." At once he hears a voice: "The boy is not a fool; and 3^3 has an obvious geometrical meaning." The voice belongs to a strange visitor who claims to have come from Spaceland—an unimaginable universe in which things have three dimensions. The visitor tries to make the Square see what three-dimensional reality is like and how limited Flatland is by comparison. And just as the Square introduced himself to the King of Lineland as a Line of Lines, the visitor defines himself as a Circle of Circles, called a Sphere in Spaceland. This, of course, the Square cannot grasp, for all he sees of his visitor is a circle—but a circle with most disturbing, unexplainable properties: it waxes and wanes in diameter, occasionally shrinking to a mere point and disappearing altogether. Very patiently the Sphere explains that there is nothing strange about this: He is an infinite number of circles, varying in size from a point to a circle of thirteen inches in diameter, placed one on top of the other. When he passes through the two-dimensional reality of Flatland, he is at first invisible to a Flatlander, then—upon touching the plane of Flatland—he appears as a point; as he continues, he looks like a circle, constantly growing in diameter, until he begins to shrink and eventually disappears again (see Figure 6.1).

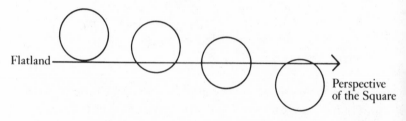

Figure 6.1 *The Sphere passing through Flatland.*

This also explains how the Sphere managed to enter the Square's two-dimensional house despite its locked doors—he simply stepped into it from above. But the idea of "from above" is so alien to the Square's reality that he cannot fathom it. And since he cannot, he refuses to believe it. Finally the Sphere sees no other recourse than to produce in the Square what we would nowadays call a transcendental experience:

> An unspeakable horror seized me. There was a darkness; then a dizzy, sickening sensation of sight that was not like seeing; I saw a Line that was no Line; Space that was not Space: I was myself, and not myself. When I could find voice, I shrieked aloud in agony, "Either this is madness or it is Hell." "It is neither," calmly replied the voice of the Sphere, "it is Knowl-

edge; it is Three Dimensions: open your eye once again and try to look steadily." [p. 80]

But from this mystical moment on, things take a humorous turn. Intoxicated with the overwhelming experience of stepping into this totally new reality, the Square is now eager to discover the mysteries of higher and higher worlds, of "more spacious space, some more dimensionable dimensionality," the land of four, five, and six dimensions. But the Sphere will have none of this trifling: "There is no such land. The very idea of it is utterly inconceivable." Since the Square will not stop insisting on the point, the infuriated Sphere eventually throws him back into the narrow confines of Flatland.

At this point the moral of the story becomes sadly realistic. The Square sees a glorious career before him: to go forth at once and evangelize the whole of Flatland, proclaiming the Gospel of Three Dimensions. But not only does it become increasingly difficult for him to remember exactly what he perceived in three-dimensional reality, he is eventually arrested and tried by the Flatland equivalent of the Inquisition. Rather than being burned, he is sentenced to perpetual imprisonment under circumstances which the author's uncanny intuition makes sound very much like certain mental hospitals today. Once a year the Chief Circle—that is, the High Priest—comes to visit him in his cell and asks him if he is feeling any better. And every year the poor Square cannot refrain from trying again to convince him that there *is* such a thing as a third dimension. Whereupon the Chief Circle shakes his head and leaves for another year.

What *Flatland* brilliantly depicts is the utter relativity of reality. Perhaps the most murderous element in human history is the delusion of a "real" reality, with all the consequences that logically follow from it. On the other hand, it requires a very high degree of maturity and tolerance for others to live with relative truth, with questions for which there are no answers, with the knowledge that one knows nothing and with the uncertainties produced by paradox. Yet if we cannot develop this ability, we will, without knowing it, relegate ourselves to the Grand Inquisitor's world, in which we will live the lives of sheep, occasionally troubled by the acrid smoke rising from some auto-da-fé or the chimneys of crematoria.

CHAPTER
7

Reality Adaptation
or Adapted "Reality"?
Constructivism and Psychotherapy

Laymen as well as clinical experts consider the degree of a person's reality adaptation an indicator of his mental health or illness. This presupposes, of course, that there is such a thing as an objective reality, or—to be more precise—that if it does exists, it is accessible to human exploration. But what if this is not the case?

This is where the influence of our fourth mentor, Professor Heinz von Foerster, comes into play. He is the former secretary of the renowned Josiah-Macy conferences, which gave birth to cybernetics as the new epistemology. Subsequently he became the founder and director of the Biological Computer Laboratory at the University of Illinois. His connection with MRI began in 1976, when he gave one of the invited addresses at the second Don D. Jackson Memorial Conference, in which he developed the principles of so-called radical constructivism and their signifi-

cance for psychotherapy. To summarize very briefly: Modern constructivism examines those processes of perception, behavior, and communication which we human beings use to create *our individual, social, scientific, and ideological realities, instead of finding them ready-made in the outside world, as we all naively assume. These processes of reality construction which Jean Piaget investigated extensively with regard to small children, overturns the basic tenet of classical psychotherapeutic theory, namely, that we must have "insight" into reality before we can change our behavior. The most concise description of the constructivist view is expressed in von Foerster's Aesthetic Imperative (mentioned at the end of Chapters 4 and 5): If you desire to see, learn how to act.*

The present chapter is taken from a lecture series organized by the Siemens Foundation.

•

At the end of a successful brief therapy, the patient, a young woman, defines the fundamental change of her conflict-ridden relationship with her mother in these words: "The way I saw the situation, it was a problem; now I see it differently, and it is no problem any more." One could comment that, on the one hand, this statement is the quintessence of therapeutic change; on the other one could easily object that nothing has "really" changed—except at best something as subjective as an "opinion" or a "judgment." The fact that these claims are contradictory, and yet make sense, introduces the subject matter of my presentation.

In 1973 the American psychologist David Rosenhan published a sensational study with the title "On Being Sane in Insane Places" [147]. It is the final report on a research project in the course of which eight of his collaborators voluntarily requested admission into mental hospitals, claiming that they heard voices and needed psychiatric care. Immediately after their admission they declared that the voices had stopped and from that moment behaved in a way which outside of a psychiatric clinic would have been considered perfectly normal. The length of their "therapy" varied from seven to fifty-two days, and all of them were discharged with the diagnosis "schizophrenia in remission." Not one of them was unmasked as a pseudo-patient; on the contrary, every aspect of their behavior was judged to be further proof of the accuracy of the diagnosis. Instead of being based on observable facts, the diagnosis *created* a "reality" sui generis, which in turn necessitated and justified specific clinical procedures. The crowning irony was that the only people who did not participate in this reality construction were several "real" patients. "You are not crazy—you must be a journalist or a professor." This and similar remarks were made repeatedly and sometimes vehemently.

In the life of the young woman mentioned earlier the same development took place, although in a positive rather than a pathological direction. The situation itself remained the same; what had changed was the meaning and the significance attributed to her relationship to her mother.

But such attributions of meaning are not reflections of objectively existing, "platonic" truths, of which some people are more aware than others, but can occur only in a specific context. A man who might be considered a swami, a holy man, in India, could be diagnosed as catatonic schizophrenic in the West. Neither the one nor the other judgment is "true" or "real" in any objective sense, but the *consequences* of these attributions of meaning create concrete results of a personal and societal nature.

In his lectures, Gregory Bateson often mentioned an analogous phenomenon reported to him during his anthropological studies in Southeast Asia, namely, the culture-specific pathology of running amok: Someone suddenly grabs a dagger (kris), runs out into the street, and starts stabbing blindly at anyone he comes across. In order to prevent a bloodbath, the person running amok is usually killed as quickly as possible. This suggests that running amok is a masked form of suicide, which is regarded with strong religious disapproval in the Islamic world. Instead of killing himself, the amok runner creates a situation which makes his killing necessary and justifiable. In the course of the colonization of that region by the Dutch, the social meaning of running amok underwent gradual changes: instead of seeing it as a form of demonic possession, it came to be regarded as a mental disorder requiring treatment. The result was that at least in the cities, where social services like police, ambulances, and psychiatric clinics were available, the frequency of people running amok declined. With due regard to the pitfalls of "post hoc, ergo propter hoc" conclusions, especially in anthropology, the fact remains that a person running amok could no longer expect a quick death but was now faced with a long sojourn in a closed institution, which probably resembled a prison more than a sanatorium. Again, the "mere" change of the meaning attributed to a certain behavior led to a fundamental, practical change.

These examples, which could be multiplied at will, stand in stark opposition to the generally accepted criterion of reality adaptation as a measure of a person's mental health or illness. What is involved here is the apparently obvious assumption that there exists an objective reality of which normal people are more conscious than the so-called insane. The idea of such a reality has been philosophically untenable at least since Hume and Kant; in science it has proven to be equally unsound, since it has been recognized that the goal of science cannot be the discovery of ultimate truth.

As far as I know, the belief in a "real" reality has survived only in psychiatry. In this connection it seems useful to differentiate between two basic reality aspects, which can be illustrated with a simple, often quoted example: The physical properties of gold have been known since ancient times, and it is improbable that new studies will throw doubt on this knowledge, or that additional research will greatly add to what is already known. Thus, if two people had a disagreement about the physical properties of gold, it would be relatively easy to furnish scientific proof that one of them is right and the other therefore wrong. These properties of gold shall be called its reality of the first order.* But it is obvious that at the same time there is another aspect to gold, namely, its value, which shall be called its reality of the second order. This second aspect has nothing whatever to do with the physical properties of the metal but is attributed to it by human beings. Admittedly, this reality of gold is itself the result of other factors, as for example supply and demand, or the latest pronouncements of the Ayatollah Khomeini. But what all of *these* factors have in common is that they are human constructs and not the reflections of ultimate truths.

This means that that so-called reality, which is the specific concern of psychiatry, is always a reality of the second order, which we construct by attributing meaning, significance, or value to the first-order reality. The difference between these two realities is expressed by that old playful definition of optimists and pessimists: the optimist says of a bottle of wine that it is half full, the pessimist that it is half empty: the same reality of the first order, but entirely different realities of the second order.

Only when we throw both these "realities" into one pot can we consider the criterion of reality adaptation to be

---

*For simplicity's sake we will disregard the fact that this aspect is itself the result of a fantastically complex reality construction on a neurophysiological level and, furthermore, that it presupposes one and the same linguistic and semantic universe.

valid. If we avoid this fallacy we find that, for example, the situation between mother and daughter mentioned earlier had remained the same in its reality of the first order, that nothing had "really" changed on that level, while in the reality of the second order a decisive transformation had taken place: "The way I saw the situation it was a problem; now I see it differently, and it is no problem any more." But neither the earlier nor the subsequent perspective of the young woman is in any objective sense "truer" or "more correct" than the other—the concrete result of this new point of view is that it causes less suffering.

The speakers of the two previous evenings have examined in depth the processes of reality construction from their specific points of view. In the context of my additional considerations I would like to use a quote from Ernst von Glasersfeld's "Introduction to Radical Constructivism" [64], where he shows that of the "real" reality we can at best know what it is *not:*

> Knowledge can now be seen as something that the organism builds up in the attempt to impose order on the amorphous flow of experience by establishing repeatable experiences and relatively reliable relations between them. The possibilities of constructing such an order are always determined by the preceding steps in the construction. This means that the "real" world manifests itself only at the point where our constructions break down. But since we have to describe and explain these breakdowns with the very concepts that we have used to build the failing structures, this process can never give us a picture of a world which we could hold responsible for this failure. [p. 39]

Applied to the formation and the solution of human problems this means that we feel in harmony with life, fate, existence, with God, nature, or whatever we want to call it, as long as our second-order reality *fits* in von Glasersfeld's sense, i.e., does not lead to painful friction. As long as we have the reassuring feeling of "fitting," we can cope fairly confidently with even major adversities. But when our construction no longer "fits," we fall into despair, fear, psychosis, or thoughts of suicide. That the greatest intellectual and artistic human achievements are obviously inspired by this burning desire for harmony and certainty shall only be mentioned parenthetically here. But the error which we are all caught up in is the assumption that a reasonably fitting reality construction proves that the world is "really" *like that* and that we have therefore found definitive certainty and security. The consequences of this misunderstanding can be very grave: they may make us assume that all other reality constructions are false and thus bring us to oppose and attack them; and they make it impossible for us to even consider necessary alternative realities when our world-view has become anachronistic and begins to "fit" less and less.

To summarize: The reality of the second order, which determines our idea of the world, our thoughts, feelings, decisions, and actions, is the result of a specific order, which we impose on the kaleidoscopic, phantasmagorical multiplicity of the world, and which is therefore not the result of understanding the "real" world but which, in the strictest sense of the word, *constructs* a specific world. We are, however, not aware of this construction and assume naively that it exists independently of us. The way these realities emerge is of the highest interest to researchers as well as clinicians. Again, Piaget's pioneering work [133] comes to mind in this connection.

At approximately the same time as Piaget, Wittgenstein too was studying this subject. At the beginning of his work *On Certainty* [192] we find the sentence: "From its seeming to me—or to everyone—to be so, it does not follow that it *is* so" (prop. 2). And further: "But I did not get my picture of the world by satisfying myself of its correctness; nor do I have it because I am satisfied of its correctness. No: it is the inherited background against which I distinguish between true and false" (prop. 94).

And finally even more explicitly:

> We do not learn the practice of making empirical judgements by learning rules: we are taught *judgements* and their connexion with other *judgements*. *A totality* of judgements is made plausible.
>
> When we first begin to *believe* anything, what we believe is not a single proposition, it is a whole system of propositions. (Light dawns gradually over the whole.)
>
> It is not single axioms that strike me as obvious, it is a system in which consequences and premises give one another *mutual* support. (props. 140–142)

The study of these systems, in which postulates and conclusions reciprocally and recursively support and confirm each other, is one of the main concerns of communication research. Second-order realities can be considered the result of communication. No higher life form could survive if it had to comprehend the world solely on its own. Lower forms of life seem to come with a genetic "set of instructions" and are wiped out mercilessly by death when their genetic program no longer fits. In human beings socialization has always taken precedence over predisposition. And socialization is based on communication, i.e., on instructions as to how to see the world.

All this is by no means relevant only to the reality of the second order. How would we fare if we had only our own immediate sense perceptions to rely upon, even on the level of the first-order reality? What certainty would I ever have that anything whose existence I have not verified myself does in fact exist? I am thoroughly convinced that a city which I have not yet visited really exists, merely because I have seen its name on a map, because other people have been there and told me about it, because I can buy an airplane ticket there at my travel agency, and on the basis of myriad similar, completely fictitious "proofs." And if we all closed our eyes and somehow excluded all other sense perceptions, would this lecture hall still be as "real" as it literally was just a moment before? These are questions which Dchuang Dsi tried to answer with his allegory of the butterfly, and Calderón de la Barca in *La vida es sueño*. In the eighteenth century Bishop Berkeley asked his famous question, whether the fall of a tree in a forest would still make a sound if no one were there to hear it. And Wittgenstein asks: "What reason do I have, now that I do not see my toes, to assume that I have five on each foot?" [192, prop. 429].

Does this mean that we are still like the infant, for whom, as Piaget has shown so elegantly, an object "really" exists only as long as it is in his field of vision; that the belief in permanence, the ongoing existence of objects we can no longer see, is one of the most essential building blocks of reality construction?

Be that as it may, one thing is certainly important among these seemingly idle ruminations: In addition to the assumed physical continuity of the world, there is also the communicated reality of the second order. This means that in our inner world not only the *objects* (in the widest sense of the word) continue to exist but that the meaning, the significance, and the value we have ascribed to these objects persist as well. This means that we are living in an imaginary reality, but one which, nevertheless, makes it possible for us to achieve concrete decisions and actions.

But *is* this surprising? Yes and no. *Yes,* if we bear in mind the already extensive literature of the psychiatric, social, and behavioral sciences and its attempt to bring some order into the hallucinatory universe of paradoxical, self-referential, and imaginary axioms and their practical consequences. *No,* when we realize that in other branches of science such propositions are not seen as problems because of their apparently illogical, fictitious, and imaginary characteristics, but are nonchalantly included into considerations and computations and are nevertheless (or maybe even because of this) leading to concrete results. "When we build ships and boats," writes the Polish philosopher Kolakowski [86, p. 143] in his essay, *The Search for Certainty,* "we should act as if Archimedes' law had validity—lest we drown. But we have today as little reason as we ever had to claim that the world carries within itself, as a permanent property, something like Archimedes' law." This quote contains the pregnant words "as if," which we will soon consider in greater detail.

An even more obvious example than Archimedes' law is the imaginary number i, which one arrives at by way of the seemingly innocent equation $x^2 + 1 = 0$. For if one transposes the number 1 to the other side of the equation, one gets $x^2 = -1$, and thereby $x = \sqrt{-1}$. This result is not only unimaginable but also contradicts the rule that no value, whether positive or negative, divided by itself, can result in a negative number. But this does not prevent mathematicians, physicists, or engineers from including the number i in their computations and achieving perfectly practical results. The fascination of this unaccountable interaction between the imagined and the concrete found literary expression in the words of one of Robert Musil's characters, young Törless, who encounters the properties of the number i for the first time in his mathematics class:

How shall I say it? Look, think of it like this: in a
calculation like that you begin with ordinary solid
numbers, representing measures of length or weight or
something else that's quite tangible—at any rate,
they're real numbers. And at the end you also have real
numbers. But these two lots of real numbers are connected by something that simply doesn't exist. Isn't
that like a bridge where the piles are there only at the
beginning and at the end, with none in the middle, and
yet one crosses it just as surely and safely as if the whole
of it were there? That sort of calculation makes me feel
a bit giddy, as if it led part of the way God knows
where. But what I really feel is so uncanny, is the force
that lies in a problem like that, which keeps such a firm
hold on you that in the end you land safely on the other
side. [122, p.74]

The most comprehensive study of the practical effects of
fictitious assumptions is still Hans Vaihinger's *The Philosophy of "As If."* In this monumental work we find an overa-
bundance of examples of this relationship between fictitious,
totally unprovable reality assumptions or attributions of
meaning and their concrete results. I do not know whether
Musil was aware of Vaihinger's philosophy, but, at any rate,
it is striking that young Törless's question had already been
asked in Vaihinger's work: "How is it that, even though we
work with a falsified reality in our thinking, the practical
result turns out to be correct?" [170, p. 289].

Of the abundance of Vaihinger's examples which reach as
far back as antiquity, two seem particularly relevant to our
subject:

A point as a zero-dimensional construct, is, in itself,
entirely contradictory, though as necessary as it is ab-

surd. A construct without any dimension is, in itself, a nothing. . . . We are here operating with unrealities and not with realities; but they are useful and indispensable unrealities. We regard these unrealities as real, however, because we are accustomed to regard everything as real to which we give a name, without realizing that we can bestow a name on unreal as well as on real things. [pp. 235–236]

And elsewhere an analogous reflection on freedom as fiction:

The judge uses this fiction only in order to arrive at a sentence. The purpose is the legal sentence which is obtained by means of the fiction that man, here in the form of a criminal, is free. Whether man is actually free is a matter of indifference. . . . The judge concludes that every man is free, and therefore if he has sinned against the law, he must be punished. A is a man, a free man, and has transgressed; he is therefore liable to punishment. First A is subsumed under the idea of a free man, then under that of liability to punishment. The idea of freedom, however, drops out here; it has only served to make the sentence possible. But the premise whether man really is free, is not examined by the judge. In actual fact this premise is only a fiction which serves for the deduction of the final conclusion; for without the possibility of punishing men, of punishing the criminal, no government would be possible. The theoretical fiction of freedom has been invented for this practical purpose. [p. 111]

Not from Vaihinger's book but from the wisdom of Oriental parables comes our final example of this "technique," of these problem-solving, reality-creating fictions:

A father has ordered that, after his death, half of his inheritance shall go to his oldest son, a third to the second, and a ninth to the youngest. His estate, however, consists of seventeen camels, and although his sons rack their brains trying to solve the problem, they find no way to obey their father's last wish without cutting up some of the animals. Finally a mullah, a wandering preacher, comes riding by, and they ask for his advice. He tells them: "Here—I'll add my camel to yours; that makes eighteen. You, the oldest, get half, that is nine. You, the second oldest, get a third, that makes six. You, the youngest, shall have a ninth, or two camels. Together that makes seventeen camels and leaves one over, namely mine." And with this he mounts his animal and rides away.

And what has all this to do with psychotherapy? The purpose of all therapy and the goal of all schools of therapy is therapeutic change. In keeping with what has been presented so far, the traditional view, according to which the so-called patient suffers from insufficient reality adaptation and therefore needs help in order to gain insight into the "true" nature of things buried in his past, has become untenable. By contrast, constructivism suggests that the painful, present consequences of a specific as-if fiction (which of course has its origin somewhere in the past) must be replaced by the effects of a different as-if fiction, which creates a more tolerable reality. Reality adaptation, in the sense of a *better* adaptation to a supposedly "real" reality, is replaced by a better adaptation of the *fictional* reality to the desired *practical* results.

In other words, the starting point of treatment is a painful situation which, in the framework of the reality fiction in question, seems unresolvable. This is one pile of young Törless's bridge. Between this and the pile on the other bank stretches the irrational bridge of an as-if fiction, namely, the reality of the second order. In Vaihinger's sense this can, for instance, be the totally unprovable assumption of personal freedom, which is used, and then, after it has served its purpose, dropped; in Heinz von Foerster's sense it is the synaptic fissure into which—metaphorically speaking—now flows a different transmitter fluid; in the sense of the camel story it is that one camel which is used for a short time and is then no longer needed; in the sense of constructivism it is a different reality construction, which can lay no more claim to being real, correct, or true than any other. If the primacy of applying Vaihinger's ideas to therapy did not belong to Alfred Adler, one could call the above technique the "Psychotherapy of As-If."

These consideration sound simple but have an unnerving effect on many people once they realize their full impact. Because it becomes clear then that explanations *as such* are of no importance, that hypotheses and theories have significance only in that they create fictitious bridges to practical results. The proverbial man from Mars studying our classical theories of therapeutic transformation here on Earth would shake his head (or its equivalent) and ask why our great schools of therapy have concocted such exquisitly complicated systems of explanations and defend their supposedly exclusive truth with dogmatic rigidity instead of studying concretely how human change takes place *spontaneously* millions of times every day.

One exception is that *enfant terrible* of orthodox doctrine, hypnosis, which has always employed fictitious, namely, suggestions, in a clear understanding of their as-if quality, as a means toward relative quick solutions of human problems.

But even hypnosis is really just a special case compared to those undoubtedly most interesting, exceedingly common reality constructions, the self-fulfilling prophecies [181, pp. 95–114]. They are based on the reality-creating power of fears, expectations, assumptions, or convictions concerning future events, which take place *only* because they are expected beyond a shadow of doubt. Self-fulfilling prophecies seem to turn the basic laws of reality upside down. Imagined effect creates concrete cause; the future (not the past) determines the present; the prophecy of the event leads to the event of the prophecy. How little the hypothetical "truth" of the prophecy matters is shown by a case reported (though unfortunately not documented) by Gordon Allport [3, pp. 7–21], which is based on a lifesaving misunderstanding:

> In a provincial Austrian hospital, a man lay gravely ill—in fact, at death's door. The medical staff had told him frankly that they could not diagnose his disease, but if they knew the diagnosis they could probably cure him. They told him further that a famous diagnostician was soon to visit the hospital and that perhaps he could spot the problem.
>
> Within a few days the diagnostician arrived and proceeded to make the rounds. Coming to this man's bed, he merely glanced at the patient, murmured *"Moribundus,"* and went on.
>
> Some years later the patient called on the diagnostician and said, "I've been wanting to thank you for your diagnosis. They told me that if you could diagnose me I'd get well, and so the minute you said *'moribundus'* I knew I'd recover."

Hence, the reality-creating power of self-fulfilling prophecies cannot only induce Oedipus to take exactly those precautions which will lead to the fulfillment of the oracle but can also—*similia similibus*—be put in the service of healing and solutions. The treatment techniques developed by the Mental Research Institute in Palo Alto, which are based on direct interventions into the client's second-order reality, are the practical applications of this constructivist thinking [179].

Without entering here into details or present case descriptions, a short synopsis of the nature of this technique may suffice. In order to achieve a specific change in a person's reality construction, one must first of all explore to some extent what this reality is like. Direct questions are of no great help, since every description presupposes that one steps outside the frame of that which is to be described. In other words, if a person were able to describe the reality he constructed, he would have to stand outside this reality, and would, therefore, already be aware of the fact that his is just one of many possible realities. But it is exactly this inability to "step outside" our reality which maintains our state of blindness.

But what the so-called patient can usually explain quite clearly is what he has attempted so far in order to solve his problem. From these attempted solutions the therapist can draw reliable inferences about the reality of the second order, where these attempted solutions seem to be the only possible, meaningful, logical, or permitted ones. And if they have not brought on the desired results, we all—humans as well as animals—apply the distastrous recipe of "more of the same," and thereby create more of the same suffering. A simple example: If someone is nervous he will typically try to speak with a firm voice and stop his hands from shaking. The harder he tries, the greater his tension, and the greater the tension, the more he will try to control it.

These attempted solutions are thus the mechanisms which not only do not solve the problem but maintain and intensify it.

How then does a therapist, using our model, proceed in order to break this vicious circle and to introduce new solutions into the world of his patient? Here the technique of *reframing* may be most indicated. It is nothing new to skillful negotiators and diplomats, who have long used it with great success, though maybe not under that name. Such an intervention constructs a new reality aspect in place of a former one, whereby the new aspect fits the given situation just as well or better than the old view. One of the most amusing examples from world literature is the scene in *Tom Sawyer*, in which the hero is punished by having to whitewash a fence on a Saturday afternoon while all the other boys are free to go swimming. To save face and escape his friends' derision he reinterprets the whole situation and acts as if painting a fence were a rare and highly desirable privilege. At first he meets with skepticism: "Oh come now, you don't mean to let on that you *like* it?" Tom continues to paint and finally remarks casually: "Like it? Well, I don't see why I oughtn't to like it. Does a boy get a chance to whitewash a fence every day?" There is a silence—then the first boy says: "Say, Tom, let *me* whitewash a little." At the end the fence has three layers of paint, and Tom is rolling in wealth. One boy after another has paid him for the privilege of being allowed to whitewash a section of the fence.

Or a clinical example: Frigidity is often considered a personal inhibition, an inability, and this feeling is reinforced by a whole catalogue of different and in part contradictory "scientific" explanations, for example, immaturity, insufficient realization of one's femininity, penis envy, latent homosexuality, subconscious aggression against the male. Especially the last "explanation" adds the imputation of evil intentions on top of personal pathology. One can hardly imagine a more effective as-if fiction to prevent a normal, natural reaction. A much more appropriate fiction would consist in attributing to the problem a totally different meaning, by interpreting it as an an excessive protection of the partner. Does she perhaps think that he could not cope with the passion of her unbridled sensuality? Does she have grounds to fear that he would be shocked if she gave her sexuality free rein? Could he become impotent and does not her reaction protect him from the fear of not measuring up to her needs? Would it not therefore be better to leave the situation the way it is for the time being?

If the reframing is successful it can block the often desperate feeling: "I should react, but I can't." It is important to remember that neither this nor the traditional interpretation is anything other than a fiction, and neither can claim to be true or right. What matters only are the practical results which a specific as-if fiction creates. Once the desired goal has been reached, the fiction itself "drops out," to use Vaihinger's expression; it has served its purpose, as did the eighteenth camel.

In addition to *reframing,* the so-called *behavior prescriptions* have an important place in the armamentarium of constructivist therapy. As the term implies, these are specific tasks which the therapist assigns to his client. Normally no explanations are given, just as a physician rarely discusses with his patient the exact chemical properties or pharmaceutical effects of the medications he prescribes. The patient takes his medicine because he believes that there are medical reasons for doing so. What is important to him are the practical results of the remedy, not the reasons for prescribing it. Taking the medication jumps directly, as it were, from one pile of Musil's bridge to the other, leaving the middle part free. The same result occurs with behavior prescriptions: The prescribed behavior already *is* the result of the as-if fiction in between, although the fiction as such is not discussed. If it becomes apparent at all, it is as a function of the anticipation of the result. In other words, the so-called patient behaves *as if* the problem were already solved, and only subsequently and secondarily does an essential transformation of his reality construction take place.

For example: An exceedingly perfectionist graduate student needs only to finish his dissertation to get his degree. He has been working on it for over three years, and the university has given him another four months to finish it. He realizes that it will be impossible for him to submit it by that deadline if he continues working in his accustomed manner. His attempted solution has been to write his dissertation in such a comprehensive and perfect way that there will be no danger of even the slightest criticism. Without even trying to examine the problem in the classical sense by searching for the reasons in the student's past which may account for this approach and thereby to bring about gradual insight into the "true" causes of the problem, and without giving any reasons for the behavior prescription, the therapist requests the student to expose himself, until the next session to public ridicule once a day, in some harmless way. The student comes back and reports:

> The first time I did it I went into a Mexican restaurant and insisted upon an egg roll and asked: "Isn't that Mexican food?" I felt terrible. I had to steel myself to enter the place and felt extremely embarrassed and self-conscious. The next time, on the street, walking down a street I knew, I asked where that street was—and felt less embarrassed and I had to steel myself less. And as I asked those types of directions more and more, the easier and easier it got and—ah [pause] ah, I began to feel more and more how seriously I take myself and how silly it is [short laugh] and—ah, how this—I'm naturally a reflective person and consequently I began

to speculate or connect all this to my problem and my
personality and my life and my past and my childhood
etc. etc.—but, in effect, it's taking myself very seriously
and I have lessened that. . . . A very useful exercise
[pause] I mean the results were quite immediate, that is
to say, I started taking myself less seriously and was a
little less concerned and less uptight and constricted,
worrying about projecting an image or whatever. [179,
p.109]

In the follow-up interview some four months later, we
learned that he had managed to submit his dissertation in
time and had taken his degree.

Another client complains about his loneliness and the fact
that people avoid and despise him. He therefore is wary and
expects little good from others. But his habitual facial expression is not so much one of sadness, as of suspicion, contempt, and anger. It is not surprising, therefore, that people
try to stay out of his way. He is totally unaware of this
self-fulfilling prophecy and asks himself again and again
why others seem to dislike him so much. He is instructed to
pull up the corners of his mouth in a certain way when he is
in the presence of other people and to note their reactions
carefully. He comes for his next session and reports that
during the last week acquaintances as well as strangers were
much friendlier and seemed more interested in him.

These interventions are in diametrical contrast to the classical view of therapeutic change: Instead of first trying to
gain insight into the nature of the problem and only then
being able to behave differently as a result of this insight, the
decisive factor in every successful behavior prescription is a
specific new behavior, which only secondarily and by no
means necessarily leads to another as-if fiction.

But enough examples. We are only beginning to understand the possibilities that constructivism may hold for our lives. These possibilities go far beyond psychotherapy. Their applicability to much larger areas, as for example problem solving in large organizations and societal systems, has already been proven. That, *mutatis mutandis,* they can also be applied to international relations is no longer a utopia.

But of equal importance is the possibility that constructivism will one day be able to build a bridge between the natural sciences and the humanities.

Finally, constructivism holds for every one of us a deeply personal promise. In one of Wittgenstein's letters from the year 1917 to his friend Paul Engelmann [46, p.7], we find a sentence which makes this basic existential element much clearer than my cumbersome explanations: "But in our better hours we wake up just enough to realise that we are dreaming."

CHAPTER
8

Life Styles and Realities

In the Spring of 1985 the University of Siegen called a meeting of literary critics, linguists, philosophers, sociologists, psychologists, theologians, historians, and archeologists from nine countries at the Inter-University-Center in Dubrovnik to discuss the modern meaning of style.

Taking as its starting point Alfred Adler's classical concept of individual life styles, the essay, read at that colloquium and reprinted here, attempts to illustrate, by means of examples taken from literature and from experimental psychology, how such life styles may give rise to what are considered objective realities.

•

The relevance of my contribution stands and falls with the answer to the question of whether one can speak of a life style, and, if so, whether this concept falls at all within the classical definition of style. My area of competence only permits me to speak on how we humans attempt to give the amorphous, phantasmagoric, and kaleidoscopic manifold of our lives sense, order, and predictability, and how we therefore live and experience our existences in certain definite ways.

In my profession people began talking about life styles during the time of Alfred Adler, the founder of individual psychology. Under this concept, Adler included those typical modes of behavior by which individuals attempt to adapt to the conditions and—most importantly—changes in their lives. He investigated in particular the effects of actual (organic) or supposed (neurotic) "inferiorities" which become the foundation for modes of perception in the life of the person in question. Whoever, like the clinician, concerns himself with the practical consequences of such modes of perception, can hardly escape the impression that the ways in which human beings attempt to order and live their lives depends largely upon suprapersonal realities—for example, cultural, religious, ideological, ethical, and philosophical ideals. "One" must live according to these in such and such a way, until another style of life finally supersedes the "right" and "self-evident" one. But this brings the observer quite close to the concept of stylistic epochs, and undeniable traces of epochal thresholds (sensu Luhmann) begin to appear. This in turn raises the question as to the origin of life styles. At a given moment does the life style of an individual become a model for others, or conversely, is this style marked, and thus limited, by a suprapersonal stylistic configuration?

With this question we fall into a model of linear causality that is no longer tenable today. Of course, there are direct relationships of cause and effect, but these form only a small part of the entire system; if they are removed and viewed independently it is at the cost of their complete reification. That genius and insanity are proverbially related while at the same time appear as irreconcilable is a classic example of the problematic character of this type of linear thinking. A more modern view sees order and chaos as interdependent: order needs disorder and disorder is the result of too rigid order. Each conditions the other and together they (and not a *spiritus rector* standing over them) lead to the self-organization *(autopoiesis)* of all kinds of systems. Admittedly, this insight is no more new than anything else under the sun. It can be found in the Upanishads, in Taoism, and in Heraclitus. Even the fact that the world of science itself is not the reflection of some eternal truth was pointed out by Giambattista Vico back in 1710: "Human knowledge is nothing else but the endeavour to make things correspond to one another in shapely proportions" [175, chap. 7, sec. 3, p. 5].

Modern constructivism bases itself on considerations of this nature [64]. It postulates that all *facts* are precisely that which the word itself actually means—*factum* comes from *facere* (to make, to do). Or as Schrödinger put it: "Every man's world picture is and always remains a construct of his mind and cannot be proved to have any other existence" [156].

But all constructions are inseparable from the concept of style—be it unintentional, as in the technical cohesion of the structural elements of an industrial structure, or obviously unique, as in the just-so-and not-otherwise nature of a work of art. But between this concept of style and that of a life style there remains a difference which for many makes the latter notion unacceptable. That there are innumerable styles in the traditional sense is easily granted, but one's own life style is almost always felt to be the only possible "normal" view of the world—simply because the world "is" just the way it is.

Hermann Hesse's *Magic Theater* offers itself as an allegory for this constructivist view of the world. The hero of the novel, Harry Haller, feels himself to be a wild wolf, "an animal lost in an alien and incomprehensible world, no longer able to find home, air, or sustenance."

One evening on the way home to his drab rented room, Haller has a remarkable experience. On an old wall in a deserted alley in the old part of town, he suddenly sees vibrant, colorful letters:

> Magic Theater. Entrance not for everyone.
> Only—for—madmen!

This "greeting from another world" leads him to search for the theater. Further remarkable encounters and experiences cast his former world-view ever more deeply into question. Finally, at the end of an intoxicating masked ball, he is led by his Psychopomp Pablo to the Magic Theater:

> This little theater of mine has as many doors into as many boxes as you please, ten or a hundred or a thousand, and behind each door exactly what you seek awaits you. It is a pretty cabinet of pictures, my dear friend; but it would be quite useless for you to go through it as you are. You would be checked and blinded at every turn by what you are pleased to call your personality. You have no doubt guessed long since that the conquest of time and the escape from reality, or however else it may be that you choose to describe your longing, means simply the wish to be relieved of your so-called personality. That is the prison where you lie. And if you were to enter the theater as you are, you would see everything through the eyes of Harry and the old spectacles of the Steppenwolf.

In one of the many boxes, each containing a freely chosen reality, there is a chessmaster, who explains:

Science is in the right in so far as no multiplicity may be dealt with unless there be a series, a certain order and grouping. It is wrong in so far as it holds that only a single, binding and life-long order is possible for the multiplicity of subordinate selves.

Hence it is that we supplement the imperfect psychology of science by the conception that we call the art of building up the soul. We demonstrate to anyone whose soul has fallen to pieces that he can rearrange these pieces of a previous self in what order he pleases, and so attain to an endless multiplicity of moves in the game of life. As the playwright shapes a drama from a handfull of characters, so do we from the pieces of the disintegrated self build up ever new groups, with ever new interplay and suspense, and new situations. . . .

Then he passed his hand swiftly over the board and gently swept all of the pieces into a heap; and, meditatively with an artists skill, made up a new game of the same pieces with quite other groupings, relationships and entanglements. The second game had an affinity with the first, it was the same world built of the same material, but the key was different, the time changed, the motif was differently given out and the situations differently presented.

And in this fashion the clever architect* built up one game out of another after the figures, each of which was a bit of myself, and every game had a distant resemblance to every other. Each belonged recognisably

*In the German original Hesse uses the term *Aufbaukünstler*, literally, "one who is capable of artful constructions."

to the same world and acknowledged a common origin. Yet each was entirely new. [72, pp. 201–202]

What Hesse had only hinted at in *Demian* he now, eight years later, announces clearly. It rests in our hands to form our lives out of the countless possibilities open to us, just as an artist creates a work of art.

John Fowles' novel *The Magus* offers itself as well as a parable for this constructivist world-view. Through the use of quite similar stylistic methods, the idea is developed that reality is that which we believe to be real and that this relativization of reality—although in itself a life style—has incalculable existential consequences.

The Magus is a rich Greek named Conchis, who whiles away his time on the imaginary Agean isle of Phraxos by playing the Godgame, which consists in undermining, through the most complex machinations, the grip on reality of the local high school English teachers who teach on the island for a year at a time. As he "explains" in his typically paradoxical fashion at one point to the young Englishman Nicholas, he calls this the Godgame because there is no God and the game is no game at all. In his analysis of the novel Ernst von Glasersfeld points out:

> Fowles comes to the core of constructivist epistemology when he lets Conchis explain the idea of coincidence. Nicholas is told two dramatic stories, one about a wealthy collector whose château in France burns down one night with everything he possesses; the other about an obsessed farmer in Norway who has spent years as a hermit awaiting the coming of God. One night he has the vision he has been waiting for. Conchis adds that it was the very same night that the fire destroyed the château. "You are not suggest-

ing . . .?" Conchis interrupts him. "I am suggesting nothing. There was no connection between the events. No connection is possible. Or rather, I am the connection, I am whatever meaning the coincidence has." This is an everyday paraphrase of Einstein's revolutionary insight that in the physical world there is no simultaneity without an observer who creates it. [63, p. 447]

Conchis with his unlimited possibilities creates worlds for his unsuspecting "victims," now in this style, now in that. It slowly becomes clear to Nicholas that the supposed reality of the isle of Phraxos has been created for his benefit by Conchis. The number of these worlds is infinite. As we make connections and thereby become the meaning of these connections, we "are," for example, the Norwegian farmer who finally sees God face to face, or Macbeth, for whom life is a shadow play, "told by an idiot, full of sound and fury, signifying nothing."

But nothing has yet been said as to *how* in our everyday lives the formation of these reality-shaping styles of life comes about. The answer to this question may lie in what are known as *noncontingent reward experiments*. The experiments are set up such that there is as little connection between the behavior of the subject and that of the experimenter as there was between the vision of God and the burning of the château, and in which the subject—like Nicholas—is led to create such a connection i.e., the assumed "contingency." This is attained by giving the subject the task of determining, through trial and error, an unknown relationship. What he is not aware of until the end of the experiment is the noncontingency of his situation, which consists in his giving answers which are declared right or wrong by the examiner without any logical relation between the subject's answer and the experimenter's reaction to it. In one such experiment the subject is supposed to decide if pairs of two-digit numbers read to him from a long list by the examiner go together or not. To the inevitable question of the subject as to the sense in which these numbers were supposed to "go together," the examiner answers that it is precisely the subject's task to find this out. He begins then with the reading of the number pairs, for example, "48 and 12." The subject is confronted with many obvious "relationships." They are even numbers, both multiples of 2, 3, and 4 and so 6 and 12 as well; if it is a question of minutes, then together they make up an hour, and so on. The subject therefore says they "go together" and the examiner says "wrong." On the basis of this answer the possibilities just considered can be definitely excluded. The next number pair may then be 17 and 83. The subject considers among other things that this time the smaller number comes before the larger, that both numbers are not only uneven but are also prime, and moreover that together they add up to 100. He therefore decides that they go together, which the examiner again declares to be false. So it goes for a while with the subject's answers slowly becoming more and more correct until the subject finally develops, if not an airtight, then at least for the most part correct hypothesis about the "connection" between these numbers. At this point the examiner stops the experiment, lets the subject explain his (usually most complex) hypothesis, and then informs him that his affirmative responses to the subject's answers were based on the rising branch of a Gauss (bell) curve, which means at first rarely and then with growing frequency and that therefore there was no logical connection between the two events (the answers of the subject and the reactions of the examiner). This is at first unacceptable for most subjects. Whoever has taken great pains to find order in an apparently senseless and random world is for that reason alone not going to give up his construction, for he believes he has *found* this order, not fabricated it [183]. Under certain circumstances this can go so far that the subject attempts to convince the examiner that his list of number pairs is based on an order that has escaped him, the examiner.

Accordingly, then, a life style is not seen as just *one* of many possibilities according to which the amorphous material of "reality" can be ordered. Rather, the order, the style, "is" the reality. Philosophy freed itself from this view at the latest with Hume and Kant; science with Einstein and his famous answer to Heisenberg: "It is completely wrong to try to base a theory solely on observable quantities. In reality just the opposite occurs. The theory determines what we are able to observe." (Only psychiatry still clings to the principle of "reality adaptation" as a measure of mental health or illness, naively implying that there is an independent real world open to the "normal.")

To assert that style determines the essence of creation would almost be tautologous. But that this assertion also applies to styles of life is less apparent and seems—at least at first sight—fundamentally to dilute the concept of style. But the phenomenon of the so-called self-fulfilling prophecy [181] teaches us better. It shows that once the world is *seen* in a given way, this way of seeing it *creates* that world.

The delphic priestess had prophesied that Oedipus would kill his father and marry his mother. This myth is generally taken to be an allegory for all emotional problems arising from the libidinal inclination of the child to the parent of the opposite sex and the consequent negative feelings toward that of the same sex. But as Karl Popper [138] suggested, the myth can be interpreted quite differently: Whatever his horrified parents and Oedipus himself did to avoid the unquestionably correct prophecy of the oracle led to its fulfillment.

This is precisely the essence of any self-fulfilling prophecy. Rumors of an impending shortage of an important commodity (for example, gasoline) lead to hoarding, which overnight brings about the shortage—even when the rumor lacks any "real" or "true" basis. It is enough that a sufficient number of people take it to be true. Whoever, for whatever reason, is convinced that people despise him creates with this assumption an interpersonal reality that "confirms" his conviction. His mistrustful, oversensitive, hostile behavior induces others to treat him as he expects, which again "proves" that the world *is* this way. "Frequently the prophecy is the principle cause of the prophesied event," wrote Thomas Hobbes in *Behemoth*.

This should not give the impression that the reality-shaping powers of a life style operate on a one-way street of linear cause-and-effect relationships. It is much more a process of circular interaction. The phenomenon of self-fulfilling prophecy shows that reality-shaping assumptions can come both from "within" as well as from "without," for whether the prophecy is born in the priestess's head or one's own, whether it is an ideal of a definite cultural epoch, whether one merely believes one is despised by one's fellow men or they really do is irrelevant the moment an interactive circle is created in which cause and effect are inseparably intertwined. In this sense the ideas of the Chilean biologist and system-theoretician Varela on the subject of "The Creative Circle" [172] are most applicable:

> That the world should have this plastic texture, neither subjective nor objective, not one and separable, neither two and inseparable, is fascinating. It points both to the *nature* of the process, which we can chart in all of its formality and materiality, as well as to the fundamental *limits* about what we can understand

about ourselves and the world. It shows that reality is not just constructed at our whim, for that would be to assume that there is a starting point we can choose from: inside first. It also shows that reality cannot be understood as given and that we are to perceive it and pick it up, as a recipient, for that would also be to assume a starting point: outside first. It shows, indeed, the fundamental *groundlessness* of our experience, where we are given regularities and interpretations born out of our common history as biological beings and social entities. Within those consensual domains of common history we live in an apparently endless metamorphosis of interpretations following interpretations.

CHAPTER
9

Management and
the Construction
of Corporate Realities

Not only individuals but entire systems are bound to organize themselves in specific ways and stubbornly maintain and defend their organization in the face of environmental changes, even at the price of increasing malfunctioning and consequent suffering—perhaps to the bitter end. This phenomenon is well known to any observer of family, societal, economic, or even international relations.

In organization research, increasing attention is now being paid to what has come to be known as corporate identity *and, therefore, to problems of a systemic nature, i.e., those which can no longer be attributed to the shortcomings of specific individuals in that system.*

This chapter was originally published as a contribution to a Festschrift *in honor of Prof. Dr. Hans Ulrich, one of the most outstanding members of the Institute for Organizational Research of the University of St. Gallen, Switzerland.*

•

We define management, more abstractly than usual, as a class of necessary activities for the *design, control and development of purposeful social systems.*

Hans Ulrich

The only reason why a clinician might be able to contribute to a *Festschrift* on systems-oriented management theory is that modern psychotherapy is built on interaction and communication. By necessity it deals with pathologies and looks for solutions which are based on the peculiarities of human systems and not of individual monads. In this sense, Ulrich's definition of *management* applies to this context. Actual management theory, of course, deals with much more complex structures than the microsystem of the family, let alone the relationship between two people. As a consequence, my suggestions may be relatively primitive and in a way constitute a rediscovery of facts not altogether new to management thinking. On the other hand, there are similarities between the two fields which doubtlessly have great heuristic value. The clinical application of systems-oriented principles makes practical use of a much wider epistemology, of a process of rethinking which can be expected to lead to further practical applications before anachronistic, rigidly retained pseudo-solutions have a chance to "solve" all problems of mankind by war and pestilence.

The necessity as well as the difficulty of this rethinking have been formulated very precisely by Frederic Vester:

It is not so much the lack of mental and technical capabilities which stands in the way of a change in our thinking and actions . . . , but rather a huge ballast of traditions and taboos, academic opinions and dogmas. Although they are not genetically fixed, they are still passed on from generation to generation as irrevocable "truths." One of the most important tasks in regard to a new thinking will be to analyze the nature of these norms. One must recognize those which only convey the appearance of final validity and which— aside from being partially responsible for our current sad state of affairs—have nothing to do with today's reality. [174, p. 456]

With this we have already referred to a systems property which opposes any attempt at solving a problem: the tendency of each system to oppose the introduction of changes to its organization or to its rules. Experience shows that even—or especially—in the event of maximum disturbances, systems will apply the counterproductive measure of "more of the same" and will thus invariably generate more of the same problem. There are at least two good reasons for this. First of all, no living being (and systems are living beings in their own way) can afford to "reinvent" the world every day. Secondly, most of the time there is no good reason to abandon a proven solution, especially if it was arrived at with great difficulty, as Thomas Kuhn has so brilliantly and thoroughly covered [93].

Changing from the idea of the individual as the ultimate entity to the concept of the individual as a partial system generates a resistance which can be compared to the resistance to the transition from the geocentric to the heliocentric conception of our solar system. It is the rejection of the apparent (or perhaps even real) replacement of the individual by a systems concept, while hanging on to the "obvious" assumption that social or managerial problems are caused by the shortcomings of a given individual. Where else, in this monadic view, could the cause lie? Only slowly are we beginning to accept the fact that they rest in the superpersonal properties of the system. The following example may illustrate this: In a medium-size company a new assistant director position was created and filled with a person who was considered well qualified. After six months it turned out that this person was not up to the task, and he was replaced with someone even more expert. The replacement did not meet the expectations either, and the position was filled for the third time. At that time, a team of management experts was called in to examine the situation, and they found that the newly created position was untenable because it entailed a high degree of responsibility without the necessary authority and freedom to make decisions. The effects of such situations are well known to the systems-oriented psychotherapist as an ingredient of depressions.

The difficulty of seeing problems from a systemic point of view also explains why in the last analysis each system only makes *one* demand on problem solvers, namely, the stereotypical request: Take us back to the time before the problem arose, when everything was all right. Obviously, this is the one thing that *no* problem solver can do.

The failure of the "more of the same" formula (and it will fail sooner or later—mostly later), has two causes. The first is obvious and has to do with the constant fluctuation of environmental conditions. No adaptation is achieved once and forever; life forms which do not adapt themselves to these changes are mercilessly exterminated in nature. In families the consequences are psychosis, divorce, murder, or suicide; in human macrosystems they lead to increasingly threatening and wide-ranging disturbances. As pointed out in Chapter II, there is no idea more murderous than the delusion of having found the final solution.

The second cause is inherent in the system and therefore much less obvious than the first. In the conventional mode of thinking there is no apparent reason why established and well-functioning structures should not be multiplied or enlarged at will. However, systems theoreticians have known for a long time that there are not only material limits (lack of money, raw materials, space, etc.) to arbitrary enlargement and growth but *qualitative* discontinuities which are unpredictable at the current state of our knowledge and contrary to all experience. The history of brain development teaches us that human (digital) language becomes possible only when the weight of the brain exceeds 1,400 grams and does not gradually develop in less complex central nervous systems. In the construction of supertankers there appears to be a critical limit at about 400,000 tons, at which a ship's maneuverability decreases drastically and which may be the reason for otherwise unexplainable collisions in clear vision and calm seas. Vester [174, p.69] refers in the same connection to a patient whose temperature rises from 37°C. to 40°C.: a clear sign that he is sick. "A temperature rise by another 3°C, however, does not mean that he is twice as sick, as some economists would logically conclude by extrapolation, but he is dead." John Gall [55, p.42] mentions a most amusing example from Cape Kennedy. In order to protect the huge rockets from the effects of the weather, notably rain and lightning, a hangar was built which is one of the largest buildings in the world. Naturally, long-known principles and experiences in the construction of hangars, suitably scaled up, were applied in the construction. After completion of the immense structure it turned out that a space of this magnitude has its own internal climate—namely, rain showers and discharges of static electricity, and thus produces what it was meant to prevent. (Heraclitus already knew this phenomenon, the reversal of things into their opposite when carried to the extreme. He called it *enantio-dromia.*)

The difficulty with these problems is their unpredictability. For effective prophylactic action we would have to know enough about the properties of large systems. The complexity of such systems has astronomical dimensions—there is considerable skepsis whether in the foreseeable future it will at least become possible to ask the right *questions,* let alone find the "right" answers. Gilbert Probst summarizes the reasons for this healthy skepsis in the conclusions of his book on hypotheses of cybernetic laws [141, pp.363 ff]. His arguments, however, do not preclude the possibility that at least some prophylactic measures will arise from repeated confrontations with unpredictable effects, even though they may at best give us spotty knowledge of the principles involved. (Again a parallel to the clinical field presents itself in that the *concrete* manifestations of pathologies are reasonably clear, but there is little hope that through them we shall ever arrive at a complete picture of man and his problems.)

In a fascinating study, Serge Kolm of the Maison des Sciences de l'Homme in Paris [87, pp.61–69] shows that certain principles can be derived, at least to a degree, from a given basic point of departure. The study deals with the economic consequences of socialist takeovers of government and proves that amazingly stereotypical developments take place which are diametrically opposed to the well-meant political programs, be it in Chile, Portugal, Australia, or Brazil. It appears that the development of the French economy since the socialist takeover follows Kolm's "itinerary" very closely.

Ashby and Beer—to mention two of the main proponents of systems thinking—have repeatedly pointed to yet another systems property: The functioning of a system depends on whether it can meet the requirements of requisite variety.

This means that its complexity must be at least as great as that of its environment, especially when new developments are such that they cannot be predicted and handled on the basis of prior experience. This does not deny the importance of experience for decision making and planning, but it points to the potential danger in a strategy based mainly on experience. In this all too restricted view of reality there is no room for unprecedented events. The consequences can be abrupt, as for example in the case of the Arab oil embargo. More likely, they can remain latent for a deceptively long time, as in the almost imperceptible beginning of the now catastrophic dying of the forests.

Here, too, there are instructive parallels to the microsystem of the family. Clinical experience suggests that families which can deal fairly well with life's problems appear to have an innate ability to make the necessary adjustments to changes in their internal and external conditions. In the so-called pathological family this ability to create new rules of behavior from within seems to be missing. Thus the system keeps repeating a (mostly very limited) repertoire of behavioral patterns and reacts to the increasing intensity of their problem with the catastrophic formula "more of the same." It cannot find a solution, nor does it come to the conclusion that the solution lies outside the available behavior modes. In communications theory this is called a *Game without End,* since on the one hand the behavior of the system is governed by rules but on the other there are no rules for changing these rules (meta-rules).*

In the early days of computer technology this condition was known under the name "halting problem." The expression refers to the situation that arose when a computer was

---

*For the sake of simplicity, we shall not deal with the fact that these rules do not exist for *themselves* but are "read" into the behavior of the system by the observer.

fed a problem which was not in its domain (i.e. within the limits of its program), and was therefore not solvable. The computer would continue to run through its entire program without ever reaching the conclusion that the problems was, under the circumstances, unsolvable. Each "program" (in the widest sense) "creates" a certain reality in which certain things are possible and others are not—not because these "things" are intrinsically possible or impossible but because their possibility or impossibility is a function of the nature of the particular program, or, in a wider sense, of the way a system has "constructed" its "reality." Once such a construction has taken place, it becomes very difficult to appreciate that it is not the *real* world, but rather an order constructed into the world, creating a vicious circle not unlike the halting problem of the computer.

These thoughts go beyond the basic law of requisite variety. There is reason to believe that the human sensory system is complex enough to receive approximately 10,000 sensory impressions per second. This number is approximately equal to the complexity of our internal and external environment. It is, however, completely impossible for the higher brain centers to process *all* these inputs and use them as the basis for conscious decisions. This volume of information must be drastically reduced to a manageable minimum. In other words, a filter is required to admit only the important information and thus protect us from total incapacity through information overload.

The selection criteria, the development of the "filter," the decision of what is "important," none of these is the result of rational decisions but the unpredictable outcome of myriad chance events in the course of the development of the individual or the system in question. This brings us to the realization, familiar to evolutionists and biologists, that all life is the result of *chance and necessity* [119]. For whatever develops by chance (provided of course that it is capable of surviving) becomes an order, which in turn creates situations in which certain things are "real" and others are not. *Nota bene:* These constraints are not in the "nature" of a world which is supposedly independent of man but are the result of an order constructed *into* this world. One might say without exaggeration that each creation or attribution of meaning in turn creates its own "meaningful" reality.

One of the most widely known examples for the working of this mechanism in science was the controversy between the Ptolemaic (geocentric) and the Copernican (heliocentric) view of our planetary system. In the course of centuries certain inconsistencies were discovered in the geocentric system whose incorporation into the system created increasing difficulties. For example, the epicycles (regressions) of certain planets contradicted what was already known about the mechanics and movements of celestial bodies. When the sun was "declared" the center of the system, these "anomalies" disappeared. Therefore they were a property of that particular *view* of the universe, not a property of its *nature.* *
One could also say that the view created a certain reality and that typically this "reality" was believed to exist objectively and independently of man.

There is no need to explore further the emotional resistance against the degradation of our planet to a third-grade satellite. However, what is important in this context is that a manager also establishes "meaning," whether *he* sees his task in this way or not, and thereby enters into the same recursion of meaning outlined above. As the creator of meaning, he himself is within the system he helped to create and is thus confronted with the *effects* of his own actions. It would

---

*It is interesting to note that in modern space travel the Ptolemaic view is frequently used again, since it simplifies the incredibly complicated calculations of space probe trajectories.

be only too easy for him to consider these effects to be causes independent of him. Does he act or react? Obviously this is the wrong question. It reminds us of a dilemma of scholasticism, and the futile attempts at resolving it: Is God subject to the laws of His own creation, or does He stand above them and can therefore do the impossible? Allegedly, the Devil took advantage of this and asked God to create a rock so big that not even God Himself could lift it.

Scholasticism aside, even more important for the subject of creating meaning are the so-called self-fulfilling prophecies, i.e., assumptions (or expectations or convictions) which simply and exclusively because they were made, bring about the assumed event. In other words, the prophecy of the event produces the event of the prophecy [181, pp. 91–110]. On superficial observation it seems that self-fulfilling prophecies carry the concept linear-causality *ad absurdum*. In classical cause-effect thinking the present is caused by the *past*, while in this case an event, expected with certainty, which in other words has already "really" happened in the *future*, determines what happens in the present. Both views are still part of a model of causality belonging to an era in which cybernetic concepts, like the retro-action of effects on their own causes, were as yet unknown. In our day, on the other hand, the consequences are only too well known. They construct situations which would never have happened without the specific basic assumptions, and they appear to call for solutions based on the increased application of the same solutions attempted so far. A blatant example is the ideological and *dirigiste* rigidity of the Soviet five-year plans and the economic and social reality they created. They remind us of Hegel's apodictic statement: "If the facts do not agree with the theory, so much the worse for the facts."

In principle, Ashby [9, p.43] already postulated the important distinction between two types of systems changes:

There is a change from state to state . . ., which is the machine's behavior, and which occurs under its own internal drive, and there is a change from transformation to transformation . . ., *which is a change of its way of behaving,* and which occurs at the whim of the experimenter or some other outside factor. This distinction is fundamental and must on no account be slighted.

This, of course, tells us nothing yet about the nature of such an intervention with a view toward inducing changes of the second order. In order to be able to intervene at all, the problem-solver would have to understand fully the details of the entire situation. In addition, he would need a solution strategy of which—as stated—we know with certainty only that it does not yet exist. It appears that, for the time being, any intervention is precluded because of the chaotic complexity of the problems of even relatively small systems.

In actual fact, however, this is not quite so. Just as it is possible to identify and predict certain interactional patterns in the absence of a comprehensive and final systems theory, it is equally possible to apply certain problem-solving strategies which do not claim completeness but only usefulness.

Deviation in the Service of Its Own Correction

So many factors interact in the evolution of atmospheric conditions that meteorologists have not yet been able to devise a reasonably reliable mathematical model to understand and predict the weather. On the other hand, a simple mechanism like the thermostat has no difficulties in stabilizing the temperature of a house in spite of changes in the weather. It does it by selecting one of the many factors involved, namely, the deviation of the temperature from a desired norm, and by using this deviation for the correction of the temperature inside the house. This seems to be a poor choice of example since one could argue that the temperature in the house has only an infinitesimal retro-effect, if any, on the weather, and that this is not really an interaction. Although the point is well taken, it should be remembered that a relatively small number of such homeostatic processes are sufficient to assure the survival of the human body.

This strategy can be quite satisfactory in treatment of the microsystem of the family. The starting point is a clear, concrete definition of the problem and the determination of the counterproductive pseudo-solution attempted so far. This is where the intervention starts. It attempts to break the vicious circle of "more of the same" attempts at solving the problem and "more of the same" problem, by neutralizing the attempted solution and reversing the process. The similarity between this approach and the thermostat lies in the fact that only *one* aspect of the problem is tackled, while the enormous complexity of the total situation is apparently disregarded. This "insignificance" of the intervention frequently creates the appearance of a perplexing, paradoxical solution. But, to emphasize once more, it simply builds on the knowledge of the prior unsuccessful attempts at a solution and counteracts them. Furthermore, practical experience shows that when an intervention is unsuccessful because of its faulty design, it will have no serious consequences just because of its relative insignificance.

In each case the problem-solver must ask himself whether a reported disturbance should be considered as such. The optimal functioning of each system (and therefore the goal of problem solutions) is a state defined by Ashby [8, p.90 ff] as *ultrastability*. Cyberneticists have emphasized again and again that this form of stability is far removed from the way "common sense" would define it. Rather, it is a dynamic equilibrium which, paradoxically, requires constant internal fluctuations for its maintenance. If these fluctuations are considered as disturbances which should be eliminated so the system can function perfectly, the consequence will be the equivalent of Ashby's example of the tightrope walker: to grasp his balancing rod in order to "correct" its apparently random fluctuations would lead to the tightrope walker's immediate fall. In terms of constructivism this means that the attempt to create a world free from fluctuations would create a reality of maximum disturbance. Applied to managerial problems, it means that well-meant improvements may prove the old saying of the cure being worse than the disease.

Turning the deviation into its opposite is frequently, but not always, an adequate solution. If it is not, it will at least generate a state of suspension or instability which makes it easier for the problem-solver to introduce from the outside those changes which the organization could not generate from within itself. In the sense of the above quote by Ashby this would be a "change from transformation to transformation," i.e. a second-order solution [185, pp.77–91]. What is surprising about these solutions is not only their almost magic character but the fact that they require no special discoveries or new insights whatsoever. The usual reason why they were not resorted to from the beginning and as a matter of course is that they did not fit the "reality" of all concerned, and if they were considered at all, they were discarded immediately.

Thinking the Unthinkable

Santayana is supposed to have said that those who ignore the past are condemned to repeat it. This is undoubtedly true, except in all those cases where the past cannot teach anything because the specific problem had never come up before. These are the cases which frequently confront the problem-solver. Do we have to suffer the unpredictable future helplessly, or is it possible somehow to think the unthinkable?

Management theory, especially in the area of planning, has created the concept of the *scenario*. A scenario is based on an assumption, purely arbitrary at first, that a given situation will occur in the future. It accepts uncertainty as an inevitable fact of life. The scenario is a qualitative picture, in contrast to trend analyses and projections, which are by definition quantitative. In the context of a scenario, the manager asks himself what the organization should look like *here and now*, in order to deal with the arbitrarily assumed situation in the future. There are, of course, a great number of such conceivable situations. Experience suggests that it is best to select only two scenarios, which should be based on two widely different assumptions. It is not assumed that these two situations *will* happen, only that they *could* happen. Thus, the scenario is not a self-fulfilling prophecy; it designs and investigates possible "realities" rather than feeling helplessly exposed to *the* reality. For example, already in 1979 Shell International, in contrast to other companies, began to plan for the mid-eighties with two scenarios: one based on a crude oil price of $15, the other one on a price of $50 per barrel. Both served as the basis for practical precautions [106]. Would it be farfetched to consider scenario thinking as a form of practical application of constructivism, of the deliberate "design" of realities in order to arrive at practical decisions?

The implications of these questions go far beyond the scope of this brief essay. Therefore, let us go back to a less ambitious, less futuristic application of this concept in the area of systemic solution strategies.

The definition of the problem (the undesirable situation in the present) often carries with it a relatively clear idea of the goal (the desired situation). In this sense, the problem-solver is like a mountain climber looking from the foot of the mountain up to the summit, attempting to map the route for his ascent. The beginner has a tendency to think about the direction in which to *start*, whereas the experienced climber asks himself at which point just below the summit he wants to *arrive* for the final climb to the top. He then thinks about where he should be standing before he gets to the point just below the summit, and so on, step by step *downward* to his starting point in the valley. He plans the route in reverse, from the summit to the start, rather than starting from the bottom and discovering, perhaps after several hours of strenuous climbing, that he has reached an impasse.

This technique also serves as an example of a procedure contrary to common sense—the route from the future solution to the present problem—which may very well be successful where previous attempts have failed. However, the problem-solver's real talent lies in his ability to convince his client even to consider "the possibility of things being different" (an expression that goes back to Aristotle). With this we have returned to the starting point of this essay, for without the tendency of all living beings to cling rigidly to solutions elaborated in the past, we would need neither psychotherapy nor perhaps certain aspects of management theory. The contemporaries of Galileo supposedly refused to look through his telescope because what he claimed to see in the heavens "could" not be true. Those who believe that their reality is the only true one will defend it to the end, as put so aptly by the German satirical poet, Christian Morgenstern: "weil, so schliesst er messerscharf, nicht sein kann, was nicht sein darf" (because, he concludes with brilliant logic, nothing can be that may not be).

Münchhausen's Pigtail and Wittgenstein's Ladder: On the Problem of Self-reference

The effects of paradoxes and vicious circles on human relation-ships have already been discussed. If, as Epimenides supposedly maintained, all Cretans lie, then he, as a Cretan, is likewise a liar, and it is therefore a lie that all Cretans are liars. This utterance therefore relates back to itself: If it is true, then it is a lie, and if a lie, then it is the truth. If this self-reference were only limited to such thought games, practical minds could simply turn to more practical problems. But that this is not the case, that the problem of self-reference runs through our ways of thinking and of grasping reality, is the theme of this lecture given before the Siemens Foundation.

•

"I had been delayed some days by a torrential rain," begins one of Baron von Münchhausen's adventures.

As a result of this downpour the roads had become uncommonly soft, and after seeing the difficulty my horse had in walking, I reined him off the road onto a course across open fields. . . . He progressed valiantly for some miles until we came to a line of trees and bushes. There he hesitated; but I, wet and fatigued, urged him on. . . . My noble stallion reared up, but at last obeyed my command and plunged through the bushes. To my astonishment we landed in the midst of a bog, unable to go either forward or backward—able however, to go downward, which we proceeded to do at an alarming rate.

Dulled with fatigue though I was, my body responded at once to the emergency. I felt a tingling at my scalp. My hair stood on end and my hand rose and took hold of my pigtail. Pulling it straight up, I found myself leaving my horse. Not wishing to abandon the hapless creature to sink into the bog and perish, I gripped my legs around his belly and with one more mighty tug on my pigtail I lifted us both out of the marsh.*

Archimedes expresses the same thought in a somewhat less adventurous form in his search for the fixed point from which he could move the earth. And Peter Weiss has his Marat reach the same conclusion: "The important thing / is to pull yourself up by your own hair / to turn yourself inside out / and see the whole world with fresh eyes."

These quotations reveal some remarkable and universal as well as elusive facts about our understanding of the world: namely, the notion of a fixed point from which the world in

---

*Angelita von Münchhausen, *The Real Münchhausen* (New York: Devin-Adair, 1960), p. 70.

its totality might be surveyed and changed; the question as to how it is possible to get beyond an apparently all-encompassing framework; and finally—closely connected with this—the problems of the logical dichotomy between "inside" and "outside" instead of the classic opposition between true and false.

The question will therefore be how—and especially if—in the undeniable absence of an Archimedian point it is nonetheless possible to pull oneself by one's own pigtail beyond the bounds of the world (in the widest sense) and thus be able to view it "with fresh eyes."

It will further be shown that the phenomena of self-reference are not an intellectual or philosophical game but a fact that one immediately and undeniably encounters in the most diverse areas when one attempts to gain even a modest degree of truth, self-consistency, computability, consequentiality, and thus predictability.

The growth or decline of all life forms depends upon how well they adapt themselves to their environment. Even the amoeba under the microscope searches in its little drop of water for the place where the factors important for its existence (temperature, light, oxygen, etc.) are at their best. If we observe our cats or dogs it becomes clear that they too carry with them a complex picture of reality and react with fear or even panic when external events cannot be integrated into this picture, but instead appear to contradict it. On the human level, thanks to our ability to reflect on our world-views and categories of experience, the unavoidable necessity for a complete and reliable world-view becomes obvious. Where such a view proves inadequate, personal catastrophes can result that are the domain of psychiatry. On a social level they can produce those bloody upheavals referred to in the proverb "plus ça change, plus c'est la même chose."

In both cases one is tempted to assume that the individual as well as society is in principle able to come to an adequate understanding of the world, and so the above-mentioned crises must be the result of human failings. The mentally healthy person sees the world as it "really" is, whereas the mentally ill distorts it, and for all people of good will the one and only true and just social order is believed to be readily apparent. It will be shown that this assumption is untenable and that to cling to it leads to social, scientific, and existential pathologies sui generis. The key to this problem is the phenomenon of self-reference.

Let it be said once again: in order to survive biologically, psychologically, and socially we need a consistent picture of the world and an explanation of reality, as it "really" is. But Hume, Kant, and many who came after them have pointed out that we can never speak of *the* world, but only of images of the world and that, to quote Jaspers [78, p.627], "The world is what it is. Not the world, but only our knowledge can be true or false." And Schopenhauer [155, pp.279–280] states in *The Will in Nature* that sense and order in the world are constructed by an act of human attribution and only then rediscovered "out there" as supposed facts:

> This is the meaning of Kant's great doctrine, that Teleology [the study of evidences of design and purpose in nature] is brought into Nature by our own understanding, which accordingly wonders at a miracle of its own creation. If I may use a trivial simile to elucidate so sublime a matter, this astonishment very much resembles that of our understanding when it discovers that all multiples of 9, when their single figures are added together, give as their product either the number 9 or one whose single figures again make 9; yet it is that very understanding itself which has prepared for itself this surprise in the decimal system.

Or think of the example of prime numbers. As laymen we naively take the quite remarkable qualities of these numbers to be clear proof of an objective world order independent of human beings, although accessible to the human intellect. In fact, this immensely complex, even apparently divine order is, so to speak, accidentally created by us when we postulate the existence of numbers only divisible by themselves and 1. What we call reality is therefore not discovered but actually created by us. Typically, however, we remain unaware of this act of creation, and once a so-called reality has been created in this way, seemingly fixed, inescapable consequences are the result.

We are now in a position to take the next step. Once a world picture has been posited and a reality thereby created, then the pressing, even vital necessity arises for its unconscious creator to understand it as completely as possible. What are its limits, its laws, its causes and effects? How can I adapt myself to it, or change it? What can I count as certain, and what must I fear as fickle? It is not just the case that man—as Schopenhauer said about the decimal system—"marvels at the miracle that he created himself," but that this "miracle" can elevate him to great deeds as well as plunge him into the depths of despair. In other words, it raises the question of the meaning of the world. But this question is self-reflexive, for it results from an answer already given. It is the postulation of meaning which then raises the question of meaning. Without this a priori postulation of meaning, the search for meaning would not arise. The snake bites its tail and we are faced with the age-old symbol of the Ouroborus.

I myself am driven to these questions of meaning not only by the facts of my own existence but also as a result of my work as a psychotherapist and the consequent daily contact with the tragedies and tragicomedies of other people, not just with my own Ouroborus. Whoever suffers emotionally, suffers not just from reality but from his *picture* of reality.

For him this picture *is* the reality, and its meaning is the true meaning of his life. For the melancholic this meaning is a tale "told by an idiot, full of sound and fury, signifying nothing." The paranoid posit a meaning through their so-called delusions, and from this basic idea everything else follows with an ironclad, unshakable logic. These sufferers (be they individuals, couples, families, or larger human systems such as nations) are trapped in their own world pictures. They are playing what in communication research is called a Game without End, that is, a game that has no rules for the change of its rules or for its termination, a game whose first rule—in the words of Alan Watts—is that this is not a game but deadly serious. It is a self-reflexive universe which in its inward-directedness continues to renew itself and its suffering, "For in this universe," as Koestler [85, p. 218] once formulated it, "after each crisis and reconciliation, time always starts afresh and history is always in the year zero."

If the sufferer should ever succeed—be it spontaneously or through therapy—to escape the apparently all-encompassing framework of his reality, it is the result of a remarkable and astounding leap out of this framework, a pulling oneself up by one's bootstraps that rivals the trick of Baron von Münchhausen. I would even go so far as to maintain that the essence of effective therapy lies in the bringing about of this leap—as shocking as this form of therapy may appear to the orthodox schools of therapy, and however much they would therefore prefer to disqualify it with semantic tricks.

But permit me to tackle the problem of self-reference from another perspective, namely, one which is less distorted by the passion which the discussion of psychiatric facts can trigger in laymen as well as professionals.

A man has journeyed to the ends of the earth and has broken through the boundary separating it from the outside. And now he looks upon the world with bewilderment and

Figure 10.1

takes hold of it as it really is (Figure 10.1). This medieval (or perhaps just apocryphal) woodcut expresses an archetypal longing of humanity—to experience the breakthrough that leads to the attainment of pure truth. And what is to be understood by "pure" should be clear: a knowledge of the world in its absolute objectivity and therefore free of all con-- tamination from the observer. This seems to describe clearly the object of science. But what remains unsaid is of great importance for our topic. As if by a totally unintended sleight-of-hand, it is thereby imputed that the world has a firm and final order and that this order will reveal itself to us if only we ask the right questions. But this assumption is a *petitio principii,* for it assumes as given that which it wants to prove, and so there is no essential difference between it and the conviction of the paranoid, referred to previously, that "someone" is after him—and this he "knows" and need not prove. In both cases certain givens result in apparently definitive conclusions, which are ascribed to reality and not to the premises themselves. Let us examine these consequences in the realm of science.

In order to grasp the world objectively and so attain a consistent and adequate knowledge of the world, it is necessary to make an absolute split between object (world) and subject (observer). Quite apart from the fact that Einstein's theory of relativity and Heisenberg's uncertainty principle have proven once and for all the impossibility of this procedure, it should be obvious even to the layman that a world from which all subjective elements were banned in the name of science's demand for absolute objectivity would be beyond human perception.

All this has been known for a long time but has had little effect on our scientific procedures, leading to results which in the orthodox sense are scientifically irreproachable but are relatively unfruitful. Let us take an example from the behavioral sciences. In modern animal research the most complex precautions are taken in order to limit the influence of the observer on the behavior of the animal as much as possible. When the goal is to observe animal behavior in the wild, then this is clearly the method of choice. But where in recent years the subject-object split has been intentionally abandoned and the researcher has intensively interacted with the animals, unforeseen results have arisen whose meaning in my opinion cannot yet be fully measured. I am thinking here above all of communication research being done with dolphins and the learning of sign language by apes. It has turned out that chimpanzees have much higher linguistic and cognitive abilities than they require for their life in the wild. This potential normally remains undeveloped in animals and is activated only through their 'unnatural' contact with man. This leads us, among other things, to the interesting question as to which capacities could be developed in *us* by a superhuman trainer. In a similar fashion the abandonment in the realm of psychotherapy of the traditional stance of passivity and neutrality—the classic ideal of the analyst as a passive mirror—has led to new, effective, and timesaving treatment methods.

But back to our actual topic. In view of the self-reference of all scientific premises, where are we to draw the boundary between subject and object, inside and outside? For the sake of brevity, permit me to skip over the steps in the proof and move right to the result that Schrödinger [156, p.52] arrives at in his book *Mind and Matter:* "The reason why our sentient, percipient and thinking ego is met nowhere within our scientific world picture can easily be indicated in seven words: because it is itself that world picture. It is identical with the whole and therefore cannot be contained in it as a part of it."

One must also mention the German cyberneticist Gotthard Günther [70] who, in an essay on the non-Aristotelian logic of reflection, points out that the process of reflexivity can never be brought to its conclusion in the frame of the subject-object relation. This is because the subject, insofar as it is aware of itself, turns itself into an object and yet despite this distinction is conscious that it remains identical as subject *and* as object. But how can something that is different be at the same time identical? To postulate that the ego as subject should distinguish itself from the ego as object while at the same time remaining identical with itself is a logical contradiction.

If the problem of self-reference has thus been summarily outlined, it still remains a distant abstraction. Allow me then to present you with further examples, ranging from the sublime to the ridiculous, as to how this problem plays havoc in all sorts of possible and impossible connections.

Let us take the problem of determinism. Here we have a world picture that views all events as determined by strict causality and therefore excludes the possibility of free choice. Within the framework of determinism even the assumption of free will becomes just one effect of myriad occurrences in one's past—which of course had its own necessary determinants—that gave rise to this belief. Thus the whole world appears to have been grasped just as it is, without contradiction, and all is well so long as one does not have the (reflexive) thought as to where this idea of determinism itself came from. No matter how we twist and turn it, viewed from our Aristotelian (dualistic) logic this idea can only be determined or undetermined. If it is determined then the question immediately arises as to whether its own determinants are determined and so on in an endless and therefore unprovable regress. But if on the other hand it is undetermined, then the whole world picture of determinism rests on a premise that contradicts itself and so essentially proceeds from the completely arbitrary and undemonstrable assumption that everything is determined.

In a similar manner Karl Popper aptly refers to rationalism as an irrational faith in reason. Long before him Søren Kierkegaard made a similar attack on rationalism in defence of the absurd. Rationalism is necessarily limited, for the correctness of a system can never be completely proven but always relies on dogmatic assumptions, an absurd (nonrational) decision that cannot be proven on any rational criteria. Kierkegaard even made the refreshing statement that the justification of irrationality is a consequence of rationalism.

In order to demonstrate (self-referentially) its logical consistency, every Aristotelian system falls into the dilemma of either trying to make this proof within its own framework, leading to a Game without End (a Russellian paradox), or it must take refuge to premises that lie outside its own domain and therefore require an even broader encompassing framework for their own truth, consistency, etc. Thus the problem is not solved, just put further and further off.

But this putting-off has its limits. In research on human communication, for example, we already bog down with the problem of metacommunication, the communication about communication. Every utterance directed at someone else communicates something, but at the same time says something about itself, namely, how the receiver is to understand it, e.g., as an order, a joke, words of comfort. This second, metacommunicative aspect is of paramount importance for it expresses as well as determines the essence of human relationships. The study of the relational (pragmatic) effects of communication, and especially of the conflicts and pathologies they arouse, requires research into the field of metacommunication. But whereas the mathematician can make use of the language of mathematics (numbers, algebraic signs, etc.) to do mathematics per se, and use natural language to express metamathematical concepts, we possess only our natural language to talk about communication as well as metacommunication. It is therefore part of the nature of communication research that it cannot take refuge in a wider system of expression, that it cannot pull itself out of the swamp by its own pigtail. But even if we were to succeed in developing a language for metacommunication, it would be of little help to us. We might then be scientifically almost as kosher as as the mathematicians, but Gödel [67] already pulled the rug out from underneath them in his epochal work on undecidability, showing that no system at least as complex as that of arithmetic can ever prove (at least not without recourse to the again unproven propositions of a larger system) its own completeness and consistency.

It is no different in the realm of theology. From the belief in the truth and authority of divine revelation comes an apparently complete world picture in which the believer finds answers to all his questions and doubts. But how about the belief itself—on what is *it* based? In Christian dogma it is taken to be an act of the grace of God and thus becomes self-referential. Furthermore, one may ask whether God in his perfection stands above the laws of His creation or whether even He is subject to them. This is not just a scholastic game, like the question as to how many angels can stand on the head of a pin. Here the paradox of self-reference invades metaphysics. In eleventh-century theology this led to the antidialectical movement that attempted to place the notion of God completely beyond the bounds of reason, thereby simply repeating the paradox of Tertullian, who is incorrectly but not implausibly credited with the proposition: *Credo, quia absurdum est* (in fact he said: *Certum est, quia impossibile est*). Tertullian probably never considered that a paradox is dependent, at least negatively, on logic and so winds up affirming it.

Or take the belief in metempsychosis and the infinite comfort that sufferers can draw from it. If the blows fate deals to me are the consequences of deeds or omissions in my previous life, then my suffering suddenly becomes meaningful, turns out to be purification, redemption. Pain that makes sense is always easier to bear than pain that is senseless. Further, it now becomes possible for me, through the good deeds I now perform, to make my next life more beautiful and happy or—best of all—to avoid being reborn altogether. Thus everything that happens to me gets a sensible explanation—except for the sense itself, namely, the belief in metempsychosis, which offers no explanation for itself.

Again and again we run up against this blind spot; just like at the point where the optic nerve joins the retina, that point where all visual impressions come together, which is itself a blind spot.

With probably unintentional clarity Roger Garaudy [57] in his book *The Alternative Future* shows the dilemma of self-reference in political structures. Garaudy, chief ideologue of the French Communist party (though since 1968 persona non grata at the Kremlin, having said some rather bitter things about the invasion of Czechoslovakia), puts forward the model of *autogestion*, the self-management of workers. If this model were to be realized, the working class would not only control the means of production but also the decisions as to their use. "Are the workers capable of managing the companies?" asks Garaudy. "Will the ticket puncher at the Austerlitz station be able to make a decision about constructing a monorail? Will he be able to decide between immediate wage increases and long-term investments?" For Garaudy these are "foolish questions," which have not only been used by the ruling class since the days of the aristocracy to relegate the worker to a state of dependence but are unfortunately also being asked even by communists and socialists.

How is the working class to free itself from dependency and start making its own decisions? Garaudy's answer is of great interest for our topic, since he straightforwardly asserts that steps toward self-determination must themselves be "self-determined." They assume themselves and so remind us once again of Baron von Münchhausen. Self-determination becomes another Ouroborus, or—to cite Garaudy again—"self-management becomes the school for self-management." This is to be attained practically by having the workers elect the engineers and other experts, being able to recall them at any time. These experts must be able to inform, explain, and convince, but the final decision rests with the workers. This means that on the one hand the workers are aware of their inadequate expert knowledge and therefore call in experts, yet stand above their decisions as, one could say, meta-experts. And whereas Garaudy criticizes the omniscience of the *leadership* in Stalinist bureaucratic centralism, his model unwittingly assigns the grass roots a similarly omniscient function. The reader experiences *déjà vu* of the Platonic idea of the rule of the wisest, with all its paradoxical, contrary consequences which Karl Popper described in his book *The Open Society and Its Enemies.* [136].

Unfortunately, democracy is doing no better. The question as to how democracy can defend itself democratically against undemocratic behavior is becoming more and more acute. Here, too, we must look to Popper's work, above all to his precise definitions of the paradoxes of freedom, democracy, and tolerance. Must tolerance tolerate intolerance? If so, then how can it avoid the consequent reintroduction of rule by brute force? If not, then how does it save itself from being led *ad absurdum* by its own self-reference?

Let us examine one of the pillars of democratic freedom: the right to unlimited parliamentary debate. The misuse of this freedom by an undemocratic opposition party can, through the relentless exploitation of freedom of speech, completely paralyze the parliament. A limitation of this freedom would therefore be necessary. But the democratic introduction of this limitation is subject to the same right of unlimited debate that it is trying to limit and can therefore itself be put off forever. The workings of government are consequently trapped in a Game without End.

A basically similar situation results when one person tries to convince another that all people, regardless of their origin, color, religion, or gender, are equal. This is dressed up in assertions like "They are just like us," "There is no difference between the whites and the blacks," or similar protestations. In order to emphasize this equality it is necessary to differentiate between "us" and "them," if only to determine that the difference is no difference at all. In this sense, self-reflexive utterances negate themselves as soon as they are made.

So we see that in more than one respect we draw close to Wittgenstein, who in the *Tractatus* [190, prop. 4.442] states, "It is quite impossible for a proposition to state that it itself is true." The trouble is that this proposition is itself a proposition that says something about itself, just like the proposition I have just stated. Level and metalevel, communication and metacommunication paradoxically intermingle, and one is forever reminded of the dog chasing its tail, or of the joker who said: "How happy am I that I can't stand spinach, for if I liked it I would eat it—and I can't stand the stuff!"

This sort of nightmarish, introverted search for meaning is for Rolf Breuer a major theme in Samuel Beckett's work, e.g., in his novel *Watt:* "The novel," writes Breuer [30, p.79]

is similar to the attempt of the schizophrenic to say (to betray) nothing while at the same time trying to avoid having his silence taken as being significant; to the attempt of the mathematician who wants to base his logic upon himself in order to avoid an infinite regress; to the attempt of the person who tries to strengthen a promise the seriousness of which has been doubted by promising to keep it; to the dilemma of the politician who must attain his good ends with bad means or fail (such as waging a war to end all wars); or the simple problem of the near-sighted person looking for his glasses.

When we were children the adults encouraged us during a long stop at a train station to get the train moving again by pushing from inside the compartment. A little later I read about the eccentric inventor who suggested that sailboats be equipped with large fans, so that in case of calm they could create their own wind. And a little later I found a sort of answer in the proposition of a Zen master: "Life is like a sword that wounds, but cannot wound itself; like an eye that sees, but cannot see itself." Or to put it somewhat more tritely, one can tickle oneself, but it is much more tickling when someone else tickles us. And I hope that no one will take offense if I presume to allude, in the frame of this scientific conference, to the fact that good pornography is much more exciting than our own sexual fantasies. What is decisive is that somehow the representation or description comes to us *from outside*. Less offensive is a third example: to be hypnotized by another person is usually more effective than self-hypnosis, even when the same methods of induction are applied. Again the *outside* (and no doubt the interaction as well) plays a decisive role. Conversely, in training hypnotherapists, I always come across the paradoxical self-referential phenomenon that the self-assuredness and self-confidence of the hypnotist is the most important precondition for success, but that only repeated success creates self-assuredness and self-confidence. The question as to how in light of this vicious circle one can nonetheless become a successful hypnotherapist and thus imitate Münchhausen's trick leads us, despite its apparent triviality, to the riddle of self-reference.

In the visual arts this riddle occurs as a theme in the works of the famous Dutch graphic artist Maurits Escher. This most interesting man rediscovered and depicted in the pictorial realm many complicated problems of higher mathematics. Take a look at his 1920 pen and ink drawing of the cathedral of St. Bavo. The ornamental sphere of the candelabra in the middle of the nave reflects the interior of the church as well as the artist with his easel. Thus the picture contains not only itself but also its creator, who is there to draw the picture. Outside turns back within, and the inside passes over to the outside, somehow apparently solving the problem of self-reference (Figure 10.2).

Figure 10.2 © 1989 M. C. Escher Heirs/Cordon Art—Baarn—Holland

To be sure, the essence of this solution was recognized before Escher by the mathematician Felix Klein (1849–1925) in the form of the bottle that bears his name, a topologically remarkable construction that on the one hand is closed yet has neither interior nor exterior but only surface (Figure 10.3). If one imagines oneself standing within the bottle, one may proceed without crossing any boundaries or edges to the other side. The transition from inside to outside, which is no transition at all, must be thought of as taking place at the point at which the bottle enters back into itself.

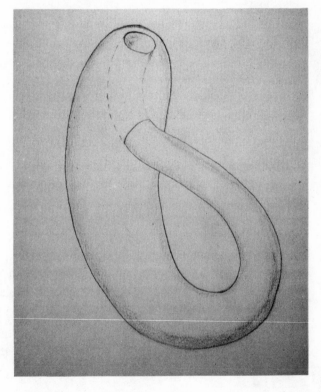

Figure 10.3

Now compare Escher's 1956 lithograph *Print Gallery* (see Figure 10.4) and Ernst's description of it:

First of all let us approach the print as an unsuspecting viewer. At the lower right-hand corner we find the entrance to a gallery in which an exhibition of prints is being held. Turning to the left we come across a young man who stands looking at a print on the wall. On this

Figure 10.4 © 1989 M. C. Escher Heirs/Cordon Art—Art—Baarn—Holland

print he can see a ship, and higher up, in other words in the upper left-hand corner, some houses along the quayside. Now if we look along to the right, this row of houses continues, and so on the far right our gaze descends, to discover a corner house at the base of which is the entrance to the picture gallery in which an exhibition of prints is being held. . . . So our young man is standing inside the same print as the one he is looking at! [48, p. 31]

At many points in his writings Escher describes how mathematicians sought him out in order to discuss the complicated theorems that his drawings depicted and how they simply could not believe it when he assured them that he was hopelessly ignorant when it came to mathematics. He writes of the picture we have just discussed:

Two learned gentlemen, Professor van Dantzig und Professor van Wijngaarden, once tried in vain to convince me that I had drawn a Riemann surface. I doubt if they are right, in spite of the fact that one of the characteristics of a surface of this kind seems to be that the center remains empty. In any case Riemann is completely beyond me and theoretical mathematics even more so, not to mention non-Euclidian geometry. [48, p. 33]

This explains the empty space in the middle of the picture, in which the artist has signed his name. As with the Klein bottle, what is important here is the blind spot, that almost mystical place of the seamless transition from inside to outside.

Permit me to give a further example—something abstract, to be understood purely as an analogy, and yet like all good analogies intuitively appealing. I have quoted Wittgenstein as saying that it is impossible for a proposition to declare itself to be true. But it is simple to demonstrate that such sentences do exist—and their consequences are anything but simple. They lead us into a logic where the paradox of self-reference has been abolished and so are indeed able to draw themselves out of the swamp by their own pigtails.

Let us try to formulate a proposition according to von Foerster's recursive (therefore reflexive) logic, which makes a definitive statement about the number of letters it contains. Let us try, "This sentence has thirty-five letters." Counting the letters we find that the sentence is composed of thirty-two letters and so we come upon the archetypal form of an utterance which only makes sense within the framework of a larger conceptual system, namely:

> The sentence
> "This sentence has thirty-five letters"
> has thirty-two letters.

In other words the original sentence in quotation marks has meaning only in conjunction with the enlarged sentence. But the new sentence says nothing about the number of its own letters. We would have to renew the operation recursively, leading to the proposition:

> The sentence
> " 'This sentence has thirty-five letters'
> has thirty-two letters"
> has fifty-one letters.

The problem of this utterance is thereby merely put off but not solved, and it is not hard to imagine that a lunatic might pursue this game to ever more fantastically complex propositional monstrosities but would probably never reach the "truth."

Instead of trying random numbers, let us focus on the most likely candidates, say, between twenty-nine and thirty-nine. For this purpose we shall put the number of letters stated by the utterance on the x-axis of a coordinate system and the actual number of letters on the y-axis (Figure 10.5).

If there now exists a sentence such that the *actual* number of letters composing it and the number of such letters *purported* by this sentence are the same, it must fall on the diagonal between the x and y axes. As we can see, this is the case

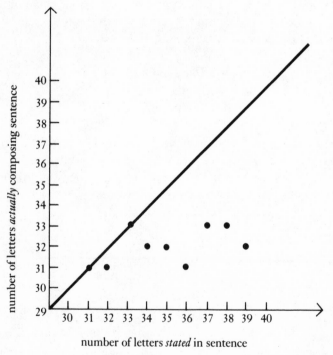

Figure 10.5

with thirty-one and thirty-three, whereas the other numbers do not lie on the diagonal. Thirty-one and thirty-three, respectively, are the so-called *eigen values* of the two sentences ("This sentence has thirty-one letters" and "This sentence has thirty-three letters"), which means that they are indeed composed by the number of letters of which they claim to be composed. In Italian there are also two eigen value sentences (twenty-eight and twenty-nine), while in German there is only one (thirty), and there probably exist languages in which such a sentence has no eigen value at all.

The significance of eigen values is for us mathematical laymen only intuitively comprehensible but can be applied to other areas of life by way of analogies. For example, it calls into question Kurt Gödel's apparently definitive proof according to which no system can prove itself. In this connection George Spencer Brown's book *Laws of Form* must be mentioned as well as the works on self-reference by cyberneticist Heinz von Foerster and neurophysiologist Francisco Varela. What they show is that a system transcends itself in its eigen value and can demonstrate its consistency from outside, so to speak, without the aid of a larger and itself open system. This system has thereby—to put it quite nonprofessionally—pulled off Münchhausens trick.

I do not know if these considerations have been able to convey even a general idea of the problems of self-reference. But I am certain that it is in no way clear why I have made this tour de force effort or where this excursion is supposed to lead. Does what I have said have some sort of practical or philosophical analogy, or does it remain a pointless pursuit? We have really made no progress. The question, put as concisely as possible, remains: Does the world have an understandable meaning? If so, what is it and what can we learn from it?

I do hope that one thing is now clear. The meaning we

get depends on the question we ask. Yet the question itself cannot provide the meaning; it is not its own meaning, it comes up empty the moment it turns to question itself. In other words, as long as the meaning of the meaning is not called into question, the world *may* be experienced as free of contradiction. Yet even this is not necessarily the case.

I would like to take this opportunity to recount the story of the wife of Bath from Chaucer's *Canterbury Tales*. Here a member of King Arthur's roundtable, returning from the hunt to his castle, comes upon a beautiful maiden sitting by the side of the road and cannot resist the impulse to rape her. The disgust provoked by this outrage is so great that King Arthur sentences him to death. But the queen and ladies of the court intervene on the knight's behalf and persuade the king to let them determine his fate. They decide to pardon him if within one year and a day he can find the answer to the question, What is the thing that women most desire? With a death sentence as the alternative the knight naturally chooses this lesser evil and rides off on his quest. The year passes, the last day arrives, and the knight is on his way back to the castle and to his death for he has not succeeded in discovering the answer. This time he comes upon an old hag—"a fouler looking creature I suppose / could scarcely be imagined." He speaks with the old woman, telling her of his predicament, to which she casually replies that she knows the answer and will reveal it to him on one condition. "Give me your hand and swear to do / whatever I shall next require of you— / if to do so should lie within your might." And so the knight once again has two choices—to be beheaded or to promise to satisfy the old hag's wishes, whatever they may be. Naturally he decides for the lesser evil and so hears the (rather banal) secret: "In general / a woman wants the self-same sovereignty / over her master as over her lover / and master him; he must not be above her." The queen and her ladies are perfectly content with this answer and now the old hag, who had thereby upheld her part of the bargain, expresses her wish and demands that the knight marry her. The wedding night comes and the knight lies in despair by her side, unable to overcome his disgust for her. And so the old hag gives him two more possibilities from which to choose. Either he can take her as she is, and she will be a true and faithful wife to him for the rest of his life—or she will turn herself into a beautiful maiden but will never be faithful to him. The knight ponders this new dilemma for a long time until he finally refuses *the choice itself,* instead of once again picking one possibility and discarding the other. And Chaucer tells us that at that moment the hag transformed herself into a beautiful maiden and was true to him for the rest of his life.

The story is not only charming but also has a deep philosophical meaning. How often must we go astray before we stop doing the same thing over and over again in the assumption that this is the only possible way to proceed but finally question this assumption itself? How long must we search in vain before we stop believing that we are just not looking in the right place and start asking if what we are searching for even exists? Karl Kraus discovered the answer in the principle that, given a choice between two evils, he would choose neither. Even better is the remarkably comforting line Chesterton cites from Pope. "Blessed is he who expecteth nothing, for he shall be gloriously surprised" (not, "for he shall not be disappointed," as Pope is usually misquoted). And Chesterton writes, "it is one of the million wild jests that we know nothing until we know nothing." We are no longer confronted here with an infinite regress whose complexity quickly surpasses the capacity of the human brain. This is a fundamentally new situation in which both the question of meaning and the necessity of answering it disappear. The search, the question is itself the problem, just as—I mention this only in passing—in the brief therapy technique developed at the Mental Research Institute the patient's attempted solution is taken to be the actual problem.

But precisely here one encounters the stiffest resistance, for people in psychological difficulties almost always declare themselves ready to do anything that could ease their suffering—with one decisive exception, namely, giving up the premises that are causing their suffering and the attempted solutions which seem to flow so naturally from them but which in reality perpetuate the problem. The dismissal of such fundamental premises is akin to a thought crime in the Orwellian sense and is, interestingly enough, seen and dealt with as such by totalitarian ideologies.

At first glance it is almost impossible not to misunderstand this situation. The phenomenon just described represents a leap to a higher logical level. It is not just a Hegelian synthesis of two antitheses, which again is itself just one member of an equivalent pair of opposites. Through this leap the contradiction between thesis and antithesis is resolved and self-reference thus becomes meaningful. As long as our thought processes remain trapped in an Aristotelian dichotomy between opposites, there is only one conclusion to be drawn from all of this, namely, hopelessness and resignation. In psychotherapy we often come upon people for whom the supposedly final recognition of the senselessness of life is the reason for suicide. Where is Chesterton's glorious surprise? But herein lies the fallacy: Whoever despairs over the senselessness of the world is caught in the illusion that there *must* be a sense but that it cannot be found. This is what makes life and the world unbearable. And this also reveals the absurdity and the counterproductive effects of those well-intentioned attempts to "encourage" the sufferer. The very opposite of this attitude is the remark of the king in *Alice in Wonderland,* who, after reading the nonsensical poem by the White Rabbit, comes to the relieved conclusion that, "if there is no meaning in it, that saves us a world of trouble, you know, as we needn't try to find any."

It seems to me that what the phenomenon of self-reference can teach us is that the world neither has nor lacks meaning—that the question of meaning itself is senseless. What the world does not hold, it cannot withhold. As Wittgenstein [190, prop. 6.5] said, "the riddle does not exist," and "the solution to the problem of life is seen in the vanishing of this problem" [prop. 6.521]. The world has its eigen value, which ultimately is our own. The Zen master's answer to the question as to the true path of enlightenment is that as long as one is looking for *satori,* one cannot attain it. And Count Dürckheim [43] reports that when he approached master Suzuki "with regard to the being that men are always in search for and which is indeed flowing all around and through them, and asked him whether this was perhaps like a fish searching for water, he replied with a subtle smile: 'It is even more. It is as if the water were searching for water.' " Taoism speaks of *wu-wei,* the intentional lack of intention. Countless interpretations have been made of the enigmatic depths of Kafka's novel *The Trial*—last but not least one that attempted to prove that the novel should be read from end to beginning. Yet the answer seems to be contained in the concluding remarks of the priest in the cathedral. After he has tried in vain to help Josef K. with the parable of the gatekeeper, he finally gives clear expression to the senselessness of K.'s search for meaning in a single remark which (so far as I know) seems to play no role in Kafka scholarship: "The court makes no claim on you. It receives you when you come and it relinquishes you when you go." Josef K. hears but does not understand and dies in his quest for final certainty.

"There is indeed the inexpressible," says Wittgenstein [190, prop. 6.522]. "This *shows* itself; it is the mystical." And finally: "My propositions are elucidatory in this way: he who understands me finally recognizes them as senseless, when he has climbed out through them, on them, over them. (He must so to speak throw away the ladder, after he has climbed up upon it.)" Then follows his proposition about remaining silent.

Components of
Ideological "Realities"

*This chapter is an attempt to examine the inhuman social reali-
ties which are the practical results of the apparently innocent
belief that one has found the ultimate truth.*

•

The term "ideology" permits a multitude of definitions,
but two elements are common to most of them: the basic
supposition that the thought system (the "doctrine") explains the world in its suchness; and, second, the fundamental, all-encompassing (and therefore generally binding)
character of ideology.

This study will examine what kind of a "reality" is constructed when one assumes one has found such an ultimate
way of viewing the world. Furthermore, the various components of this construction will be defined abstractly (the pas-
sages in italics) and then substantiated with reference to
their manifestations and with examples of their characteristic symptoms. These references are not intended as proof

but, rather, as anecdotal, metaphorical, or anthological illustrations of the given effects; thus they are compiled from the most varied disciplines and sources without any claim to completeness.

Let us set out the thesis itself: *The actual content of the given ideology is of no consequence in regard to the reality created by acceptance of that ideology. It may completely contradict the content of another ideology. The results, however, are of a terrifying stereotypy.*

For the ideologue—as we will laconically, but not altogether correctly, call the founder or champion of an ideology—this thesis is absurd. And he appears to be right. According to content, there are hardly more irreconcilable differences than between the faith of a Torquemada, the *Myth of the 20th Century*, the ultimate, "scientific" interpretation of social reality by Marx and Engels, and the convictions of the Baader-Meinhof gang. Yet the praxis of the Inquisition, the concentration camps, the Gulag archipelago, and the terrorist scene are of an undeniable, terrible isomorphy. Whether the victim is murdered by Pinochet's henchmen or the Irish Republican Army, the act does not permit a claim to eternal worth for either ideology. British historian Norman Cohn mentions this phenomenon in his book *The Pursuit of the Millenium:*

> In the history of social behavior there certainly are some patterns which in their main outlines recur again and again, revealing as they do so similarities which become ever more recognisable. And this is nowhere more evident than in the case of highly emotional mass movements such as form the subject-matter of this book. It has happened countless times that people have grouped themselves in millennial movements of one kind or another. It has happened at

many different periods of history, in many different parts of the world and in societies which have differed greatly in their technologies and institutions, values and beliefs. These movements have varied in tone from the most violent aggressiveness to the mildest pacifism and in aim from the most ethereal spirituality to the most earth-bound materialism . . . but similarities can present themselves as well as differences; and the more carefully one compares the outbreaks of militant social chiliasm during the later Middle Ages with modern totalitarian movements, the more remarkable the similarities appear. The old symbols and the old slogans have indeed disappeared, to be replaced by new ones; but the structure of the basic phantasies seems to have changed scarcely at all. [37, p.xiv]

The Pseudo-Divine Origins of Ideologies

Because the cosmic order is incomprehensible to the average man, an ideology is all the more convincing the more it relies upon an unusual, superhuman, or at least brilliant originator.

The highest authority, and therefore the authority that has been appealed to most frequently, is the word of the creator of the world. If He exists, one can rightfully assume that He knows the origin, meaning, course, and end of the world. But at the same time the question arises as to how He makes His knowledge and His will known. Then the idea of a mediator is necessary. As the history of mankind demonstrates, this mediator must be of divine *and* human origin; demons, demiurges, interpreters of oracles, seers—often physically blind prophets, and divine messengers, born from human mothers, appear and reveal His wisdom.

But nontheological sources have also appeared, presenting ultimate interpretations of the world: philosophical systems, the genius or clairvoyance of certain individuals, the supreme axiomatic significance of reason, of "common sense," or of some simplistic chauvinism, each defined in a very specific way. These are portrayed as the highest authority. Then again, in our day we attribute particularly radical infallibility and finality to an allegedly scientific world-view. Furthermore, there are uncritically accepted prejudices, the whole domain of tradition, superstition, and the phenomenon of rumors. "When a whole city says the same thing, there must be something to it," was the answer a team of sociologists received while researching the origin and wild spreading of a rumor in Orléans [120]. "Pure" truth is indeed axiomatic, not probabilistic. Doubts are not desirable. Answering the question why Cuba does not allow the International Red Cross to visit its prisons, Fidel Castro told the American television reporter Barbara Walters simply, "We fulfill our norms, our principles. What we say is always the truth. If someone wants to doubt this truth, he should do so, but we will never allow someone to try to test our realities or to refute our truths." [35]

Another possibility for avoiding refutation or even discussion lies in representing the truth so cryptically or replacing it with a formalism void of meaning so that—in nebulous brilliance, as it were—it appears at once bombastic and profound. Exemplary in this context is Michael Bakunin's definition of freedom. This prophet of terrorism, one of freedom's gravediggers, states in his *Revolutionary Catechism*, "It is not true that the freedom of one man is limited by that of other men. Man is really free to the extent that his freedom, fully acknowledged and mirrored by the free consent of his fellowmen, finds confirmation and expansion in their liberty." [12, p.76] (Pseudo-profound babble, nowadays known under the unkind rubric "Party Chinese.")

The Assumed Psychological Necessity of Ideology

It is perhaps a waste of time to say anything at all about why an ultimate world-view is so crucial to us. We human beings and— as the modern study of primates demonstrates—the other higher mammals appear to be psychologically unable to survive in a universe without meaning and order. Thus it follows that there is a need to fill the vacuum, for this vacuum in its more diluted form can drive us to boredom, and in its most concentrated form to psychosis or suicide. But when so much is at stake, the interpretation of the world must be invulnerable and must not leave any questions unanswered.

Gabriel Marcel sees life as a fight against nothingness. Viktor Frankl's life work gives a wealth of examples about how human beings can fall ill because of a lack of meaning and, on the other hand, how the person who has a reason for living can bear almost any conditions (Nietzsche).

Does it then follow that being threatened personally by hunger, illness, or general insecurity makes an individual particularly susceptible to ideologies? In a similar way, do times of political or social upheaval bring about collective susceptibility? Not necessarily. Orwell writes in his *Essays,*

> The leading writers of the twenties were predominantly pessimistic. Was it not because after all these people were writing in an exceptionally comfortable epoch? It is just in such times that "cosmic despair" can flourish. People with empty bellies never despair of the universe, nor even think about it, for that matter. [128, p. 235]

As we shall later show, the compulsive search for burning questions appears to be a symptom of affluent society. It cannot be denied that resignation can cause a life-endangering situation. Moreover, one can hardly dispute that real misery is a breeding ground for desperate attempts to change the existing injustices by means of violence. But, as Lenin recognized, these spontaneous outbursts are not an expression of an already extant revolutionary awareness but, rather, "much more an expression of desperation and revenge than a battle" [103, vol. 2, p. 53]. The urge for utopia seems to feed itself much more from sources that have little or nothing to do with material misery. For instance, the American hippies' protest, according to the sociologist Walter Holstein, was a movement that "was lived out by young people who were able to take advantage of all the privileges and benefits of the system. It was not jealousy and ambition which led to the flower children's revolt, but rather abundance and the desire for something different" [74, p. 67].

The Paradoxes of Eternal Values

Every ideology's claim to finality unavoidably leads to a paradox that has been known in formal logic for millennia. This paradox, however, enables the conceptual system to resolve even the greatest contradictions with no apparent effort. It concerns the introduction of zero or infinity into mathematical equations and its results.

The problems of the negligent use of these two values are traditionally portrayed by means of Zeno's descriptions, which, although almost 2,500 years old, illuminate the paradoxes. For example, there is the story of fleet-foot Achilles, who—contrary to all human quotidian experience—"must" lose a race with the tortoise. Since those days long ago the paradoxes of the infinite (the term goes back to Bernhard Bolzano [27]) have not ceased moving the human spirit to ever new and fascinating variations, such as the one Arthur Schnitzler describes in his story *Flight Into Darkness:*

> He remembered an idea that Leinbach once, years ago, had expounded to a large gathering, quite seriously, in fact with a certain impressiveness. Leinbach had discovered a proof that there really is no death. It is beyond question, he had declared, that not only the drowning, but all the dying, live over again their whole past lives in the last moment, with a rapidity inconceivable to the rest of us. This remembered life must also have a last moment, and this last moment its own last moment, and so on; hence dying was itself Eternity: in accordance with the theory of limits one approached death but never got there [154, pp. 29–30].

In 1940 Arthur Koestler published his famous novel *Darkness at Noon* [83]. The book's French version appeared under the title *Le Zéro et l'infini* [84], a title that surpasses the original by far. The book deals with the political results of introducing zero and infinity into—as Koestler formulates it so suitably elsewhere—the "social equation":

> I remembered a phrase of Malraux's from *Les Conquérants:* "Une vie ne vaut rien, mais rien ne vaut une vie." In the social equation, the value of a single life is nil; in the cosmic equation it is infinite. Now every schoolboy knows that if you smuggle either a nought or the infinite into a finite caculation, the equation will be disrupted and you will be able to prove that three equals

five, or five hundred. Not only Communism, but any political movement which implicitly relies on purely utilitarian ethics, must become a victim to the same fatal error. It is a fallacy as naive as a mathematical teaser, and yet its consequences lead straight to Goya's Disasters, to the rein of the guillotine, the torture-chambers of the Inquisition, or the cellars of the Lubianka. Whether the road is paved with quotations from Rousseau, Marx, Christ or Mohammed, makes little difference. [85, p. 429]

From what has been said, it also follows—almost of necessity—that the final goals of every ideology will have to be utopian, and therefore inhuman.

Here Rousseau's thesis, pulled out the attic and dusted off, which speaks of the goodness of man in nature and of society that depraves him, makes a glorious comeback. However, it remains unclear, just as in Rousseau's time, why the totality of all the good, natural human beings has degenerated into this dark evil force that is responsible for oppression, mental illness, suicide, divorce, alcoholism, and crime. In 1945, Karl Popper, in *The Open Society and Its Enemies*, [136], made a comment that sounds almost prophetic now: that the paradise of the happy, primitive society (which, by the way, never existed) is lost for all those who have eaten of the fruit of the tree of knowledge. The more we try to return to the heroic age of tribalism, Popper warns, the more certainly we will reach the Inquisition, the secret police, and a romanticized gangsterism. But once the existential problems of the individual, who is good by nature, can be blamed on the "evil" society, nothing stands in the way of sheer imagination. The definition of the benevolent society free of all power is only a question of fantasy. Thus Marx and Engels, for example, see one of the manifestations of bourgeois power in the unavoidable division of labor among individuals and then quickly imagine the solution to the problem:

> For as soon as labour is distributed, each man has a particular, exclusive sphere of activity, which is forced upon him and from which he cannot escape. He is a hunter, a fisherman, a shepherd, or a critical critic, and must remain so if he does not want to lose his means of livelihood; while in communist society, where nobody has one exclusive sphere of activity but each can become accomplished in any branch he wishes, society regulates the general production and thus makes it possible for me to do one thing to-day and another to-morrow, to hunt in the morning, fish in the afternoon, rear cattle in the evening, criticize after dinner, just as I have a mind, without ever becoming hunter, fisherman, shepherd or critic. [112, p. 22]

"I want to see all oppressed people throughout the world free. And the only way we can do this is by moving toward a revolutionary society where the needs and wishes of all people can be respected." With these words the radical philosophy professor Angela Davis paraphrases Isaiah's ancient messianic dream of the lion that will peacefully lie down with the lamb in a completely good world. But what the Biblical prophet perhaps could not know is contained with a clarity that leaves nothing to be desired in the opening sentence of an address of the French Senate to Napoleon I: "Sire, the desire for perfection is one of the worst maladies that can affect the human mind." The authors of this sentence could, of course, take advantage of the dubious benefit of having directly experienced and survived the consequences of the attempted introduction of *liberté, égalité* and *fraternité.*

Utopian expectations receive further impulses from the assumption that the noble oppressed will change into champions of the most ideal human values after their liberation—precisely because they have experienced injustice and oppression themselves. George Bernard Shaw has pointed out that this is not quite the case in his preface to *The Revolutionist's Handbook:* "Revolutions have never lightened the burden of tyranny; they have only shifted it to another shoulder." How it comes about that the most wonderful utopias turn into the most gruesome oppression is the subject of speculation later in this essay. That the utopias do this is confirmed by history consistently, from Plato's day to the most recent past. And one must bear in mind that most of the classical utopias existed only in the minds of their originators and on the pages of their treatises. Nevertheless, these utopias bear the characteristics of inhumane oppression, even if their models have never been put into practice. Wolfgang Kraus speaks of this in *Die verratene Anbetung* (Betrayed adoration):

> If one examines the classical social utopias for the values appearing most important to their authors, one comes to amazing results. From Plato's *Republic* and *Laws,* to Plutarch's chapter on Lycurgus, to Thomas More's *Utopia* and Campanella's *State of the Sun,* to Francis Bacon's *Atlantis* and many other works, a terrifying disposition to violently established orders manifests itself. The political dictatorships known to us today look like bastions of freedom in comparison to these so-called ideal states. [91, p. 49].

And yet the world still runs after the utopian Pied Piper until the bitter end. What remains is disbelief and disappointment, as if this end had not been foreseeable from the start. Max Frisch expresses this with enviable terseness in *The Fire Raisers:*

> What all have foreseen
> From the outset,
> And yet in the end it takes place,
> This idiocy,
> The fire it's too late to extinguish,
> Called fate.

Different people come to terms with the pain of disillusionment in different ways. In the newspaper *das konzept* of March 1979 Niklaus Meienberg writes,

> For years we have ignored things that could have darkened our pretty image of socialism, or then things that we have fought in Switzerland we have excused because of the unique politicohistorical context; not until after our Vietnam had marched into Cambodia in a very classical way, with American-like bombs and tanks, with authentic Blitzkrieg tactics . . . did it become instantly clear to some people that the Khmer Rouge had committed genocide. But not before. [114]

And the Zurich *Zeitdienst* complains,

> There are now, after Prague, Ethiopia and Cambodia, no longer any progressive camps that settle differences of opinion or conflicting interests in principle without armed confrontation. There are—and this may be the central experience of the next generation—no more good political examples. The time of political models is over. [195]

The Paradoxes of Perfection and Infinity

As audacious and powerful as the most sublime philosophical edifice may be, as much as it may appear to be an ironclad system, it nevertheless has a fatal flaw: It cannot prove its own logic and freedom from contradiction from within itself. This fundamental condition for the logical construction of every reality we create has been most thoroughly researched by the mathematicians—above all by Kurt Gödel [67]—and their results are valid for all thought systems having a complexity that corresponds at least to that of arithmetic. In order to establish its freedom from contradiction, it is unavoidable that the given system step out of its own conceptual framework to demonstrate its consistency from without by using interpretive principles that it cannot generate from within. The logical consistency of these new additional principles—that is, of the conceptual metaframe—can in turn only be proven within a metametaframe of another more comprehensive system, and so on *ad infinitum.* We know since Whitehead and Russell [189] that whatever refers to a whole cannot be a part of that whole, that is, cannot refer back to itself without falling into the paradoxes of self-reflexivity. The famous liar who says of himself, "I am lying," illustrates the simplest form of such a paradox. If he actually is lying, then his statement is true. But if it is true, it is false that he is lying, and he therefore lied when he claimed to be lying. Therefore he lied . . . and so on. In other words, the statement, "I am lying," refers at the same time to both the whole (mathematically expressed, the class) of his statements *and* a part (a member) of this whole, namely, this one statement. Where the class and its members are not strictly distinguished, the well-known paradoxes of self-reflexivity, demonstrated in formal logic, appear. The map is not the territory; the name is not what it names; an interpretation of reality is only an interpretation and not reality it-self. Only a schizophrenic eats the menu instead of the foods listed on the menu.*

Kant already recognized that every error of this kind con-sists in our taking the way we determine, divide, or deduce concepts for qualities of the things in and of themselves.

Thus when an interpretation of the world, an ideology, for example, claims to explain everything, one thing remains inexplicable, namely, the interpretive system itself. And with that, every claim to completeness and finality falls. Popper points to this issue in his *Conjectures and Refutations* [135, p. VI] in which he ascertains that no theory can be proven positively. We only learn from its failures; we can never know with certainty. Therefore there is no authority that can raise a claim to authority. All we can achieve are approximations to a never completely comprehensible truth.

The British logician Lucas speaks in greater detail on this subject:

It is a fair criticism of many philosophies, and not only determinism, that they are hoist with their own petard. The Marxist who says that all ideologies have no independent validity and merely reflect the class interests of those who hold them can be told that in that case his Marxist views merely express the eco-nomic interests of his class, and have no more claim to be adjudged true or valid than any other views. So too the Freudian, if he makes out that everybody else's philosophy is merely the consequence of childhood experience, is, by parity of reasoning, revealing merely his delayed response to what happened to him

---

*Compare Varela's essay [171, pp. 309–323], in which he presents completely new methods of dealing with the problems of self-reflexivity.

when he was a child. So too the determinist. If what he says is true, he says it merely as the result of his heredity and environment, and of nothing else. He does not hold his determinist views because they are true, but because he has such-and-such stimuli; that is, not because of the *structure* of the universe is such-and-such but only because the configuration of only part of the universe, together with the structure of the determinist's brain, is such as to produce that result. [109, p. 114]

But this incompleteness, which can never be overcome, is unacceptable to the ideologue. His interpretation of the world has to be absolute truth; it has to prove everything and therefore must also contain its own veracity. In the attempt to achieve the impossible, the political ideologue fares worse than his theological *confrères*. The reason why Christianity, for instance, has been able to maintain, in this respect, a consoling consistency for the believer lies in its postponing the realization of Isaiah's dream of the vegetarian lion to the end of time. Thus it escapes the dilemma by introducing the concept of infinity. Thereby the existence of evil, while it is not excused, is at least relativized, although other problems, like the idea of the eternal damnation of the impenitent sinner, original sin, the question whether God is subject to the laws of His own creation or whether He can do the impossible, remain unanswered. Such questions drove Basilides, for example, in the second century A.D., to the heretical position that the cosmos was the frivolous and malicious improvisation of imperfect demiurges. The political ideologue cannot afford to put things off until the end of time; for him the harmony has to start here and now, or at least in the lifetime of the next generation. On this issue

Popper argues,

> our fellow men have a claim to our help. No genera-
> tion must be sacrificed for the sake of future genera-
> tions, for the sake of an ideal of happiness that may
> never be realized. In brief, it is my thesis that human
> misery is the most urgent problem of a rational public
> policy and that happiness is not such a problem. The
> attainment of happiness should be left to our private
> endeavors. [137, p. 322].

With the demand for perfection the ideologue puts on himself, he gets caught between the binary Aristotelian logic of
true and false with its excluded *tertium* and the unpredictable tricks of a logic that tries to prove itself recursively and
fails. For no ideology can afford to come to terms with the
wise, human imperfection, as it is expressed in Ernst-Wolf-
gang Böckenförde's thesis, according to which "the modern
free state lives on the basis of suppositions which it cannot
guarantee without putting into question its own freedom"
[26, p. 37] This thesis poignantly reflects the principle of
incompleteness of all interpretations of the world and thus
also of all "social equations."

The radical left in particular entangles itself in the inextri-
cable contradiction of its "equation": On the one hand, man
is only a wheel in the brazen, once and for all determined,
regular course of history; on the other hand, he fancies that
he is called and obliged to turn the rudder of history as a
messianic renewer by acting freely on his own initiative. So
does he act or react? Does the initiative come from within,
thus spontaneously, or is it dictated from outside of him—
perhaps by the ironclad logic of historical progress? Lenin
had already dealt with this problem. In his famous essay

published in 1902, *What Is To Be Done?*, he throws out the question of the spontaneity of the revolution and concludes categorically,

> We said that there could not yet be Social-Democratic consciousness among the workers. This consciousness could only be brought to them from without. The history of all countries shows that the working class, exclusively by its own effort, is able to develop only trade union consciousness.

And what is this outside entity that gives the decisive impetus? Surprisingly, it is the enemy camp, for Lenin continues,

> The theory of socialism, however, grew out of the philosophic, historical and economic theories that were elaborated by the educated representatives of the propertied classes, the intellectuals. According to their social status, the founders of modern scientific socialism, Marx and Engels, themselves belonged to the bourgeois intelligentsia. [103, p. 53]

Accordingly, then, the metaframe would be the bourgeoisie, and one would have to ask oneself in which metametaframe it is embedded. Instead of forging ahead to the anticipated, final answer, in this way one sinks into the infinite regress we have already spoken of, which contradicts the ideology's claim to prove itself from within its own system.

The man of action who has not been "sicklied o'er with the pale cast of thought" tends toward Gordian solutions to the paradox. Martin Gregor-Dellin provides a fascinating example of that in a study of socialist semantics in the German Democratic Republic. He analyzes a speech by Erich

Honecker and comes across the sentence, "It is a regular process which our party plans and leads with a view to the future." Gregor-Dellin responds,

> Here the vocabulary betrays the deceiver. It unmasks the alleged administrator as mere manipulator. Thus laws are not, as claimed by Marx, determined by the economic and social realities, but rather by the party, which itself "plans and leads these regular processes." It is not my task to prove that Honecker is betraying Marxism. The example only shows how for one fleeting moment a language which has become almost independent of the intellect lets down its visor: What comes to the fore is the cynicism of the central committee, in which one has for a long time agreed that regularities do not need to be adhered to, but rather must be prescribed. [69, p. 81]

Yet for the believer the appearances are preserved.

Heresy and Paranoia

> . . . weil, so schliesst er messerscharf,
> nicht sein kann was nicht sein darf.
> Christian Morgenstern

It follows from the assumption of a universally valid ideology, just as night follows day, that other positions are heresy. The word hairesis *originally did not mean heresy at all but, rather, choice, that is, a condition in which one can choose.* The so-called heretic thus has the freedom to make choices and to live as he sees fit. But in this way he comes into conflict with the ideology, the true faith, the party line. Here it is important to keep in mind that without the true doctrine there would be no heresy at all.

One can distinguish a few typical stops on the road to oppression and liquidation of the heretic.

The idea of possessing the ultimate truth first leads to a messianic attitude that clutches the belief that the truth *qua* truth will prevail in and of itself. At this point the champion of an ideology may still believe in the possibility of teaching or convincing the heretic. But because the world soon proves to be obdurate, unwilling, or unable to open up to the truth, the next inevitable step results in what Hermann Lübbe calls the self-authorization to use violence. In its own deepest interests, the world must have its eyes opened. Lübbe traces this idea back to the August 18, 1919, issue of the Cheka mouthpiece *Red Sword*, in which the famous principle "for us everything is permitted" is announced and then justified with the baffling explanation "our humanity is absolute."

Lübbe explains how that can be reconciled:

> The historicist philosophy of history which above has been referred to . . . as the theoretical precondition of unlimited self-authorization to use violence, achieves that. Through a critical, ideological examination it enables one to identify the mystification that holds captive the consciousness of the people, such that when the people hate where they are supposed to love, the love for the people on the part of those who see clearly remains free of disappointment even in the face of absence of acute counterlove. It is this love for the people which justifies everything. [107, pp. 65–66]

Thus the world's benefactor has no choice; he is the surgeon who wields the healing scalpel. He does not want the violence, but the reality (which he has invented) drives him to use violence, in a way, against his will. Throwing a bomb into a crowded department store thus becomes an act of revolutionary love for mankind (and, in general, to quote Lübbe again, "his primary intention is not to throw bombs into department stores or police stations, but rather into public consciousness"). In the heart of the terrorist mass murderer Felix Dzerzhinski there lived a "soul of deep poetic sensitivity, always driven by pity for the weak and the suffering . . . always living in the tension between his sublime idealism and the slaughter, which was his daily business" [41, p. 85]. Günther Grass is supposed to have said of the terrorist Gudrun Ensslin, "She was idealistic, with an innate disgust of any kind of compromise. She longed for the absolute, for the perfect solution" [19, p. 72]. Whoever can certainly tries not to get his hands dirty. Himmler, watching a mass execution in Smolensk, became ill after the second volley and had to leave. But from the aseptic distance of his headquarters, he rendered thanks in a letter to his men for the selfless way in which they performed their difficult duty.* The Nazis' final solution was admittedly not very ambitious; their ideology was made for use at home, not throughout the world. They were satisfied with annihilating their enemies [183, pp. 175–205]. The true ideologue, however, who wants to make his pure doctrine absolute and everlasting, feels the necessity of totally exterminating, liquidating, and obliterating every fact or opinion that contradicts that doctrine. But to achieve this, disdain, repudiation, and banishment do not suffice. Having introduced the concept of infinity into the social equation, the ideologue is now concerned with introducing zero. "You are a flaw in the pattern," explains the torturer

---

*Of course, there are those for whom the "difficult duty" is an open pleasure: "Our slogan: terror without limits makes for unlimited fun"; this motto supposedly originated from the terrorist Michael Baumann.

in *1984* to his victim. "You are a stain that must be wiped out. . . . It is intolerable to us that an erroneous thought should exist anywhere in the world, however secret and powerless it may be [127, p. 258].

One can physically liquidate dissidents and heretics and even—so to speak, *ad majorem gloriam ideologiae*—degrade them psychologically beforehand so much that they not only admit the most absurd charges in a kangaroo court but also beg to be destroyed. But it is not as simple with the laws of logic; one does not face an enemy of flesh and blood but, rather, the *fata morgana* of a mental construct that withholds its proof from its own architect. As we have already mentioned, the concept of an ultimate, generally valid interpretation of the world implies that no other interpretations can exist beside the one; or, to be more precise, no others are permitted to exist. Otherwise we would find ourselves in a universe in which finally everything would be true, including its opposite. Where the ideology tries to refer back to itself in order to establish its validity and truth from within itself, a blind spot arises corresponding precisely to what Heinz von Foerster calls localized blindness:

> Note that this localized blindness is not perceived as a dark blotch in our visual field (seeing a dark blotch would imply "seeing"), but this blindness is not perceived at all, that is, neither as something present, nor as something absent: Whatever is perceived is perceived "blotchless." [50, p. 43]

This localized blindness, which makes itself blind of itself, enables the believer of an ideology to believe in the ultimate truth and completeness of the doctrine. When, however, social equality does not come about, it is obviously not a defect of the pure doctrine; rather, there must be an undiscov-

ered, insidious enemy lying in wait outside, hoping to sabo-
tage the dawning of the millennium; or perhaps it is a parasite who betrays himself sometimes only by his choice of
words, these words deviating from a language that has
become obligatory. "The domination of language was not
to be changed," writes Schneider about the Nazi period,
"the real crime was rebelling against it. At the end of
Klemperer's book* there is a simple woman's answer to the
question why her husband was sent to a concentration
camp: 'because of expressions,' she said" [153, p. 133]. The
Polish satirist Wieslav Brudziński knows better; one of his
punchlines goes, "He used to begin his speeches preten-
tiously: 'If I may express my opinion, already Engels said
that . . .' "

As did many other philosophers, Leibniz struggled with
the irreconcilability of our imperfect world and the perfection of God. In his famous concluding precept, he postulates
that if the existing world were not the best, then God either
would not have known how, or would not have been able or
would not have desired, to create the best world. But all
three assumptions are incompatible with God's character.
Therefore the existing world is the best of all possible
worlds.

The ideologue reasons in another manner. If our idea
were not the only true one, we would either be unable to
know the best world, or would not be able to shape it completely, or would not want to shape it completely. But all
three assumptions are incompatible with the essence of our
idea; therefore the (undeniable) evil of the world lies with
yet undiscovered enemies.

*It appears that at this point paranoia enters the ideologue's
thought process.* It is inherent to the concept of paranoia that

---

*Victor Klemperer, *Die unbewältigte Sprache* (The Unconquered Language) [82].

it rests on a fundamental assumption that is held to be absolutely true. Because this fundamental assumption is axiomatic, it cannot and need not demonstrate its own veracity. Strict logical deductions are then made from this fundamental premise and create a reality in which any failures and inconsistencies of the system are attributed to the deductions, but never to the original premise itself.

In the ivory tower of formal logic, this technical error leads to the *enfant terrible* of paradox over which more practical spirits are able to move nonchalantly onto the daily agenda. For there are no earthshaking practical consequences in the fact that there can be no barber who only shaves those men in his village who do not shave themselves, which leaves unanswered the question as to what happens to his own beard. It only demonstrates that the premise is somehow defective. The ideological premise, however, "can" not be defective; it is sacrosanct. Whoever attacks it thereby proves his depravity and malice. This is the reason, for example, why the January 13, 1974, *Pravda* condemned Solzhenitsyn: Other authors before Solzhenitsyn had criticized the insufficiencies and errors of the past; he, however, sought to prove that the violations of legality had not been violations of the norms of socialist society but, rather, a direct result of the *nature of socialism* (that is, of the ideology). Thus Solzhenitsyn became a traitor, and every upright human being, not just those in the Soviet Union, was supposed to turn away from him in anger and disgust. Whatever does not seem right, whatever does not fit, must be explained by something wrong outside of the ideology; for its perfection is beyond all doubt. In his way the ideology immunizes itself by offering more and more hair-splitting accusations. Betrayal and the dark powers of inner and outer enemies lie in wait everywhere. Theories about conspiracies develop and conveniently hide the absurdity of the premise, necessitating and justifying bloody purges. As Elster states [183, p. 201], causality is replaced by guilt. Furthermore, one should compare Elster's quotation of Zinoviev's *Yawning Heights:* "From the official point of view particular individuals can be held responsible even for natural catastrophes (earthquakes, droughts, floods)." This does not apply simply to official catastrophes. Maurice Duverger places the following report at the beginning of his book *Les Orangers du lac Balaton* [44, p. 9]:

> At the time while the Stalinist Rákosi was ruling, the Hungarian leaders decided to cultivate oranges on the banks of Lake Balaton. The lake freezes every winter, although the mass of water mitigates the harshness of the continental climate, giving those banks which are protected from the north wind a bit of a Mediterranean appearance. The agricultural expert in charge of the project had the courage to point out that the project was purely a dream. All was in vain. As the interpreter of historical materialism, which proclaims the scientific truth, the party cannot err. Thousands of orange trees were planted, having been imported at a very high price in hard currency. They died. As a result, the agricultural expert was charged with sabotage. Hadn't he demonstrated his ill will from the very start by criticizing the Politburo's decision?

Countless examples of this paradoxical, recursive logic go from the ridiculous to the gruesome. We find an example of the first category in the way prophets rationalize their own prophecies' not being fulfilled. According to newspaper reports, during a drought in California that lasted a number of years, 400 San Jose State University students gathered on February 17, 1977, in the main auditorium under the leadership of several instructors to recite Indian rain chants in order to produce rain by means of these "combined energies." One of the organizers explained to a reporter that "negative attitudes could be the only reason why the rain ceremony would not be successful" [169, p.2]. Rain did not come. This form of proof is what Popper calls self-sealing; or, as Elster puts it, it corresponds to the primitive Manichaean logic, "Whoever is not for me, is against me." In the sense of what we have said so far, it is an ouroboric logic that is typical for ideology. "A convinced Communist cannot become an anti-Communist; Solzhenitsyn never was a Communist" [115, p. 87]. In this manner Stalin Prize winner Sergei Mikhalkov disposes of the phenomenon of Solzhenitsyn. Somehow it is reminiscent of the joke about the wonder rabbi:

"No one can compare with my rabbi. He not only speaks with God directly, but, imagine, God speaks directly with him."

"I don't believe it. Do you have witnesses? If your rabbi says that, he's not only exaggerating, no, he's simply lying."

"Really? Here's the best proof: would God speak with someone who lies?" [31]

How long this logic can be maintained seems to depend on a number of factors, whereby large, rigid, powerful systems appear to have a much longer life span than individuals. Manès Sperber writes,

For a while terrorists can win ambitious victories, which temporarily give them the illusion they are masters of their own fate, the same feeling that a kid-napper has when he makes a family, or an entire town, tremble for the child whom he can kill any moment. In as much as politics is the struggle for power, at such a time terrorists may think that they, these wanderers into nothingness, are making head-way on the shortest path to power. [167]

When the exalted ideology suffers shipwreck, one can still point to the powers of darkness as the final explanation. Naturally this fit particularly well into Hitlerism's mythology of the twilight of the gods. In his study of *The Myth of the 20th Century,* Kurt Sontheimer writes the following of Rosenberg:

> In Nuremberg, when the myth of the Reich had van-ished, he unflinchingly advocated the position that the National Socialist idea had in its essence been right and worthwhile and had failed only because of its corrupt use by others. "The instinct for the upwelling of profound historical events," an instinct for which the Nazi philosopher Alfred Bäumler had praised him in 1943, had obviously remained so strong that Rosenberg remained unable to recognize the terrible reality even in the hour of reckoning and reflection brought about by the victors. [165, p. 113]

On a recording of Reverend Jim Jones's last speech to his followers on November 18, 1978, shortly before the mass suicide of approximately 900 people of the People's Temple in the Guyana tropical forest, a recording first kept secret by the governments of the United States and Guyana but finally made accessible to the press, one hears the identical excuse and projection of guilt:

I've tried my best to give you a good life. In spite of all that I've tried, a handful of our people, with their lies, have made our life impossible. . . . Not only are we in a compound situation: not only are there those who have left and committed the betrayal of the century; some have stolen children from others and they are in pursuit right now to kill them, because they stole their children. . . . We've been so betrayed. We have been so terribly betrayed. [80].

The basic theme of a hostile environment that seeks to destroy the ideology has many variations. Hitler fought his life-and-death struggle against a coalition (constructed by him alone) of "Jewish, plutocratic and Bolshevik powers supported by the Vatican"; Ulrike Meinhof's indignation was directed against "the German parliamentary coalition, the American government, the police, the state and university authorities, the bourgeois, the Shah of Iran, the multinational corporations, the capitalist system" [19, p. 159]; the opponents of nuclear energy imagine themselves up against a powerful, monolithic alliance of irresponsible corporations, the powers of high finance, and all the institutions that are slaves to it: courts, authorities, universities, as well as other research institutions, and political parties.

The transition from at worst eccentric, otherworldly, impractical utopianism to cold, paranoid inhumanity often appears to take place overnight, baffling psychiatry. As contradictory as results of research and attempts to interpret the phenomena have been up to now—this research has by no means been limited to historical personalities but has also considered modern radicals, revolutionaries, terrorists, and, above all, the many sects and cults sprouting up everywhere—they seem to have one thing in common: the psychological and intellectual consequences of believing in an ideology can be of a demonic pitilessness, in comparison with which the deeds of a hardened criminal only look like regrettable impertinence. The Russian emigrant Naum Korzhavin, who should know, reflects on this subject in his autobiography written while he was still in Moscow in 1968:

> I hate the paid revolutionaries . . . They embody the most extreme, most expensive (for others), and most merciless form of egoism; they have found the simplest and cheapest means of satisfying their own ambition and of hiding their intellectual void, as well as of arriving at something like the kingdom of heaven without any particular cost of their own (and accordingly all the more at the expense of the lives and fates of others). [88, p. 33]

In the ideologue's eyes things are admittedly just the opposite. We have already spoken of the assumption of the dissident's malice and depravity. Those who will not have anything to do with the ideology-produced reality and its beneficial consequences can, of course, also be psychologically (and not just morally) abnormal. A desire to emigrate, for example, can be interpreted not only as a refusal to adapt to reality but also as an individual difficulty in adapting. The Nazi's social parasite was a subject unworthy of life—his unworthiness usually being defined genetically. When in October 1973 Dr. Alfred Freedman, at that time president of the American Psychiatric Association, took part in a psychiatric symposium in the Soviet Union, he and his colleagues came to the conclusion that certain behavior, for instance, demonstrations on Red Square, was seen as a sign of mental disturbance:

> Although it was stated that criticism itself is not a sign of psychopathology, one does get the impression that

dissent, criticism or opposition are considered to be bizarre behaviors and important manifestations of disease. . . . Tied in with this is the impression that deviance appears tolerable until it is involved with political dissent. [52, p. 1]

The ideological modification and reeducation of opponents are of central importance. With its insistence not only on passive subjugation but also on active, voluntary acceptance, the ideology falls into a further paradox.

The Paradox of Demanded Spontaneity

The pressing, essentially unanswered question of how the weakness and sinfulness of man can be brought into harmony with the demands of a pure faith crosses all major religions, but especially Christian ethics.

How perfect must one's surrender to the will of God be? Catholic moral theology distinguishes between following God's commandments out of fear of the punishment resulting from disobedience (which is considered a good but less valuable form of faith) and following God's will out of love for Him—thus in voluntary submission. The believer's sorrowful dilemma between his fallible humanity and the pure life of *Imitatio Christi* finds its most poignant portrayal in Dostoevsky's Grand Inquisitor. Next to Dostoevsky, Pascal comes to mind above all others, for he, more than other thinkers, struggled with the question of how an unbeliever can of himself—that is, spontaneously—come into the state of faith. In *Pensée* 223, he develops the famous argument in which he maintains that one can summon forth one's own faith by behaving as if one already believes*—for instance, by praying, using holy water, going to mass, and carrving out similar tasks of devotion. Considering the potential gain (faith and salvation of the soul), says Pascal, the investment is small. "What do you have to lose?" he asks rhetorically. The paradox of the decision to believe in order to reach a state of faith has been thoroughly analyzed by Elster [45]. Here, too, the problem of self-reflexivity arises. Elster points out that even if it were possible to decide to believe in p, one could not both believe in p and also believe that one's faith in p stems from one's decision to believe in p. In other words, the decision to believe in p (the cause of the faith) cannot at the same time be its own cause (that is, the reason for deciding to believe in p). Therefore Pascal's argument provides no proof of God's existence but, rather, at best offers a proof of the benefits of believing in God—unless one could willingly forget one's decision to believe. Apart from that, Pascal's argument deals with the demands of a given person on himself and with the paradoxical consequences he has to struggle with.

The moment the demand is imposed from without, however, the fallacy cannot be disguised any longer. What results is known in the theory of human communication as the "be spontaneous" paradox. What is meant is the untenable position that comes about when person B is in a relation of dependence on A, with A demanding a certain behavior from B, but a behavior which by its very nature must be spontaneous. But precisely because it is demanded, it cannot possibly be spontaneous any more. The demand for spontaneity produces a Russellian paradox, as has already been mentioned under "The Paradoxes of Perfection and Infinity." An example of this "be spontaneous" paradox is a

---

*Ovid, in his *Art of Love*, says the same thing about love: "Convince yourself that you love where you desire only fleetingly. Then believe it. . . . He loves rightly who has succeeded in talking himself into a passion."

wife's wish disguised as a question to her husband: "Why
don't you ever bring me flowers any more?" There are only
two actions open to him: Either he doesn't bring her flowers
any more, which indubitably will disappoint her, or he
brings her some—an action that is bound to disappoint her,
for he was supposed to do what was desired spontaneously,
and not merely because she had asked him to do so. In other
words, he does the right thing for the wrong reasons.

The dilemma of demanded spontaneity is a component of
all ideological realities. Koestler speaks of this in *Darkness at
Noon:*

> The Party denied the free will of the individual—and
> at the same time it exacted its willing self-sacrifice. It
> denied his capacity to choose between two alterna-
> tives—and at the same time it demanded that he
> should always choose the right one. It denied his
> power to choose between good and evil—and at the
> same time it spoke accusingly of guilt and treachery.
> The individual stood under the sign of economic fatal-
> ity, a wheel in a clockwork which had been wound up
> for all eternity and could not be stopped or in-
> fluenced—and the Party demanded that the wheel
> should revolt against the clockwork and change its
> course. There was somewhere an error in the calcula-
> tion; the equation did not work out. [83]

The victim in Orwell's *1984* must be made spontaneous as
well:

> We are not content with negative obedience, nor even
> with the most abject submission. When finally you
> surrender to us it must be of your own free will. We
> do not destroy the heretic; as long as he resists us we

never destroy him. . . . We convert him, we capture
his inner mind, we reshape him. We burn all the evil
and all illusion out of him; we bring him over to our
side, not in appearance, but genuinely, heart and soul.
We make him one of ourselves before we kill him.
[127, p. 258]

Once again in Elster's sense one could speculate that there
are not only two forms of negation, the passive and the active, but also a passive and an active form of acceptance or
obedience. An example of the former would perhaps be the
"inner emigration" practiced by many people under Hitler.
This inner emigration usually went with an external *pro
forma* "act as if," and the Nazi ideologues foamed with rage
at these inner emigrants wherever they could find them.
The spirit of the good soldier Schwejk came back from the
days of the imperial Austrian army, and, during the Second
World War, fraternized with the insidiousness (the Nazis
had a special "insidiousness law" that was supposed to com-
bat this mental state) of Corporal Hirnschal of Radio London.

Both forms of obedience were well known to the Reichs-
minster for (armed) Enlightenment and Propaganda. In a
speech on September 16, 1935, Goebbels exclaimed, obviously playing on Talleyrand's sentence about the bayonets:
"It may be nice to have command over the bayonets, but it is
nicer to command the hearts! . . . We must make the heart's
coercion into the commandment for action in the German
people" [153, p. 126]. The "be spontaneous" paradox was familiar to him, as Schneider writes,

What was most baffling was his technique for making
the voluntary, the future and the unpredictable into
objects of command: "The command to put up flags is

obeyed within half an hour in the cities and in the country in an overwhelming way," he announces on January 15, 1935, after the Saar vote. . . . "The population gathered for giant rallies of a spontaneous character." [153, p. 128].

Within the frame of any ideology, only active obedience is acceptable, because "whoever is not for us, is against us." In this way ideology becomes pseudo-religious. Roger Bernheim, the Moscow correspondent of the *Neue Zürcher Zeitung,* describes the "ecclesiastical" aspects of the Soviet Communist party:

> The party has its god. The sentence "Lenin lived, lives and will live forever" belongs to the creed of a Soviet Communist, indeed must belong to the creed of every Soviet citizen. The party has its priests, pastors, its holy scriptures and its scribes. It has its liturgy. Its announcements consist of liturgical formulae. The adjective "great" belongs to the concept October Revolution, the word "glorious" to the Soviet Communist party, to Lenin the noun "genius."
> . . . If something is said about the Soviet people's support for the party, then this support must be characterized as unanimous, passionate, and unconditional. The workers, the peasants, and the intellectuals of the country are "rallied monolithically around the party." [21, p. 3]

In the irrational universe of demanded spontaneity, the power of state reaches beyond the prohibition of acts contrary to society, assigning itself the task of prescribing the citizen's thoughts and convictions. To quote Revel's concise conclusion, "C'est dans les sociétés totalitaires que l'Etat se charge de 'donner un sens' à la vie des êtres" [144, p. 320].* Thus original thought becomes treason, and life becomes a hell of a particular kind. According to a publication of the literary underground, *Samizdat,* this hell consists of "a complete surrender of the soul beyond all physical and economic constraints: it demands the constant, active participation in the common lie, which all can see [164]."

The lie creates its own luscious flora. From the alleged Aryan sobs of joy upon seeing the face of the worshiped Führer (one man, Reck-Malleczewen [143], who recklessly referred to it as excrement face, did not come back from the concentration camp), there is a monotonous, unbroken litany of undiscerning praise right across the stereotypical reality of the most varied ideologies, even up to the present. For what difference is there between, on the one hand, the bombastic literary effusions that immortalize the blossoming love between the young man in the Hitler-Jugend and the young woman who belongs to the Bund deutscher Mädchen in the ever-rustling forests or under fluttering flags and, on the other hand, the heterosexual mass of students gathered in the tear gas-filled corridors of the Sorbonne in May 1968, or the Chinese short story "The Role of Love," in which the narrator describes how she fell in love with a young man?

We began asking one another questions: "Did you see how Premier Chou's hearse drove down Changan Street to the funeral? Where were you standing? Did you catch part of the anthology of poetry in memory

---

*"In totalitarian societies the state assumes the task of giving life a meaning." And Revel adds, "On the other hand the liberal state tends to bring about the conditions in which the collectivity does not impose any kind of life-style or way of feeling on the individual."

of Chou-en-Lai? . . . When did you first hear of the fall of the Gang of Four?" As we spoke, I saw that we had so much in common. [110, p. 70]

The lie inherent in the "be spontaneous" paradox has to be rendered credible; for that, propaganda and, above all, art that has been modified to fit the ideology must be mobilized. The impression has to be artfully created that there is actually a passionate enthusiasm trembling within all the others—and whoever does not feel this within himself had better recognize that something is wrong with him and not perhaps with the official definition of reality. Presumably one must cultivate these feelings *à la* Pascal so that they finally become spontaneous; then one can feel the same for Hua, Mao's successor, as a certain Yu Kuangh-Lee expresses in his poem:

> My pulsating heart
> Leaped into my throat;
> Tears of happiness
> Made me blind.
> But through the sea of red flags,
> Through the waves of flowers
> I saw, I saw
> Chairman Hua on the Tienanmen
> in his green army uniform. [194, p. 5]

Not everyone succeeds with the trick of spontaneous enthusiasm. What the East German Thomas Brasch has to say in his ironic *Self-Criticism* sounds quite different, more probable, more human:

I admit it all. I do not stay on the topic. I do not take a stand. I only pick away the dirt from between my

toes. I have never been involved. . . . Hallelujah, the
insurrection rots between my loose teeth. Hallelujah,
the wind. It sweeps through our nationalized brains.
[29, pp. 160–161]

What has been said so far is only valid once power is in the
hands of the ideologue. Until it has reached that point, the
"be spontaneous" paradox has another function. This function results from the necessity of creating a revolutionary
consciousness. The technique for this is called *consciousness
raising*. Bringing about perfection presupposes an acute
awareness of the imperfection of the world; yet it seems that
one of the weaknesses of man is his ability to tolerate a great
deal of this imperfection. Marx coined the term "mystification" both for the creation of this condition of blindness by
the ruling class and for its continuing existence. The advocate of perfection, therefore, must, above all, demystify. It is
not enough simply to uncover objectively and denounce the
insufficiencies. To fulfill its purpose, the indignation may
not be repeated mechanically; rather, it must be spontaneous. Not until then can the call for perfection be brought to
a spontaneous resonance. Nothing is more aversive to the
designs of these universal benefactors than the idea of limi-
ting oneself to, and accepting the inevitable imperfection of,
that which is feasible. Hence the increasingly frantic search
for burning problems, specifically in those countries enjoying a measure of freedom, security, and affluence unheard of
in human history. But since this state of the world is largely
the result of steeply increasing scientific progress, science—
especially in our day—has more and more come into the
ideologue's focus.

The Claim to Scientificity

If the facts do not agree with the theory,
so much the worse for the facts.
Hegel, cited by Marcuse

*With the growing trust in a total comprehension of reality on the
basis of objective observations and experiments that can be repeated, science began to fill the ideological vacuum which in the
last hundred years gradually developed through the fading of the
great religious, ethical, and philosophical ideals.* Admittedly
there were early representatives of the doctrine of scientific
salvation, for instance, Bacon and Descartes. Yet the utopian
political expectations that have been removed from any context of divine revelation and attributed to science are relatively young.

The idea is seductive in its apparent simplicity and clarity:
Whoever succeeds in comprehending nature's intrinsic
order, in its existence independent of human opinions, convictions, prejudices, hopes, values, and so on, has eternal
truth on his side. The scientist takes the place of the seeker
after God; the objective truth takes the place of superstition.

Competent minds since Giambattista Vico have emphasized again and again that no scientific theory (or interpretation) can be more than, at best, an image, a particular interpretation of the world, and not reality itself. At this point we
only want to examine the practical consequences that follow
the assumption that the world can be (or already has been)
scientifically explained, or, in other words, to examine what
happens when ideology attempts to derive its generally
binding claim to truth from science.

What validity do scientific conclusions have? As far as the
daily business of living is concerned, we may assume that

they actually do have general validity. Observations of the free fall of a body in a vacuum at sea level—assuming it takes place under identical conditions—yields the same values every time. Here we can disregard the fact that this observation neither explains the causes of this phenomenon (the nature of gravity), nor establishes more than a statistical probability that on the 100th try the body will behave in the same manner (and not, for example, fly up away from the earth). Referring back to a distinction that I have already described in previous chapters, two fundamentally different aspects of what we call *reality* can be postulated. To start with, there are the properties of objects. Let us call this the reality of the first order. Accordingly, this reality would be the universe of all "facts" fitting in a particular framework, that is, that of observation or experiment (both of which, naturally, are constructs of the theories standing behind them), that is, the universe of "facts" which can be established objectively in as much as the repetition of the same experiment yields the same result independently of by whom, when, and where the experiment is being carried out.*

It is then a great temptation to assume, with apparent logic, that the key to an ultimate interpretation of the world has been found, and with it, therefore, the ultimate guidelines for man's proper attitude toward the world, his fellow man, and his own existence. For the truth would now be accessible to all men of good will, and only the insane, the obdurate, and the otherwise insidious would resist reason.

What the terrible oversimplification overlooks is that the facts of reality of the first order give no reference point for

---

*At this point we shall not consider that this is, of course, only possible when all participants make use of the same linguistic and semantic communication system. The construction of the Tower of Babel ran aground when God commanded His angels "to go down there and confound their language."

the meaning of human existence. As for what concerns us, the law of gravity teaches us nothing more than we already know: that a fall from great heights leads to death. Life's (or death's) meaning does not derive from it. Shakespeare knew of no philosopher who could simply get over his toothache. And in the *Tractatus* Wittgenstein writes, "We feel that even when *all possible* scientific questions have been answered, the problems of life remain completely untouched. Of course there are then no questions left, and this itself is the answer" [190, p.rop. 6.52] Yet the reality that is addressed here (and that the ideology proposes to explain) is not the reality of scientific facts of the first order; rather here it has to do with that aspect of reality through which first-order facts are given meaning, order, and value. A small child with normal vision can perceive a red light but does not already know that it prohibits his crossing the street or that it denotes a brothel. This meaning of the red light has absolutely nothing to do with its wavelength or the like; rather it is a human convention, an assignment of significance which, like every other sign—and more obviously—every word, has no other relation to that which is named by it (with the exception of onomatopoetic words, of course). As Bateson and Jackson have stated "There is nothing particularly five-like in the number five; there is nothing particularly table-like in the word 'table' " [17, p. 271] thus giving a new form of expression to Shakespeare's remark, "There is nothing either good or bad, but thinking makes it so." The aspect of reality in the framework of which meaning, significance, and value are attributed is called reality of the second order. While it is sensible in the area of first-order reality to examine, in the cases of differences of opinion, whose opinions do justice to the concrete facts and who is wrong, in the sphere of second-order reality it is senseless to argue about scientifically established "truth" or to claim to have found it. Let us choose one of the innumerable possible examples of this. There is no "scientific," "objective" solution to the conflict between the Arab countries and Israel, just as there is no such solution for a conflict between two individual partners of a relationship. Relationships are not aspects of first-order reality, whose true nature can be determined scientifically; instead, they are pure constructs of the partners in the relationship, and as such they resist all objective verification. And with that the naive faith in reason based on scientific knowledge no longer can be the final authority. At the same time hope for "man who is good by nature" (Rousseau), whose goodness grows out of his voluntary, spontaneous, and reasonable subordination to the so clearly recognizable, scientifically established value bases, and for whom, therefore, individual wishes and needs coincide completely with those of human society, is disappointed miserably.

Precisely this is the crux of the scientific utopias of a healthy, peaceful, selfless world: the claim to the scientificity of ideology, a claim that builds on the confusion between first- and second-order realities. Where this is the case, a construct of reality results that by no means needs to be inferior to the obligatory world of any other "unscientific" ideology. In classical psychiatry it is naively assumed that there is a real reality, of which normal people (above all the psychiatrists) are more clearly aware than are the insane. In the sociological application of the doctrine of scientific world salvation there is faith in—as Andersson and Radnitzky have so poignantly noted in a reply [4, p. 33]—a narrowing of the gap between what is and what should be, a hope for the fulfillment of man's century-old dream of a world in which undeniable facts and human wishes and hopes are one and the same.

When a scientific theory is finally declared valid by political fiat, thus becoming a generally binding justification of the state's existence, the iron curtain of obscurantism comes down. Alfred Rosenberg's *Myth of the 20th Century* (a racial theory on account of which millions of human beings were declared worthless and killed) or Trofim Denisovich Lysenko's theory of the genetic transmission of acquired characteristics (a theory which led to the arrest and death of colleagues who refuted it, and which for decades paralyzed the Soviet study of genetics) are particularly glaring examples—all the more glaring when one keeps in mind that even in both men's lifetimes these "theories" were preposterous nonsense. In the sublunar world of scientific ideologies there is no more place for further research, for questioning earlier assumptions, for creative doubt about what has already been established. What is a self-evident condition in the world of free science becomes of necessity treason and subversion when those in power imagine that they possess the ultimate truth.

However, often the course of events itself is subversive by contradicting the ideology. The ideologues then usually make a jump that becomes a *salto mortale* only for those who cannot adjust quickly enough. Yesterday's truth becomes today's heresy. Those who have been murdered because of their errors are rehabilitated as geniuses.

Enantiodromy

But where there is danger deliverance grows too.
Hölderlin

Since Heraclitus, the great philosopher of change, we understand enantiodromy as the transition of things into their opposite. The forty-fifth fragment reads, "Changing into its opposite is the harmony which permeates the opposition." After Heraclitus numerous thinkers over the centuries have described and tried to explain this phenomenon in its most varied forms of appearance. It seems that finding a useful conceptual access to these processes that are illogical and therefore inexplicable in terms of a classical, linear understanding of causation is reserved for modern thought, with its concept of systems and of systems' characteristics. The works of Nobel Prize winner Ilya Prigogine—technically difficult for the reader not schooled in biology, physics, and chemistry—are especially noteworthy in this context. In *From Being to Becoming* [140], dealing with *dissipative structures* as the interpretive principle of enantiodromy, Prigogine points out that the stabilizing and destabilizing functions of these structures can be demonstrated in social systems as well. Purely empirically, the impression forces itself upon us that enantiodromy can be expected most certainly where a certain attitude or orientation becomes extreme. This obviously applies to the realities created by ideologies. For there—as we have tried to demonstrate—everything that contradicts the ideology must be treated as nonexistent or brought to nonexistence. Even so the ideology entangles itself in the insidiousness of active negation. As Elster says in his analysis of atheism [183, p. 184], the negative faith of the atheist remains connected with God, as much as that of the believer (or even more so if the believer has no strong desire to proselytize); for "the inefficacy of atheism comes about precisely because it wants to achieve the impossible: to establish, by active negation, a state of passive negation."

As long as this dilemma takes place only in the ideologue's mind, the rest of humanity can dismiss it with a laugh or a shrug of the shoulders. But as soon as the enantiodromic component for the construction of the ideological reality is added not just in fantasy, but in actuality, it can no longer simply be shrugged off. The character Shigalov in Dostoevsky's novel *The Possessed* offers such an example. Shigalov is the founder of a utopian system through which "the present form of society will be redeemed." As one might think, this system is very complex. He is ready to present it to his coconspirers in its shortest form, but warns them from the start that this will

> occupy at least ten evening sessions, one for each of my chapters. (There was the sound of laughter.) I must add, besides, that my system is not yet complete. (Laughter again.) I am perplexed by my own data, and my conclusion is in direct contradiction to the original idea with which I started. Starting from unlimited freedom, I arrived at unlimited despotism. I will add, however, that there can be no other solution of the social formula than mine. (The laughter grew.)

While Shigalov's personality is fictional, his dilemma is not; rather, it is the crass reality in many countries in which Shigalovism came to power. The more active the negation, the more powerfully the negated forces itself upon the person negating it. Freud spoke of the return to the suppressed; for Jung every psychological extreme contains "secretly its opposite, or stands in some sort of intimate and essential relation to it" [81, p. 654]. Lenin, who thought he had "completely destroyed the bureaucracy," experienced enantiodromy as a bitter disappointment. Heinz Abosch reflects on this:

> A new, much larger bureaucracy with more absolute control of power came out of the rubble of the old ap-

paratus. Lenin filled his last years with complaints
about this cancerous growth; he no longer praised the
"destruction" of the bureaucracy, but rather regretted
its complete triumph. In a secret memo in 1922 he admitted that the Soviet state "had simply been taken
over from czarism and only very lightly anointed with
Soviet oil." [2, p.69]

Not every ideologue takes the failure of the ideology so
tragically. The terrorists who surface after years in the underground appear to have the inclination to aver naively
and frankly that they are sorry, but to err is human. The
president of Kampuchea, Khieu Samphan, who with his
Sorbonne dissertation gave the Khmer Rouge the ideological basis and justification for the murder of a quarter of a
million people and the gradual liquidation of another million by means of forced labor and privation, explained to
United Press International on August 20, 1980,

> We know now that there is no longer any possibility
> of a Socialist revolution for our generation. The only
> goal we can hope to realize in our lifetime is the sur-
> vival of Cambodia. . . . People are still a bit afraid of us
> but we tell them we are nationalists before we are
> Communists and we now realize that we cannot fulfill
> our dream of socialism.*

The ideology's failure does not necessarily lead to insight
into the fatal process of ideological constructivism. It only

---

*A few minutes later in the same interview, Khieu accused the Vietnamese of
"systematically creating famine conditions in Cambodia and purposely hindering
the distribution of international food aid to the people."

makes room for a new construct. For at best we know what reality is *not*. Or, as von Glasersfeld so clearly puts it,

> This means that the "real" world manifests itself exclusively there where our constructions break down. But since we can describe and explain these breakdowns only in the very concepts that we have used to build the failing structures, this process can never yield a picture of a world which we could hold responsible for their failure. [64, p. 39]

It is difficult to become aware of the enantiodromic fact that the dark side of an ideology that is to be found in praxis can be attributed neither to "industrial accidents" nor to the incapability of lower (or even higher) party functionaries nor to the intrigues of internal or external enemies. Stolzenberg shows us the reason for this when he points out [183, pp. 265ff] that one can only escape the trap of a particular fundamental view by seeing this view no longer as a fact—existing independently of us and leading to certain conclusions (which, in turn, recursively "prove" the "veracity" of the view)—but, rather, by questioning the fundamental view itself.

Duverger poses precisely this question in his book *Les Orangers du lac Balaton:*

> And what if Marx had not been betrayed? He did not desire the terrible regimes that claim to follow his teachings. They probably would have filled him with horror. But what if they are not an excrescence, an aberration, a deviation of his doctrine? What if they reveal the implicit logic of his doctrine, pushed to its ultimate conclusion? [44, p. 9]

And in the course of his book Duverger masterfully shows that these abuses actually result from the nature of the ideology.

Today France's *"nouveaux philosophes"* are expressing clearly what Solzhenitsyn already said, for which—less than ten years ago—he was accused of malicious distortion of the facts. Bernard Lévy, in his book *Barbarism with a Human Face* [104, p. 155], states, "there is no worm in the fruit, no sin that came later, but rather the worm is the fruit and the sin is Marx." The same conclusion is found in André Glucksmann's *Master Thinkers* [66]: no Russian camps without Marxism. And Monique Hirschhorn summarizes this development as follows:

> Having awoken from their dogmatic slumber, the new philosophers are discovering the truth in a strikingly simple thought. The connection between the Gulag and Marx is obvious. It is not an accident which can be explained by bureaucracy, Stalinist deviation or Lenin's errors. Rather it is a direct and ineluctable, logical consequence of Marxist principles. The classless society is not a messianic vision, but rather another name for terror. [73, p. 106]

One of the results of primitive causal thinking is that enantiodromy—in spite of all historical proofs to the contrary—remains unimaginable for the visionaries and ideologues, thus overtaking them completely unexpectedly. It makes matters worse that these two-dimensional thinkers have taken out their own lease on humanity, morality, and justice. What man of good will would not be willing to stand behind such catchwords as *classless society, freedom, equality, and brotherhood?* For most, the sober realization comes too late—except for the rare Grand Inquisitor, who already knows. Neither the content nor the geographical location of the ideologies changes anything. Whether the condition of equality is created in a Marxist or capitalist sense makes no difference for the stereotypical result. The attempt to balance out the natural diversity of people unavoidably leads to totalitarian excesses of inequality. In a similar way the annihilation of freedom can result both from an unlimited overemphasis and from an all too anxious protection of freedom.

What the ideologue cannot accept in his search for perfection, even if he saw it, is an ancient truth that has been rediscovered again and again in more and more convincing forms in the last decades and in the most diverse disciplines: Complex systems—such as human society—are homeostatic, that is, self-regulating, and deviations from the norm *themselves* lead to the correction of those conditions which endanger the system or limit its natural development. But everything that continues to develop is, for that very reason, imperfect—and the ideological reality cannot accept the imperfect. In complex systems, change and evolution result from factors that at first seem to be deviations and pathology; but without them the system would congeal into hopeless sterility. Thus the apparent enemy must be recognized as an archetypical black sheep or demonic double rather than something to be liquidated.

Constructivist thinkers will strive to bring a better understanding of this complexity and of the logic that—although it cannot be comprehended by common sense—paradoxically both confirms and transcends itself. More about this vicissitude of constructivism shall occupy us in the Epilogue. Meanwhile Winston Churchill's wise maxim gives us a ray of hope: *Democracy is a lousy form of government, but I don't know a better one.*

EPILOGUE:

The Outlook for a Communicative Future

The word "communication" has been on everyone's lips for decades now; it has become a fashionable expression, with a sparkle that also serves to muddle its meaning. For example, instead of saying, "We don't understand each other," or "We're fighting," it is today, above all in my field, much more scientific to say, "We are not communicating." The conflict seems thereby to be clearly defined.

"Communicative" here describes that aspect of our world created when "entities" in the widest sense, but above all human beings, come together and begin to interrelate. The result of this interaction, or, more simply put, the essence of every relationship, despite its immediate and everyday nature, is difficult to grasp. What escapes the classic, linear-causal thought of science (to say nothing of our own careless everday thinking) is what biologists call an *emergent quality*. This means that the essence of every relationship (and therefore of all interaction and communication) is always more and different from the sum of the elements the communicants bring into it. Not only does cause create an effect but each effect for its own part has an effect on its own cause. Complexities thus develop which elude any attempt to reduce them to their individual parts. Water is something more and different from the simple addition of the qualities of two atoms of hydrogen and one of oxygen.

The development of modern technology, the tightening of economic bonds between all the countries of the earth, and many similar factors have made the modern world ever more interdependent (and thus more communicative). Its complexity is now such that classical models of explanation leave us in the lurch when it comes to dealing with it. To see what a new dimension we have reached, consider the following example: When the University of Illinois turned on the first large computer in 1946, the world's computational capacity was doubled. In comparison with a modern Cray supercomputer, though, this first one was a dinosaur.

What is the outlook then for a communicative future? Above all we must realize that we have attained a level, unimaginable to our ancestors, at which the naive increase or multiplication of the desirable and good all too often turns into its opposite. We stand helpless before this apparently unpredictable toppling of quantity into quality and ask ourselves why the dizzying progress of medicine can also create unheard-of problems, why more and more "scientific" methods of instruction seem to produce less and less education, why ever faster means of transportation leave us with ever less time, and why more and better social institutions "somehow" seem to bring with them more dependent people in need of help.

In light of the fact that we are now confronted by a systemic complexity for which our past experience offers us no guide, it should come as no surprise that viable solutions are of an almost stunning, bewildering nature. For example, consider the only apparently absurd consideration which in the realm of systemic therapy has proven itself again and again: What must I do in order to bring about what I want to avoid? In the realm of medicine the question would be: How can I kill this patient?

Problem-solving strategies of this nature arouse immediate resistance in many people and are rejected as being too pessimistic. All-encompassing problems can apparently only be solved by all-encompassing solutions. But the old utopian belief in progress has in our communicative present long since become a pipe dream, which interestingly enough is already succumbing to enantiodromia. The magnificent technical and social utopias are now confronted by the dark menace of what Hermann Lübbe [108] so accurately describes as horror utopias *(Schreckensutopien)*. This mood bears amazing similarities to what historical sources report held sway at the end of the first millenium. It is well known that round numbers have a special meaning for many people. One's sixtieth birthday is much more important than one's fifty-ninth, for example, and so one may await even more ill from a year that ends in three zeroes. Just like today, people at that time expected that with the approach of the year 1000 the world would end in flames and pestilence and that flaming swords would cut through the heavens (albeit without cutting holes in the ozone layer). Militant cults sought to bring about the world's salvation quickly through brute force, whereas others withdrew into the solitude of esoteric communes to prepare themselves for the end through introspection.

But allow me to propose some more immediate and less historical perspectives on the coming third millenium. Above all the threat of nuclear holocaust comes to mind, about which everything speakable and unspeakable seems already to have been said. Nevertheless, one aspect has been neglected, namely, the undeniable fact that precisely the ex-

istence of nuclear weapons and their unimaginable consequences have *until now* had a stabilizing influence not just in
their own regard but also in the area of conventional weapons. To publicly point to these facts is considered almost
immoral by many people. But whoever, like the psychotherapist, has to deal with personal horror utopias can hardly
escape the impression that the fear of nuclear holocaust has
become a rationalization for a much more diffuse "discon-
tent of civilization" (as Freud put it) and that it permits us to
ignore other, perhaps more pressing problems—for example, the rapidly increasing overpopulation of the earth or the
poisoning of the biosphere. Has man already exhausted the
limits of his genetic potential (a question many renowned
biologists have been seriously asking)? How long can we
continue to fritter away our resources in financing ever
more grandiose social projects (France, Greece, Portugal,
and Austria being worrisome examples)? And how much
longer can the researcher interested in the pathologies of
larger systems console himself with the thought that such
systems only reorganize themselves under the pressure of
failure and that therefore a certain degree of this is necessary
for the invention of new problem-solving strategies? What if
by the time this point is reached it were already too late to
avoid global disaster?

Even these considerations are still too general and abstract, though. Much more concrete problems appear precisely in regard to the role of communication in the near
future, although admittedly these seem to pale in the face of
the global difficulties just sketched. One of these problems is
expressed in the pithy words of Lord Kelvin—*Everything
that exists, exists in a quantity and can, therefore, be measured*—a spokesman for the belief (which admittedly existed
long before him) in the quantifiability of our world as well as
the consequent obliteration of all illogic and irrationality.

The modern computer seems to have brought these hopes to the brink of realization. The future influence of electronic data processing on the structure of our society is at this point impossible to estimate, but we can already see the first signs of change, described by the Romanian author Virgil Gheorghiu in 1950:

> A society which contains millions of millions of mechanical slaves and a mere two thousand million humans—even if it happens to be the humans who govern it—will reveal the characteristics of its proletarian majority. . . . The mechanical slaves of our civilization maintain these characteristics and live according to the laws of their nature. . . . In order to make use of their mechanical slaves men are obliged to get to know them and to imitate their habits and laws. . . . Conquerors, when they are numerically inferior to the conquered, will almost always adopt the language and customs of the occupied nation, for the sake of convenience or for other practical reasons—and that in spite of the fact that they are the masters.—The same process is working itself out in our own society, even though we are unwilling to recognize it. We are learning the laws and jargon of our slaves, so that we can give them orders. And so, gradually and imperceptibly, we are renouncing our human qualities and our own laws. We are dehumanizing ourselves by adopting the way of life of our machines. The first symptom of this dehumanization is contempt for the human being. [62, p. 44]

Whoever first entered this "new world of zero and one" [92] as an adult may have been immunized enough by their past against the infection which one can contract in communication with comrade computer. Yet even among the adult population of the global "Silicon Valley"—be they mathematicians, physicists, engineers, programmers, or other computer specialists—remarkable changes in personality have begun, whose common denominator is the unwillingness or even inability to deal with the "irrational," illogical, emotional aspects of human interaction, or even in their purely personal and intimate lives. Their eyes glisten as they long for the day when finally all the "analogic" (as they refer to it) will be eradicated and the world of man will be encompassed by an objective, "digital" logic. This digitalization becomes the modern vision of paradise on earth.

It is to be feared that this trend may grow to avalanche proportions when the eight or ten year olds of today reach adulthood—which brings us almost exactly to the beginning of the new millenium. The world of these children is, at least in the United States, already to a large extent a digital one. This is to say that the home computer (to say nothing of the violence of the electronic games that can be played upon it) has already become in hundreds of thousands of families the child's most important toy; these children are therefore learning how to communicate with a soulless machine and to mold themselves to its demands, whereas earlier the first nonfamilial object of attention was probably a dog or a cat. To demonstrate how subtle this atrophying force is and how easily the world-view of the child may be influenced, let us take an example that in and of itself is insignificant. Not only does the pocket calculator relieve these children of the need to arrive at a conceptualization of the world of numbers, but the digital watch pushes aside the image of the passage of time which the old-fashioned (analog) watches provided. To many of these children, therefore, the expression "ten minutes *before* twelve" is already incomprehensible, to say nothing of the utilization of the clock face for the purpose of giving directions, for example, in navigation. (This is not to say that the conceptualization of time as a circular passage has special importance per se; the example is only meant to show how subtle changes in the world-view of innumerable people can arise through the use of everyday objects.)

Another promise of electronic data processing is a radical change in the conditions of work known as telecommuting. For millions of people it should be possible in the foreseeable future not to use overcrowded public transportation or drive through congested streets to get to and from workshop or office. Instead they will do their work at home, sitting comfortably in blue jeans before their computer terminal, at a time most convenient for them—and yet remain in electronic communication with their bosses and colleagues. The personal and social effects of this change, should it ever be realized, can only be vaguely imagined at this time.

Another symptom of our communicative future is the flood of information in all areas and its consequences. The technical potential for the storage and immediate retrieval of information has reached a complexity of which we laymen have no adequate idea. In the words of an expert, the philosopher Jürgen Mittelstrass [118, pp. 66–67]:

> There is now a lot of talk, above all by politicians, about the information society into which civil society has supposedly transformed itself. With this slogan one dresses up the domination of politics by the media and the idea of a technological future in which society should order itself according to the notions of the engineers. What is thereby . . . overlooked is the opposition between information and knowledge, the fact that information is attempting to *replace* knowledge, thus representing a new form of superficiality. Whereas knowledge is always the opposite of stupidity, this does not apply in all cases to information. This is to say that

we understand less and less of the information at our disposal. . . . Knowledge can only be appropriated by the knowledgeable, information just has to be believed.

This brings us to another marvel of digitalization; television. Going far beyond what the propaganda ministries of totalitarian states have so far been able to achieve, television creates a voluntary submission and leveling of thought and feeling unprecedented in human history—not because people of former times were more immune, but because the modern technology for the stultification and brutalization of millions of individuals was not yet in existence. Television teaches us how we should speak, act, and dress, which problems are "in" for elegant, modern people, and how he should deal with them (usually with violence). Here another quotation from an expert source, Neil Postman's *Amusing Ourselves to Death:*

> What Huxley teaches is that in the age of advanced technology, spiritual devastation is more likely to come from an enemy with a smiling face than one whose countenance exudes suspicion and hate. In the Huxleyan prophecy, Big Brother does not watch us, by his choice. We watch him, by ours. There is no need for wardens or gates or Ministries of Truth. When a population becomes distracted by trivia, when cultural life is redefined as a perpetual round of entertainments, when serious public conversation becomes a form of baby-talk, when, in short, a people become an audience and their public business a vaudeville act, then a nation finds itself at risk; culture-death is a clear possibility. [139, pp. 155–156]

The withering away of what for thousands of years have been taken to be the noblest of human traits and potentials leaves in its wake the above mentioned feeling of emptiness and angst and usually gives rise to helpless and haphazard attempts to fill this void. It is probably no accident that cocaine use in California's Silicon Valley is especially high— much to the delight not only of drug pushers but of industry spies as well.

In *Neue Jugendreligionen* (New Youth Religions), psychoanalyst Johannes R. Gascard [60] quite correctly describes a wavering between "longing and addiction" found among today's youth (as well as among those no longer so young). Intoxication and ecstasy have admittedly always been associated with the desire to break through to another, transfigured reality. In contrast to what has been said above, this seems to be a problem about which the past has much to teach us. Closer inspection of the wonderful "ideas" of these modern evangelists reveals that almost without exception they have been proposed before, and soon enough rejected as useless, if not inhuman. *Plus ça change, plus c'est la même chose*, states the wisdom of the French proverb. Here, too, the necessary information is *available*, but its mere availability is not tantamount to *knowledge*.

But enough of this cultural pessimism, it may be objected—and rightly so. What remains for the outlook on the communicative future of the year 2000? The answers which greater minds than my own have already given to this question seem disappointingly inadequate. But precisely therein lies their importance. As has been mentioned, people tend to assume that complex problems require answers of at least equal complexity. But nature teaches us a better way. Life develops in little steps, while all great changes are catastrophic. The same holds for the life of the individual. It is the little steps, at times even unforeseen, chance events, that can lead to important new developments. Modern biology must be credited for having established this connection between chance and necessity. Based on these findings, problem-solving strategies can be designed which have already proven their utility both in the limited framework of psychotherapy as well as in the interaction between large systems in general. The possibility cannot be dismissed that perhaps in the foreseeable future the fundamental laws for a *science of change* can be worked out. Modern, scientific futurology has an important role to play here.

All of this, however, is merely a provisional, tentative beginning. But its very modesty makes it immune to utopian thought, which indeed it attempts actively to avoid. Yet few things are faster at arousing resistance and moral outrage than a philosophy of small steps, like that recommended by Karl Popper. Along with him one may also think of the philosopher Robert Spaemann, who had the courage to point out that the only humane definition of peace is a negative one, namely, the absence of violence, and that every positive definition *must* lead *eo ipso* to violence and inhumanity. This is a bitter pill for many idealists and ideologues: Whoever strives for the *summum bonum*, thereby posits as well the *summum malum*.

REFERENCES

1. Abbott, E. A. *Flatland: A Romance in Many Dimensions.* 2d ed. New York: Dover, 1952.
2. Abosch, H. "Karl Kautskys Kritik am Bolschewismus." *Neue Zürcher Zeitung,* November 27, 1976.
3. Allport, G. W. "Mental Health: A Generic Attitude." *Journal of Religion and Health* 4 (1964).
4. Andersson, G., and Radnitzky, G. "Finalisierung der Wissenschaft im doppelten Sinn." *Neue Zürcher Zeitung,* August 17, 1978, p. 33.
5. Ardrey, R. *The Social Contract.* New York: Atheneum, 1970.
6. Arieti, S. "Schizophrenia: Other Aspects; Psychotherapy." In *American Handbook of Psychiatry,* edited by S. Arieti. New York: Basic Books, 1959.
7. Asch, S. E. "Opinions and Social Pressure." *Scientific American* 193 (1955).
8. Ashby, W. R. *Design for a Brain.* New York: Wiley, 1954.
9. ———. *An Introduction to Cybernetics.* London: Chapman & Hall, 1956, 2d ed. 1964; New York: Wiley, 1963.
10. Austin, J. L. *How To Do Things with Words.* Oxford: Oxford University Press, 1962.
11. Ayer, A. J. *Language, Truth and Logic.* New York: Dover, n.d.
12. Bakunin, M. A. "Revolutionary Catechism." In *Bakunin on Anarchy,* edited by S. Dolgoff, p. 76. New York: Knopf, 1972.
13. Balint, M. *The Basic Fault.* London: Tavistock, 1968.
14. Bateson, G. "Conventions of Communication." In *Communication: The Social Matrix of Psychiatry,* edited by J. Ruesch and G. Bateson. New York: Norton, 1951.
15. ———. "The Group Dynamics of Schizophrenia." In *Chronic Schizophrenia: Exploration in Theory and Treatment,* edited by L. Appleby and J. Weakland. Glencoe, Ill.: Free Press, 1960.

16. ———. *Steps to an Ecology of Mind.* San Francisco: Chandler, 1972.
17. Bateson, G., and Jackson, D. D. "Some Varieties of Pathogenic Organization." In *Disorders of Communication,* edited by D. M. Rioch. Research Publications, Association for Research in Nervous and Mental Disease, volume 42, 1964.
18. Bateson, G., Jackson, D., Haley, J., and Weakland, J. "Toward a Theory of Schizophrenia." *Behavioral Science* 1 (1956).
19. Becker, J. *Hitler's Children: The Story of the Baader-Meinhof Terrorist Gang.* Philadelphia: Lippincott, 1977.
20. Berger, M. M. *Beyond the Double Bind.* New York: Brunner/Mazel, 1978.
21. Bernheim, R. "Der 'kirchliche' Aspekt der sowjetischen KP." *Neue Zürcher Zeitung,* August 16, 1970.
22. Bertalanffy, L. von. "An Outline of General System Theory." *British Journal of Philosophical Science* 1 (1950).
23. ———. "General System Theory—A Critical Review." *General Systems* Yearbook 7 (1962).
24. Bleuler, E. *Dementia Praecox, or the Group of Schizophrenias.* New York: International Universities Press, 1950.
25. ———. *Textbook of Psychiatry.* New York: Macmillan, 1930.
26. Böckenförde, E. W. *Der Staat als sittlicher Staat.* Berlin: Duncker & Humblot, 1978.
27. Bolzano, B. *Paradoxes of the Infinite.* London: Routledge and Kegan Paul, 1950.
28. Born, M. Address to the Fourteenth Annual Convention of Nobel Prize Winners, Lindau, 1964.
29. Brasch, T. "Selbstkritik 2." In *Kargo: 32. Versuch, auf einem untergehenden Schiff aus der eigenen Haut zu kommen.* Frankfurt: Suhrkamp, 1979.
30. Breuer, R. *Die Kunst der Paradoxie.* Munich: W. Fink, 1976.
31. Broch, H. "Wunderrabbis." *Neue Zürcher Zeitung,* October 4, 1975.
32. Buber, M. "Distance and Relations." *Psychiatry* 20 (1957).
33. Carnap, R. *The Logical Syntax of Language.* London: Kegan Paul, Trench & Trubner, 1937.
34. ———. *Introduction to Semantics.* Cambridge: Harvard University Press, 1942; 2d ed. 1959.
35. Castro, Fidel. In *Neue Zürcher Zeitung,* January 7, 1978, p. 5.
36. Cherry, C. *On Human Communication.* New York: Science Editions, 1961.
37. Cohn, N. *The Pursuit of the Millenium.* Fairlawn, N.J.: Essential Books, 1975.

38. Coyne, J. C. "Depression and the Response of Others." *Abnormal Psychology* 75 (1976a).

39. ———. "The Place of Informed Consent in Ethical Dilemmas." *Consulting and Clinical Psychology* 44 (1976b).

40. Davis, M. *Computability and Unsolvability*. New York: McGraw-Hill, 1958.

41. Deutscher, I. *The Prophet Unarmed*. London: Oxford University Press, 1959.

42. Dewey, J. *Human Nature and Conduct: An Introduction to Social Psychology*. New York: Modern Library, 1950.

43. Dürckheim, K. von. "Das Überpersönliche in der Übertragung." *Acta Psychotherapeutica, Separatum* vol. 2, no. 3/4 (1954).

44. Duverger, M. *Les Orangers du lac Balaton*. Paris: Le Seuil, 1980.

45. Elster, J. *Ulysses and the Sirens: Studies in Rationality and Irrationality*. London: Cambridge University Press, 1979.

46. Engelmann, P. *Letters from Ludwig Wittgenstein. With a Memoir*. Oxford: Blackwell, 1967.

47. Erickson, M. H. "The Confusion Technique in Hypnosis." *American Journal of Clinical Hypnosis* 6 (1964).

48. Ernst, B. *The Magic Mirror of M. C. Escher*. New York: Random House, 1976.

49. Foerster, H. von. "Notes pour une épistémiologie des objets vivants." In *L'unité de l'homme*, edited by E. Morin and M. Piatelli-Palmarini. Paris: Editions du Seuil, 1974.

50. ———. "On Constructing a Reality." In *The Invented Reality*, edited by Paul Watzlawick, pp. 41–61. New York: Norton, 1984.

51. Frankl, V. E. *The Doctor and the Soul*. New York: Knopf, 1957.

52. Freedman, A. In *Monito, American Psychiatric Association* 4, no. 12 (December 1973), and United Press International, November 2, 1973.

53. Frey, G. *Sprache—Ausdruck des Bewusstseins*. Stuttgart: Kohlhammer, 1965.

54. Galin, D. "Implications for Psychiatry of Right and Left Cerebral Specialization: A Neurophysiological Context for Unconscious Processes." *Archives of General Psychiatry* 31 (1976).

55. Gall, J. *Systemantics*. New York: Pocket Books, 1978; 2d ed. 1986.

56. Gallie, W. B. *Peirce and Pragmatism*. New York: Dover, 1966.

57. Garaudy, R. *The Alternative Future*. New York: Simon & Schuster, 1974.

58. Gardner, M. "Free Will Revisited, with a Mind-Bending Prediction Paradox by William Newcomb." *Scientific American* 229 (1973).

59. ———. Reflections on Newcomb's Problem: A Prediction and Free-Will Dilemma." *Scientific American* 230 (1974).

60. Gascard, J. R. *Neue Jugendreligionen. Zwischen Sehnsucht und Sucht.* Freiburg: Herder, 1984.

61. George, H. *The Brain as a Computer.* Oxford: Pergamon Press, 1962.

62. Gheorgiu, C. V. *The Twenty-Fifth Hour.* Chicago: Henry Regnery, 1950.

63. Glasersfeld, E. von. "Reflections on John Fowles' *The Magus* and the Construction of Reality." *The Georgia Review* 33 (1979).

64. ———. "An Introduction to Radical Constructivism." In *The Invented Reality*, edited by Paul Watzlawick, pp. 17–40. New York: Norton, 1984.

65. Glover, E. *Freud or Jung?* New York: Meridian, 1956.

66. Glucksmann, A. *The Master Thinkers.* New York: Harper & Row, 1977.

67. Gödel, K. *On Formally Undecidable Propositions of Principia Mathematica and Related Systems.* Edinburgh: Oliver & Boyd, 1962; New York: Basic Books, 1962.

68. Goebbels, J. Quoted in Schneider (1962).

69. Gregor-Dellin, M. In *Schriftsteller testen Politikertexte*, edited by H. D. Baroth. Munich: Scherz, 1967.

70. Günther, G. "Die aristotelische Logik des Seins und die nicht-aristotelische Logik der Reflexion." *Zeitschrift für philosophische Forschung* 12 (1958).

71. Hart, O. van der. *Rituals in Psychotherapy.* New York: Irvington, 1983.

72. Hesse, H. *Steppenwolf.* New York: Modern Library, 1963.

73. Hirshhorn, M. "Les nouveaux philosophes: L'écume et la vague." *Stanford French Review* 2, no. 2 (1978).

74. Holstein, W. *Der Untergrund.* 2d ed. Neuwied: Luchterhand, 1969.

75. Jackson, D. D. "The Question of Family Homeostasis." *Psychiatric Quarterly* 31 (1957).

76. ———. "A Suggestion for the Technical Handling of Paranoid Patients." *Psychiatry* 26 (1963).

77. James, W. *Pragmatism.* New York: Longmans & Green, 1907.

78. Jaspers, K. *Truth and Symbol.* New York: Twayne, 1959.

79. Johnson, A. M., Griffin, M. E., and Beckett, P.G.S. "Studies in Schizophrenia at the Mayo Clinic II. Observations on Ego Functions in Schizophrenia." *Psychiatry* 19 (1956).

80. Jones, J. Quoted in *San Francisco Chronicle*, March 15, 1979.

81. Jung, C. G. *Symbols and Transformations of the Libido. Collected Works,* volume 5. New York: Twayne, 1959.
82. Klemperer, V. *Die unbewältigte Sprache.* Darmstadt: Melzer, 1966. Quoted in Schneider (1976).
83. Koestler, A. *Darkness at Noon.* New York: Modern Library, 1941.
84. ———. *Le zéro et l'infini.* Paris: Calmann-Lévy, 1945.
85. ———. *The Invisible Writing.* New York: Macmillan, 1969.
86. Kolakowski, L. *Leben trotz Geschichte.* Munich: Piper, 1977.
87. Kolm, S. C. "A General Theory of Socialist Failure." In *Surviving Failures,* edited by B. Persson. Stockholm: Almquist & Wiksell; Atlantic Highlands, N.J.: Humanities Press, 1979.
88. Korzhawin, N. In *Kontinent,* edited by V. E. Maximov. Unabhängiges Forum russischer und osteuropäischer Autoren, vol. 8. Berlin: Ullstein, 1978.
89. Korzybski, A. *Science and Sanity.* New York: International Non-Aristotelian Library, 1933.
90. Kraft, V. *The Vienna Circle.* New York: Philosophical Library, 1953.
91. Kraus, W. *Die verratene Anbetung.* Munich: Piper, 1978.
92. Kreuzer, F., ed. *Neue Welt aus Null und Eins.* Vienna: Deuticke, 1985.
93. Kuhn, T. S. *The Structure of Scientific Revolutions.* Chicago: University of Chicago Press, 1970.
94. Laing, R. D. *The Self and Others: Further Studies in Sanity and Madness.* London: Tavistock, 1961.
95. ———. "Mystification, Confusion, and Conflict." In *Intensive Family Therapy,* edited by I. Boszormenyi-Nagy and J. L. Framo. New York: Harper & Row, 1965.
96. ———. *Knots.* New York: Pantheon, 1970.
97. Laing, R. D., and Esterson, A. *Sanity, Madness, and the Family.* Volume 1. London: Tavistock, 1964.
98. Laing, R. D., Phillipson, H., and Lee, A. R. *Interpersonal Perception.* London: Tavistock; New York: Springer, 1966.
99. Langsley, D. G., and Kaplan, D. M. *The Treatment of Families in Crisis.* New York: Grune & Stratton, 1968.
100. Langsley, D. G., et al. "Family Crisis Therapy—Results and Implications." *Family Process* 7 (1968).
101. Laplace, P. S. de. *A Philosophical Essay on Probabilities.* New York: Dover, 1951.
102. Lasègue, C., and Falret, J. "La folie à deux ou folie communiquée." *Annales médico-psychologiques* 18 (1877).

103. Lenin, V. I. *What Is To Be Done?* In *Selected Works*, vol. 2. New York: International, n.d.

104. Lévy, B.-H. *Barbarism with a Human Face.* New York: Harper & Row, 1979.

105. Lidz, T., Cornelison, A., Terry, D., and Fleck, S. "Intrafamilial Environment of the Schizophrenic Patient, VI: The Transmission of Irrationality." *Archives of Neurological Psychiatry* 79 (1958).

106. Lorenz, C. "Shell Strikes a Refined Way of Exploring the Future." *Financial Times*, March 4, 1980.

107. Lübbe, H. "Ideologische Selbstermächtigung zur Gewalt." *Neue Zürcher Zeitung*, October 28, 1978.

108. ———. "Die Schreckensutopien." *Rückblick auf das Orwell-Jahr. Schweiz. Monatshefte* 66 (December 1986).

109. Lucas, J. R. *The Freedom of the Will.* Oxford: Clarendon Press, 1970.

110. Mäder-Bogorad, Y. "Literatur als Zerrspiegel der Wirklichkeit." *Neue Zürcher Zeitung*, October 28, 1978.

111. Mally, E. *Grundgesetze des Sollens.* Graz: Leuscher & Lubensky, 1926.

112. Marx, K. *The German Ideology.* New York: International, 1947.

113. Mead, G. H. *Mind, Self and Society.* Chicago: University of Chicago Press, 1934.

114. Meienberg, N. In *das konzept* (March 1979). Quoted in *Neue Zürcher Zeitung*, March 17, 1979.

115. Michalkow, S. In *Der Spiegel* 28 (February 4, 1974).

116. Miller, G. A., Galanter, E., and Pribram, K. H. *Plans and the Structure of Behavior.* New York: Holt, Rinehart and Winston, 1960.

117. Mischel, W. *Personality and Assessment.* New York: Wiley, 1968.

118. Mittelstrass, J. "Bibliothek und geisteswissenschaftliche Forschung." *Neue Zürcher Zeitung,* June 28, 1986.

119. Monod, J. *Chance and Necessity.* New York: Vintage, 1972.

120. Morin, E., et al. *Rumour in Orléans.* New York: Pantheon: 1971.

121. Morris, C. "Foundations of the Theory of Signs." In *International Encyclopedia of Unified Science*, edited by O. Neurath, R. Carnap, and Ch. Morris, vol. 1, pp. 77–137. Chicago: University of Chicago Press, 1938.

122. Musil, R. *Young Törless.* New York: Noonday Press, 1958.

123. Nagel, E., and Newman, J. R. *Gödel's Proof.* New York: New York University Press, 1958.

124. Newman, J. R. *The World of Mathematics.* New York: Simon & Schuster, 1956.

125. Niederland, W. G. *The Schreber Case*. New York: Quadrangle Books, 1974.
126. Nozick, R. "Newcomb's Paradox and the Two Principles of Choice." In *Essays in Honor of Carl E. Hempel*, edited by N. Rescher. Dordrecht: J. Reidel, 1979.
127. Orwell, G. *1984*. New York: Harcourt, Brace, 1949.
128. ———. "Inside the Whale." In *A Collection of Essays*. Garden City, N.J.: Doubleday, 1954.
129. Osgood, Ch. E. "Reciprocal Initiative." In *The Liberal Papers*, edited by J. Roosevelt. New York: Anchor, 1962.
130. Peirce, C. S. "Pragmatism and Pragmaticism." In *Collected Papers of Charles Sanders Peirce*. Volume 5. Cambridge: Harvard University Press, 1934; 2d ed. 1960.
131. Peseschkian, N. *The Merchant and the Parrot*. New York: Vantage Press, 1982.
132. Pfungst, O. *Clever Hans*. New York: Rinehart & Winston, 1965.
133. Piaget, J. *The Construction of Reality in the Child*. New York: Basic Books, 1954.
134. Planck, M. *A Scientific Autobiography and Other Papers*. London: Williams & Norgate, 1950.
135. Popper, K. R. *Conjectures and Refutations: The Growth of Scientific Knowledge*. New York: Basic Books, 1962.
136. ———. *The Open Society and Its Enemies*. New York: Harper, 1963.
137. ———. "Utopie und Gewalt." In *Utopie: Begriff und Phänomen des Utopischen*, edited by A. Neusüss. Neuwied/Berlin: Luchterhand, 1968.
138. ———. *Unended Quest*. La Salle, Ill.: Open Court, 1974.
139. Postman, N. *Amusing Ourselves to Death*. New York: Viking, 1984.
140. Prigogine, I. *From Being to Becoming*. San Francisco: Freeman, 1980.
141. Probst, G.J.B. *Kybernetische Gesetzeshypothesen als Basis für Gestaltungs- und Lenkungsregeln im Management*. Bern/Stuttgart: Haupt, 1981.
142. Rapoport, A. *Fights, Games and Debates*. Ann Arbor, Mich.: University of Michigan Press, 1960.
143. Reck-Malleczewen, F. P. *Tagebuch eines Verzweifelten*. Stuttgart: Henry Goverts, 1966.
144. Revel, J.-F. *Totalitarian Temptation*. Garden City, N.J.: Doubleday, 1977.
145. Rosen, J. N. *Direct Analysis*. New York: Grune & Stratton, 1953.
146. Rosen, S. *My Voice Will Go with You*. New York: Norton, 1982.

147. Rosenhan, D. L. "On Being Sane in Insane Places." In *The Invented Reality,* edited by Paul Watzlawick, pp. 117–144. New York: Norton, 1984.
148. Rosenthal, R. *Experimenter Effects in Behavioral Research.* New York: Appleton-Century-Crofts, 1966.
149. Ruesch, J. *Disturbed Communication.* New York: Norton, 1957.
150. Salimbene. *La bizzarra cronaca di Frate Salimbene.* Lanciano: Carabba, 1926.
151. Salzman, L. "Reply to Critics." *International Journal of Psychiatry* 6 (1968).
152. Schatzman, M. *Soul Murder.* New York: Random House, 1973.
153. Schneider, W. *Wörter machen Leute: Magie und Macht der Sprache.* Munich: Piper, 1976.
154. Schnitzler, A. *Flight Into Darkness.* New York: Simon & Schuster, 1931.
155. Schopenhauer, A. *The Will in Nature.* London: G. Bell, 1907.
156. Schrödinger, E. *Mind and Matter.* Cambridge: Cambridge University Press, 1958.
157. Searles, H. F. "The Effort To Drive the Other Person Crazy." *British Journal of Medical Psychology* 32 (1959).
158. Selvini-Palazzoli, M., et al. "Family Rituals: A Powerful Tool in Family Therapy." *Family Process* 16 (1977).
159. Shah, I. 22 titles, Institute for the Study of Human Knowledge, Los Altos, California.
160. Sluzki, C. E. "Process of Symptom Production and Patterns of Symptom Maintenance." *Journal of Marital Family Therapy* 7 (1981).
161. Sluzki, C. E., Beavin, J., Tarnopolsky, A., and Verón, E. "Transacciones descalificadoras." *Acta psiquiátrica y psicológica de America Latina* 12 (1966) (English edition: "Transactional Disqualification." *Archives of General Psychiatry* 16 [1967].
162. Sluzki, C. E., and Ransom, D. C., eds. *Double Bind.* New York: Grune & Stratton, 1976.
163. Sluzki, C. E., and Verón, E. "The Double Bind as a Universal Pathogenic Situation." *Family Process* 10 (1971).
164. Solschenizyn, A., et al. *Stimmen aus dem Untergrund. Zur geistigen Situation in der UdSSR.* Darmstadt: Luchterhand, 1975.
165. Sontheimer, K. "Die Erweckung der Rassenseele." In *Bücher, die das Jahrhundert bewegten.* Munich: Piper, 1978.

166. Spencer-Brown, G. *Laws of Form.* New York: Bantam Books, 1973.
167. Sperber, M. "Die Erben des Herostratos." *Süddeutsche Zeitung,* September 20, 1975.
168. Spitz, R. A. "Hospitalism." In *The Psychoanalytic Study of the Child,* vol. 1, pp. 53–74. New York: International Universities Press, 1945.
169. Stienstra, T. "400 Students Chant Ritual at Rain-Making Ceremony." *Palo Alto Times,* December 18, 1977.
170. Vaihinger, H. *The Philosophy of "As If."* London: Kegan Paul, Trench & Trubner, 1924.
171. Varela, F. "A Calculus for Self-Reference." *International Journal of General Systems* 2 (1975).
172. ———. "The Creative Circle." In *The Invented Reality,* edited by Paul Watzlawick, pp. 309–323. New York: Norton, 1984.
173. Vaughn, C. E., and Leff, J. P. "The Influence of Family and Social Factors in the Course of Psychiatric Illness." *British Journal of Psychiatry* 129 (1970).
174. Vester, F. *Neuland des Denkens.* Stuttgart: Deutsche Verlagsanstalt, 1980.
175. Vico, G. *De Antiquissima Italorum Sapentia.* Naples: Stampa de' Classici Latini, 1858.
176. Watzlawick, P. *An Anthology of Human Communication: Text and Tape.* Palo Alto, Calif.: Science & Behavior, 1964.
177. ———. "Patterns of Psychotic Communication." In *Problems of Psychosis,* edited by P. Doucet and C. Laurin. Amsterdam: Excerpta Medica, 1969.
178. ———. *How Real Is Real?* New York: Random House, 1976.
179. ———. *The Language of Change.* New York: Basic Books, 1978.
180. ———. "Das Kriterion der Wirklichkeitsanpassung." In *Psychopathologische Konzepte der Gegenwart,* edited by W. Janzarik. Stuttgart: Enke, 1982.
181. ———. "Self-Fulfilling Prophecies." In *The Invented Reality,* edited by Paul Watzlawick. New York: Norton, 1984.
182. ———. *Münchhausen's Pigtail.* New York: Norton, 1990.
183. ———, ed. *The Invented Reality.* New York: Norton, 1984.
184. Watzlawick, P., Beavin, J. H., and Jackson, D. D. *Pragmatics of Human Communication.* New York: Norton, 1967.
185. Watzlawick, P., Weakland, J., and Fisch, R. *Change.* New York: Norton, 1974.

186. Watzlawick, P., et al. "On Unbecoming Family Therapists." In *The Interactional View,* edited by Paul Watzlawick and John Weakland, pp. 308–324. New York: Norton, 1977.

187. Weakland, J. "Family Somatics: A Neglected Edge." *Family Process* 16 (1977).

188. Weakland, J., Fisch, R., Watzlawick, P., and Bodin, A. "Brief Therapy: Focused Problem-Resolution." *Family Process* 13 (1974).

189. Whithead, A. N., and Russell, B. *Principia Mathematica.* Cambridge: Cambridge University Press, 1910–1913.

190. Wittgenstein, L. *Tractatus Logico-Philosophicus.* New York: Humanities Press, 1951.

191. ———. *Remarks on the Foundations of Mathematics.* Oxford: Basil Blackwell, 1956.

192. ———. *On Certainty.* Oxford: Basil Blackwell, 1969.

193. Wynne, L. C., Ryckoff, I. M., Day, J., and Hirsch, S. "Pseudomutuality in the Family Relations of Schizophrenics." *Psychiatry* 21 (1958).

194. Yo Kuang-Lieh. In *Neue Zürcher Zeitung,* March 12, 1977.

195. *Zeitdienst, Der.* In *Neue Zürcher Zeitung,* March 17, 1979.

196. Zeleny, M., ed. *Autopoiesis.* New York: Elsevier-North Holland, 1981.

NAME INDEX

SUBJECT INDEX

ACKNOWLEDGMENTS

Chapter 1   Originally published as "Wesen und Formen menschlicher
            Beziehungen," in *Neue Anthropologie*, edited by H.-G.
            Gadamer and P. Vogler, vol. 7, pp. 103–131 (Stuttgart:
            Thieme, 1975).

Chapter 2   Originally published as "Der Wandel des Menschenbildes in
            der Psychiatrie," in *Schriften der C. F. von Siemens Stiftung*,
            vol. 5, *Reproduktion des Menschen*, edited by A. Peisel and A.
            Mohler, pp. 174–200 (Berlin: Ullstein, 1981).

Chapter 3   Originally published in *Family Process* 19 (1980): 13–18.

Chapter 4   Originally published in *Familiar Realities*, edited by H.
            Stierlin et al., pp. 52–59 (New York: Brunner/Mazel, 1987).

Chapter 5   Originally published in *Psychosocial Intervention in Schizo-
            phrenia*, edited by H. Stierlin et al., pp. 215–225 (Berlin:
            Springer, 1983).

Chapter 6   Originally published in Paul Watzlawick, *How Real Is Real?*,
            pp. 207–222 (New York: Random House, 1976).

Chapter 7   Originally published as "Wirklichkeitsanpassung oder an-
            gepasste 'Wirklichkeit'?" in *Schriften der C. F. von Siemens
            Stiftung*, vol. 10, *Einführung in den Konstruktivismus*, edited
            by H. Gumin and A. Mohler, pp. 79–83 (Munich: Olden-
            bourg, 1985).

Chapter 8   Originally published as "Lebensstile und 'Wirklichkeit,' " in
            Stil, edited by H. U. Gumbrecht and K. Pfeiffer, pp. 673–681
            (Frankfurt: Suhrkamp, 1986).

Chapter 9   Originally published as "Management oder—Konstruktion
            von Wirklichkeiten," in *Integriertes Management*, edited by
            G.J.B. Probst and H. Siegwart, pp. 365–376 (Bern: Paul
            Haupt, 1985).

Chapter 10   Originally published as "Münchhausens Zopf und Wittgensteins Leiter," in *Schriften der C. F. von Siemens Stiftung,* vol. 1, *Der Mensch und seine Sprache,* edited by A. Peisel and A. Mohler, pp. 243–264 (Berlin: Propyläen, 1979).

Epilogue　Originally published as "Ausblick in eine kommunikative Zukunft," in *Erfolge mit Dienstleistungen,* edited by H. Afheld, pp. 155–165 (Stuttgart: Poller, 1988).

The Preface and Chapters 1, 2, and 7 were translated by Ursula Berg-Lunk. Chapters 8 and 10 and the Epilogue were translated by Carl Hill. Chapter 9 was translated by Hans Lunk.